MW00911260

THE CONTEMPORARY STUDY OF THE ARAB WORLD

THE CONTEMPORARY STUDY OF THE ARAB WORLD

EDITED BY

Earl L. Sullivan

Jacqueline S. Ismael

 THE UNIVERSITY OF ALBERTA PRESS

First published by
The University of Alberta Press
Athabasca Hall
Edmonton, Alberta
Canada T6G 2E8

Copyright © The University of Alberta Press 1991

ISBN 0-88864-211-3

Canadian Cataloguing in Publication Data
Main entry under title:

The Contemporary study of the Arab world

　　Includes bibliographical references.
　　ISBN 0-88864-211-3

　　1. Arab countries -Study and teaching.
I. Sullivan, Earl L. II. Ismael, Jacqueline S.
DS37.6.A2C65 1991　909'.0974927　C90-091080-1

All rights reserved

No part of this publication may be produced, stored in a retrieval system, or transmitted in any forms or by any means, electoric, mechanical, photocopying, recording, or otherwise, without the prior permission of the copyright owner.

Typesetting by The Typeworks, Vancouver, BC, Canada

Printed by D.W. Friesen & Sons, Ltd., Altona, Manitoba, Canada

∞ Printed on acid-free paper.

To
Jeanne, Mark, Erin and Colin Sullivan
and
Tareq, Shereen and Jennan Ismael

CONTENTS

PREFACE

THE ARAB WORLD is sufficiently distinctive and important to warrant specialized study. United to at least some degree by language, culture and geographic contiguity, the states and peoples of the Arab World are noted for their diversity and lack of political unity. However, they are not culturally, economically, and politically isolated; the Arab World is commonly and correctly perceived to be part of a larger whole. One consequence is that it has not been customary to focus methodological attention on Arab Studies. Thus, there are many schools and centers of Near East Studies, Middle East Studies, and Oriental Studies, but few places which specialize in Arab Studies. The Center for Contemporary Arab Studies at Georgetown University is a notable exception. Many scholars are *de facto* specialists on Arab affairs, devoting all or nearly all of their research time to questions pertaining to the Arabs. For some, including several authors in this book, when they use the phase "Middle East" they do not mean the area from Morroco to Afghanistan: they mean the Arab countries. There may be something to gain intellectually by constricting the focus methodologically in order to concentrate on the specific issues and problems facing research related to the Arab World. There may also be some weaknesses to this approach, in that it may increase parochialism, but the likely gain in increased intellectual self-awareness should be worth the risk, particularly if researchers, by virtue of this *explicit* fix on the Arabs, become more conscious of the dangers of parochialism.

Many of the chapters in this book are products of the University of Calgary's 1986 conference on the State of the Art in Middle East Studies. Only Edward Said's essay has been published elsewhere. The essay on the problem of indigenization by Morsy, Nelson, Saad, and Sholkamy, and the discussion of Arab economics by Farah are original to the book. Senior scholars, as well as several just beginning their careers, are represented in this volume. It also has a clear interdisciplinary flavor, in that its contributors include specialists in Comparative Literature, Religious Studies, Anthropology, Sociology, Economics, and Political Science.

The Contemporary Study of the Arab World is the second book to emerge from the conference in Calgary. The first one, *Middle East Studies: International Perspectives on the State of the Art,* presented a global view of the broad field of Middle Eastern Studies. This book has a narrower focus. It discusses key paradigms which have dominated the study of the Arab World from three perspectives: those which have dominated the West's thinking about the Middle East in general, those paradigms used by indigenous scholars who study the region, and finally, the paradigms which have dominated, and continue to dominate, selected fields of study within the social sciences are outlined.

The 1978 publication of *Orientalism,* by Edward Said, constitutes an important benchmark in Middle East Studies and the study of the Arab World. In that book, Said, a Professor of Comparative Literature at Columbia University, challenges the validity of much of mainstream scholarship on the Middle East. His charge is that Orientalists are motivated chiefly by a desire to control the Orient and the Orientals. He says further that, according to the Orientalists, the area can be understood properly only from the outside.

This view of scholarship as imperialism is so basic to an evaluation of paradigms in this field that the book starts with a series of essays which address issues central to the debate about the "proper" study of Arabs and Islam. The chapters in Part One, "Neo-Orientalism and the Study of Islam," are "Orientalism Reconsidered" by Edward Said and "Hermenutics of the Old and New Orientalism," by Antonio Roberto Gualtieri. Part Two, "Methodological Perspectives on the Study of the Arab World," contains two essays, one by a sociologist and the other by four anthropologists. Scholars will find this section useful and informative regardless of their discipline. Mark Kennedy opens Part Two with "Dilemmas in Middle Eastern Social Sciences: Contours of the Problem of the Relevance of Western Paradigms as Guides to Research, Policy and Practice." This is followed by "Anthropology and the Call for Indigenization of Social Science in the Arab World" by Soheir Morsy, Cynthia Nelson, Reem Saad, and Hania Sholkamy.

Part Three, "Special Topics in Arab Studies," contains essays on urban studies, women's studies, economics and economic policy, the study of foreign policy and closes with two essays on strategic studies. The opening shot is fired by Janet Abu Lughod's essay entitled "The State of the Art in Studies of Middle Eastern Urbanization." This is followed by "Old Wine, New Bottles: Reflections and Projections Concerning Research on Women in Middle Eastern Studies" by Cynthia Nelson; "Science, Ideology and Authoritarianism in Middle East Economics" by Nadia Ramsis Farah; "The Dilemma of Modern Arab Economic Thought" by Basil al-Bustany; "Biased Science or Dismal Art? A Critical Evaluation of the State of the Art of Arab Foreign Policies' Analysis" by Bahgat Korany; and "Strategic Studies and the Middle East: Periodical Literature in the United States, 1980–1990" by P. Edward Haley. If, as Edward Said charges, the point of much scholarship on the Middle East has been to aid and abet its control from the outside, it is only fitting to conclude this volume with a concern with strategic studies as viewed from the region. "Strategic Studies and the Middle East: A View From the Region" by Kamel Abu Jaber examines how Arabs may defend themselves.

ACKNOWLEDGEMENTS

THE EDITORS WISH to thank the Social Science and Humanities Research Council of Canada and the Province of Alberta Department of Advanced Education for supporting the international conference which initiated this endeavor. This book, based on selected and revised conference proceedings, is one of the outcomes of the conference. We also wish to thank The University of Calgary for Providing a publication subvention for this volume. The International Association of Middle Eastern Studies and The University of Calgary co-sponsored and hosted the conference, which was also assisted by the Department of Political Science and the Faculty of Social Work.

While the scholarly work of the contributors made this volume possible, we also wish to acknowledge their stamina and patience in seeing it through to publication. In the same vein, we cannot overlook the skill and patience of Judi Powell who took it through many revisions on the word processor, or the care of our editor, Mary Mahoney-Robson, who maintained scrupulous editorial standards.

CONTRIBUTORS

KAMEL S. ABU JABER is Professor of Political Science at The University of Jordan. He is the author of *The Arab Ba'th Socialist Party* (1966); *The United States of America and Israel* (1971) in Arabic; *The Israeli Political System* (1973) in Arabic; *The Jordanians and the People of Jordan* (1980); *Economic Potentialities of Jordan* (1984); *Political Parties and Elections in Israel* (1985) in Arabic; *The Badia of Jordan* (1987). He is a contributor to several other books including: *The Arab-Israeli Confrontation, 1967* (1969); *Government and Politics of the Contemporary Middle East* (1970); *The Future of Pastoral Peoples* (1981); *The Contemporary Mediterranean World* (1983); *Political and Economic Trends in the Middle East* (1985); *Regional Security in the Third World* (1986). He is also the editor of *Roots of Arab Socialism* (1964) in Arabic; *Levels and Trends of Fertility and Mortality in Selected Arab Countries of West Asia* (1980); and *Major Issues in the Development of Jordan* (1983). His articles have appeared in *The Middle East Journal, The Muslim World,* the *Arab Journal, Mideast, The Encyclopaedia Britannica, Orient, The Third World Chronicle, Problems of International Cooperation, The Arab Perspective* and *The American Arab Journal.* He is currently editor of *The Journal of the Arab Political Science Association, al-Reem (The Journal of the Royal Society for the Conservation of Nature in Jordan).*

JANET LIPPMAN ABU-LUGHOD is currently Professor of Sociology and History at the Graduate Faculty of the New School for Social Research, where she is Department Chair and Director of a Research Center dealing with New York. She holds graduate degrees in Planning from the University of Chicago and in Sociology from the University of Massachusetts. She has published eight books, including three on Middle Eastern cities, one on Third World urbanization, and two on American cities, as well as hundreds of articles and reviews. Her book, *Before European Hegemony: The World System A.D. 1250–1350* (Oxford University Press, 1989), recently won an award for distinguished scholarship from the American Sociological Association. *Changing Cities,* a textbook in Urban Sociology, will be released by Harper/ Collins in early 1991. She is currently researching the history and urban dynamics of the Lower East Side of New York.

BASIL AL-BUSTANY is Professor of Economics at the College of Administration and Economics, University of Baghdad. He is the author of several books in Arabic and numerous articles in English. In addition, he has served as a senior administrator with the World Bank and the Central Bank of Iraq.

NADIA RAMIS FARAH is presently Adjunct Associate Professor at The American University in Cairo and has a Ph.D. in Economics from Clark University. Dr. Farah is the author of *Religious Strife in Egypt* (Gordon and Breach, 1986); "Economic Theory and Arab Development," in Adel Hussein, Nader Fergany, Nadia Farah, et al. (eds.), *Arab Development: The Present and the Future* (Center for Arab Unity Studies, November 1984); with Edward E. Azar, "The Structure of Inequalities and Protracted Social Conflict: A Theoretical Framework," *International Interactions 7*, no. 4 (February 1981); and "The Political and Economic Dimensions of Conflict," in Nazli Choucri (ed.), *Multidisciplinary Perspectives on Population and Conflict* (Syracuse University Press, 1984), published for the United Nations Family Planning Agency (UNFPA).

ANTONIO R. GUALTIERI is Professor of Religion, Carleton University, with special interests in problems of religious diversity and comparative religious ethics. Previously, he served as a minister of the United Church of Canada and taught in the Religion Department at Vassar College. Among the journals in which his articles have appeared are: *SR Studies in Religion/Sciences Religieuses, Scottish Journal of Theology, Religious Studies, Journal for the Scientific Study of Religion, Theological Studies, Encounter, Religion and Society, Journal of Dharma, Journal of Ecumenical Studies, Canadian Ethnic Studies,* and *Dalhousie Review.*

P. EDWARD HALEY is Senior Research Associate of the Keck Center for International and Strategic Studies and Professor of Government, Claremont McKenna College and Claremont Graduate School. Formerly he served as Dean of the School of International Studies, University of the Pacific and as Director of the Keck Center for International Strategic Studies and Chairman of the International Relations Committee, Claremont McKenna College.

JACQUELINE S. ISMAEL is Professor of Social Welfare at The University of Calgary. Her research interests include the Canadian welfare state and social development/social change in the Arab World. Her publications include numerous articles and book chapters, and the following books: *Kuwait: Social Change in Historical Perspective* (1982); *Canadian Social Welfare Policy: Federal and Provincial Dimensions* (ed.) (1985); with Tareq Y. Ismael, *PDR Yemen: Politics, Economics and Society—The Politics of Socialist Transformation* (1986); *Perspectives on Social Services and Social Issues* (ed.) (1986); *The Canadian Welfare State: Evolution and Transition* (ed.) (1987); *Privatization and Provincial Social Services in Canada: Policy, Administration and Service Delivery* (ed.) (1988).

MARK C. KENNEDY is Professor Emeritus of Sociology at The American University of Cairo and received a Ph.D. in Sociology from the State University of New York at Buffalo. He is the author of: with Tullio C. Caputo, C.E. Reasons, and A. Brannigan, *Law and Society: A Critical Review* (Harcourt Brace Jovanvich, 1989); "The New Global Network of Corporate Power and the Decline of National Self Determination," *Contemporary Crisis* 12, no. 3 (1988); with Mediha El-Safty and Monte Palmer, *An Analytical Index of Social Research in Egypt*, Monographs 1 and 2, Cairo Papers in Social Science (The American University in Cairo Press, 1985); "Egyptian Youth and Justice Systems: A Rural-Urban Comparison," Cairo Papers in Social Science; Special Issue edited by Richard Lobban under the title "Urban Research Strategies for Egypt" (1983); and "The Problem of Relevance of Western Sociology in Middle Eastern Societies," *International Review of Modern Sociology* 12, no. 1 (June 1982) [Note: The editor, Dr. Man Singh Das, also published a different issue of this same journal bearing the same volume "12, no. 1" designation].

BAHGAT KORANY is Professor in the Department of Political Science, and Director of the University Program of Arab Studies, at the Université de Montreal. He has been visiting professor in many universities (Algiers, Dakar, McGill, Aix-Marseille, Harvard (visiting scholar)) and is on the editorial board of many specialised periodicals in the fields of International Relations and Development Studies. A founding member of the Organization South-South Corporation (Beijing, 1983), he has published four books and some 35 articles (in such periodicals as *Revue française de science politique, Etudes Internationales, International Journal,* and *Journal of Social Sciences, World Politics*), some of which have been translated into Arabic, Italian, Spanish and Chinese. His first book, *Social Change, Charisma and International Behavior,* was awarded the 1976 Hauchman Prize.

SOHEIR MORSY is Visiting Associate Professor at the University of California, Berkeley, and has a Ph.D. in Medical Anthropology from Michigan State University. He is the author of "Islamic Clinics in Egypt: The Cultural Elaboration of Bio-Medical Hegemony," *Medical Anthropology Quarterly* 2, no. 4 (December 1988); *Sickness, Health and Gender in the Egyptian Nile Delta: A Political Economic Ethnography* (Westview Press, 1991); and "Women and Contemporary Social Transformation in North Africa," in Rita S. Gallin and Anne Ferguson (eds.), *The Women and International Development Annual,* Vol. 2 (Westview Press, 1991).

CYNTHIA NELSON is Professor of Anthropology at The American University in Cairo and has a Ph.D. in Anthropology from the University of California, Berkeley. She is the author of "Private and Public Politics: Women in the Middle Eastern World," *American Ethnology* 1, no. 2 (1974); "The Voices of Doria Shafik: Feminist Consciousness in Egypt, 1940–1960," *Feminist Issue* 6, no. 2 (Fall 1986); and with A. Khater, "al-Harakah al-Nisa'aya: The Women's Movement," *Women's Studies International Forum* 2, no. 5 (1988); and editor of *Women Health and Development,* Vol. 1 and 7, Cairo Papers in Social Sciences (The American University of Cairo Press, 1977).

REEM SAAD is a Ph.D. candidate at St. Anthony's College, Institute of Social Anthropology, Oxford University; her doctoral thesis is entitled "Peasants Perceptions of Recent Egyptian History." She has a MA in Sociology-Anthroplogy from The American University in Cairo and is the author of *Social History of an Agrarian Reform Community in Egypt,* Cairo Papers in Social Science, Vol. 11, no. 4 (Winter) (The American University of Cairo Press, 1988).

EDWARD W. SAID was born in Jerusalem, and grew up there and in Cairo before coming to the United States for his education. He is now Professor of English and Comparative Literature of Columbia University, where he has been since 1963. His many books include *Beginnings: Intention and Method; Orientalism; The Question of Palestine; Covering Islam; The World, the Text, and the Critic; After the Last Sky.* His forthcoming books include *Musical Elaborations* (spring 1991) and *Culture and Imperialism* (late 1991).

HANIA SHOLKAMY is a Ph.D. Candidate, Department of Social Anthropology, London School of Economics, with a MA in Sociology-Anthropology from The American University of Cairo and is the author of "They Are the Government: Bureaucracy and Development in an Egyptian Village," MA Thesis, Department of Sociology/Anthropology, The American University of Cairo (1988).

EARL L. (TIM) SULLIVAN is a Professor of Political Science at The American University in Cairo. He received his Ph.D. in International Relations from Claremont Graduate School. Dr. Sullivan is the author of *Women in Egyptian Public Life* (Syracuse University Press, 1986); *The Impact of Development Assistance on Egypt,* Cairo Papers in Social Science, Vol. 7, no. 3 (September 1984); with K. Korayem, *Women and Work in the Arab World,* Cairo Papers in Social Science, Vol. 4, no. 4. (December 1981); with Ann Lesch, "Women in Egypt: New Roles and Realities," *UFSI Reports* 1986/no. 22, Africa [AML-2 '86] (Universities Field Staff International); "The U.S. and Egypt: The Potential Crisis," *Worldview* 222, no. 12 (December 1979); with D. Fixler and R. Farrar, "The Economic and Political Consequences of a Convertible Egyptian Pound," *The Middle East Journal* 29, no. 4 (Autumn, 1975).

INTRODUCTION
Critical Perspectives on Arab Studies

"ORIENTALISM RECONSIDERED" by Edward Said introduces a fundamental premise of the study of the 'other'; that is the location of the self as an existential and moral fact outside that which is to be studied (here the Orient—in particular, Arabs and Islam). In the light of the sociology of knowledge of imperialism, Orientalism accommodated itself readily to the establishment of the subject/object relationship that responded more to the culture that produced it than to its putative object. To Said, Orientalism asserts that the Orient requires investigation, even needs information about itself (i.e., cannot represent itself). The relationship is radically one of power. Scholarship and media representation of the area becomes a manner of "regularized writing, vision and study dominated by imperatives, perspectives, and ideological biases ostensibly suited to the Orient. The Orient is taught, researched, administered and pronounced upon in certain discrete ways."[1] That is to say, the portrayal of all that is Arab became racist and almost completely ethnocentric. Such is the tradition of Orientalism, according to Edward Said.

The broad issues involved in the discussion in Said's Orientalism and readdressed in the article presented here are: 1) the representation of other cultures, societies, and histories; 2) the sociology of knowledge and the relationship between power and knowledge; 3) the role of the intellectual; 4) methodological questioning involving the relationship between texts, between text and context, between text and history. Basic to any theory of interpretation is the placing of the object into the political, ethical and epistemological contexts proper to it. The line is always drawn separating

the Orient from the Occident and regarding the former as a sort of a "fecund night out of which European rationality developed."[2] This Orient is a
human creation, a fact of the social and political rather than the natural
world. Once this is recognized, and the images, fantasies, and ideological
presuppositions identified, the problem becomes the possibility of knowledge. Said writes, "no one trying to grasp it can by an act of pure will or
sovereign understanding stand at some Archimedean point outside the
flux."[3]

Orientalism, which has in the past been ruled by historicism and what
Said calls "essentialist universalism," must become a more critical field. Beginning with Said's work there are signs that the field is developing in a
new direction which comes with the consciousness raised by Said and a
few Orientalist scholars before him. In the new scholarship (that which is
truly "new" in approach, not merely "recent" applications of traditional
Orientalist methods) the scholar is more conscious of his position vis-a-vis
his object (the Orient). Much of what has appeared in the field since 1978
has been in reaction to Said's study and this has created something of a dialectic, taking the form of a discourse between supporters and critics of the
original work. "Orientalism Reconsidered," the article presented here, is a
part of that dialectic.

Progress (for there is no success as such, no point of complete understanding) lies in what Said calls a "decentered consciousness"—a direction
the field seems to be taking. There will be no center of sovereign authority,
the process will be non- (even anti-) totalizing and systematic. It will be
secular, marginal, and political only in its intent to challenge the old Orientalism, a scientific dialogue to which this book and the essays it contains
aspire to contribute. This new trend, however, also has its pitfalls. Particularly, Said thinks that as the old Orientalism is opposed and critiqued, new
anti-dominant groups of scholars will form. He makes an appropriate
comparison between Islamic and Arab Studies and Women's Studies and
asks:

... whether in identifying and working through anti-dominant critiques, subaltern groups—women, blacks, and so on—can resolve the
dilemma of autonomous fields of experience that are created as a consequence. A double kind of possessive exclusivism could set in: the sense
of being an excluding insider by virtue of experience... and second,
being an excluding insider by virtue of method. ... [4]

While Antonio Roberto Gualtieri agrees with many of Said's criticisms of the field, he points out in "Hermeneutics of the Old and New Orientalism" that there is another side to the field of Orientalism which is generally ignored by critics.

The "old Orientalism" as Gualtieri calls it, is exemplified by (to use Foucault's phrase) a "discourse of power." This view sees the purpose of Orientalism as perpetuating and justifying the economic and political domination of the East by the West. This is also Said's general view of the field, but Gualtieri accuses him of seeing the field as almost totally blind and corrupt as Said "continually stresses the subjectivist and relativist dimensions of scholarship." Moreover, he calls Said's thesis "a victim of overkill."

Gualtieri points out that Orientalism criticized the entire field, although there were Orientalists who were practicing their craft in very different ways from those pilloried by Said at that time. He cites, by way of example, the work of Wilfred Cantwell Smith. Smith parts with tradition in studying Islam from the participants' point of view. The "study of religion," Smith writes, "is the study of persons" and "to ignore the reality of people is to fail to understand the Islamic vision and Muslim history."[5] Moreover, Smith perceives "the universal humanity of eastern people," a striking contrast to Said's Orientalists and their overriding perception of the Oriental as "other." Smith also believes that his studies must, in order to be meaningful, be understandable to Muslims. Said's Orientalism was considered to be something that Europeans did for consumption by other Europeans and in no part of the process were Muslims included.

Smith's study of the Orient is "carried out on the basis of a personalist hermeneutic that lets him transcend the Western view of Islam and see it from a Muslim's perspective." One should not, therefore, believe the entire field of Orientalism perpetuates old stereotypes and ethnocentrism. How very different a study using Smith's personalist frame of reference would be from a study using the frame of reference of the conventional Orientalists.

Following these two essays on the problems raised by Said's Orientalism, the book shifts focus to macro-methodological concerns in the Social Sciences. Mark Kennedy's "Dilemmas in Middle Eastern Social Sciences: Contours of the Problems of the Relevance of Western Paradigms as Guides to Research, Policy and Practice," the opening essay of the second section of this book, examines broad questions briefly and goes into detail regarding the problem of relevance for Arab social scientists. The purpose of the chapter is to examine dominant Social Science paradigms and "portray the varying facets of this problem of relevance as they are visible in the literature issuing out of the Maghreb and Egypt today."

Kennedy begins with a brief outline of the beginnings of Western anthropological paradigms in the Middle East. Western concepts, definitions and ideas used by Westerners studying the region began with colonial rule. These Westerners fully expected their framework of analysis would be as applicable to the Middle East as it would be to Europe or North America. It may not have always been the principal Western paradigm, nevertheless, functionalism dominated the study of the Middle East from the beginning of the colonial period to the 1960s. Only when Western and indigenous scholars began to critically analyze what functionalism had achieved (or, rather, failed to achieve) did it begin to languish and ultimately fall as the preeminent framework for study of the Middle East. The key criticism was that, given its western bias, it lacked the ability to fully illuminate the Middle East.

Kennedy sees the dominant paradigms today—especially in the field of anthropology—as being a variety of Marxist and Weberian models that are in danger of becoming outmoded because of heavy criticism from the Middle East. There is one important point to be made however: the response to each framework is not uniform across the area, perhaps, he speculates, due to variations in colonial experience. There is in the Middle East then, no consensus of opinion on which Western models, if any, are relevant to Middle Eastern social scientists in their study of the region. Some say Western models are irrelevant and indigenization of social science is crucial while others say indigenization is impossible and ineffective, an issue taken up in detail by the essay which follows Kennedy's in this volume.

The most common Western paradigms, despite being often criticized, are Weberian and Marxist models. Kennedy gives a brief account of the scholarship in the Maghreb which follows those paradigms. For the interpretation of the Maghreb, Kennedy found that Marxist paradigms are "continually undergoing critical revision through more regional research into the history and present situations of the Maghreb" and that rigidity is giving way to flexibility and inventiveness. Despite revisions, Kennedy argues, Marxist and Weberian paradigms are essentially flawed in that both are Euro-centric in theory and methodology and their predictions have not been borne out in the Middle East. It is for these reasons that they are coming under increasingly intense attack. In general, Kennedy sees scholars in the Maghreb placing little value on European models because the histories of both the West and the Middle East are so radically different from their own. Instead, they believe that, to be influential in the development of society—to be relevant—new, indigenously oriented paradigms are needed.

The situation in Egypt is somewhat different. Kennedy believes Egyptian social scientists have found it difficult to be influential on a policy level, as development and planning in contemporary Egypt is tied to the interests of foreign aid agencies. Furthermore, the government controls certain forms of research.

In Egypt, the debate revolves not so much around which paradigm is relevant but, rather, "how to make relevant ideas effective in national development planning." In the Egypt of today, this involves the debate about free enterprise and the policy which, since 1974, has symbolized it: the so-called "open door" policy, which was ostensibly designed to open the country to increased trade and foreign investment. This, Kennedy argues, is important methodologically because it "moved Egypt from introverted to extroverted development," i.e., Egypt is no longer capable of self-development and must rely on foreign agencies and governments, usually American, to finance its programs.

Kennedy outlines the positions of Egyptian social science on the open door policy. While the left understandably hates the policy, the right, including what Kennedy calls neo-classical economists, like it because they believe it will benefit Egypt in the long run. Kennedy argues that the policy has been detrimental to Egypt's short-term and long-term interests. The task for Egyptian social scientists, as he sees it, has become not only to oppose the open door program but to involve themselves in the nation's development policy, to somehow become politically relevant.

The second essay in this section, written by Soheir Morsy, Cynthia Nelson, Reem Saad and Hania Sholkamy, is also concerned with the problem of relevance. It takes up the challenge of confronting what Edward Said calls "possessive exclusivism" in the first chapter of this book. The danger of the old Orientalism seems clear. In order to counter it, indigenous scholars have been called upon to develop their own paradigms and free the area from the intellectual imperialism of the old Orientalism. Is it possible, however, that there could be a threat similar to that emanating from Orientalism from the new trend toward indigenization?

"Anthropology and the Call for Indigenization of Social Science in the Arab World" by Soheir Morsy, Cynthia Nelson, Reem Saad and Hania

Sholkamy constitutes a detailed examination of current trends in the quest for indigenization. It concentrates on both the social/historical and epistemological/methodological contexts of the debate underway in the Arab World concerning strategies for the future direction of Arab social science.

The crisis which affected social science in the post-war period affected not only the intellectual centers of the world (Europe and North America) but the periphery as well. In the chapter, the authors give a detailed account of how the end of colonialism and the accompanying anti-imperialist sentiment evident in the Arab World affected Arab social science.

Accompanying the rise of national liberation movements, anti-imperialist ideologies, and the crisis in Western social science, were calls by both Arab and Western academics for indigenization of the social sciences. When scrutinized, it was found that the Western paradigm which had dominated the social sciences for so long was not universally applicable, yet scholars using it had "chosen to compromise social realities in these (Third World) societies rather than admit a limitation in its generalizing capacity."

Prior to independence, indigenous scholars were thought of by their Western counterparts in much the same manner some people think of children: they should be seen and not heard. When the Western framework began to be challenged, however, the indigenous scholars led the way and, as the authors say, "talk[ed] back at the social scientists." For the first time, Arab social scientists were able to have a say in how their area of the world was to be studied and it was their goal to indigenize the social sciences so that they would "produce more authentic knowledge." Increasing the relevance of the social sciences was also a goal and the result was a dramatic growth in new ideas emanting from the Arab World on how Arabs should be studied.

It is clear that the indigenization was not merely methodological in nature but political as well. Indigenization, the authors contend, was necessary because Western social science could no longer adequately explain Arab realities. However, intellectual decolonization was far from ideal, as political considerations tended to produce overt political criticism and indigenization was too often desired more in order to make the Arab social sciences independent of the West more than for the interest of better social science. The drawbacks of politically motivated indigenization are increased when one considers that many supporters of the movement favored using Arab/Islamic sources exclusively. The result, of course, has been that Arab social science was in danger of becoming too localized and exclusive, therefore resulting in an "us versus them" mentality, where scholarship would be categorized as to the nationality of the author.

The team which produced this essay identified two main trends in the growing interest in indigenization. The first is that of the radicals who stressed the relationship between the crisis in the social sciences and socio-economic factors. For them, social science is an agent of social change and must, therefore, be relevant if it is to be of any use. Although they seek indigenization, the radicals do not completely discount all Western models as being irrelevant. Marxism, for example, is thought by many to be the Western model most relevant to Arab society. The authors credit the radicals for their definition of the current crisis but criticize them for stressing the political nature of indigenization while ignoring methodological problems. The second trend in indigenization is the neo-traditionalist approach which requires "constructing a specific theory built on the essence of Arab civilization and rejecting the essence of Western civilization." For most neo-traditionalists, the essence which is to be captured is Islam. It is only by turning to Islamic models and rejecting secular (i.e., Western) models that Arab social science can be relevant to Arab realities, they say.

As a case study of what indigenization has meant to the social sciences, the authors focus their strongest criticism on recent Arab efforts to indigenize anthropology. They are not against making Arab anthropology more authentic; they agree fully that Arab anthropology has been out of touch with Arab social reality and needs to be made more relevant. Instead, their criticism is based on the negative effects they believe indigenization will have on the field and on the current intellectual division of labour in the world.

Among their criticisms of indigenization is that, just as the Western models were found to be lacking in universal applicability, it is very possible that an Arab paradigm may not be applicable across the Arab World. The highly localized and exclusive nature of indigenization would also pose problems, as there is a growing trend in anthropology (and other social sciences) which stresses that no society can be understood in a vacuum; a comparative approach, which seeks to understand many societies is necessary.

The authors' most potent criticism of indigenization is that the logic of indigenization leads to the conclusion that the validity of research will be determined on the basis of the researcher's nationality. An Egyptian anthropologist would thus become an "us" while a European one would become a "them"; a situation which the authors see as an interesting juxtaposition of the old Orientalist approach of creating the Orient as other. Grouping scholarship by nationality also assumes that all studies by a particular national group have more in common with each other than they do with studies in the other group. This ignores the ideological dimension: American and Egyptian Marxist anthropologists may share more perspectives than either would have with a fellow national who approaches research guided by a different ideology.

While the authors agree that Arab anthropologists have made new critiques of the field and have provided important insights, one factor most often overlooked in the indigenization debate is the role of the world order on Arab intellectuals. As the authors state, it is impossible to escape "the political economic agendas of the global centers of power." Although Arab states have achieved political independence, Arab intellectuals are still dependent on the West; therefore, the idea that you can have a distinctly Arab or Islamic anthropology covers up the reality of the "satellite nature" of Arab social sciences and gives the impression that the field is unique. Despite all the attempts at creating an indigenous social science, the West is still the major source of paradigms and the Arab World is still primarily an object of scientific analysis. This is "a manifestation of the political economy of underdevelopment of the Arab World." The authors, therefore, agree with the radicals in their assessment that an important relationship between scholarship and socio-economic factors exists.

One other attempt at indigenization is also analyzed and that is the trend toward Participatory Action Research. This is the school of thought which wants "the subject (to be) an active producer in the relations of knowledge production" so that the subject is not just an object of study but an agent of change as well. This trend mainly affects the field of development studies as it is believed that Western-dominated development programs were irrelevant in the societies they were supposedly benefiting and were instead furthering Western domination over the Third World. If the researcher can indigenize his or her work in a way to make it reflect the national interest of the subject of research rather than the interests of a foreign power, developmental projects will become of more use to the societies in which they operate.

Indigenization of Social Science has had some positive aspects but these authors have concluded that the trend toward indigenization has been useful more as a critique of western dominated theory, methodology and research than in producing a truly original alternative. They call, therefore, for a dialogue between indigenous and nonindigenous scholars, as "self conscious intellectuals" and seek a "unifying synthesis and a creative theory, in which Self and Other could enter a discourse that reflects the values of freedom, justice and equity rather than abstract 'univeralism.' "

In many ways, the essay on indigenization constitutes the intellectual centerpiece of this volume and most of the issues it raises are taken up, one by one, in the final section of the book. Part Three of *The Contemporary Study of the Arab World* contains seven chapters, each of which draws attention to a special issue in Arab Studies. Chapters are oriented around state-of-the-art themes and try, to varying degrees, to be both descriptive and prescriptive while discussing current trends and problems in scholarship. Topics covered include urban studies, women's studies, political economy, foreign policy studies and strategic studies. Quite obviously, Part Three could have been expanded considerably, as the number of special topics and problems affecting the Arab World may be limited mainly by the imagination of researchers. Conspicuous by its absence is any example of work in the field of comparative politics, but to cover that area properly would have taken the addition of several chapters and thus was beyond the scope of this volume. This section, therefore, is but a sample of what has been accomplished in a few illustrative cases in the general field of Arab Studies.

The discussion of dominant subfield paradigms starts with an analysis of the study of the Middle Eastern city in Janet Abu-Lughod's chapter entitled "The State of the Art in Studies of Middle Eastern Urbanization." Abu-Lughod identifies and critically analyzes three main approaches to the study of the Middle Eastern city and suggests directions for future research.

The first pattern identified by the author is that of generalizing about the characteristics of the Islamic city and the mechanisms which created this form of urban life in the medieval and preindustrial eras. Abu-Lughod says the major scholars in this field are primarily Western Orientalists and modern Muslims "who are seeking, in the cities of the past, models for creating 'true' Islamic cities today." Studies of this kind are almost always based on a small number of cases and the period examined is almost always that just prior to European domination. Abu-Lughod contests the belief that a true "Islamic City" exists. This concept, she argues, often shows lack of "an understanding of the universal processes whereby cities are created and recreated and [of] a comparative perspective against which to judge what was general and what was unique about medieval cities of the Middle East. Scholars who follow the "Islamic City" approach fail to attribute features of the cities they studied to such factors as climate and technology and wrongly attribute them to Islam. In short, because of the lack of knowledge about cities in general and of the adverse affects of the dominant paradigm at the time, scholars who studied the Islamic city were, more often than not, wrong in what they claimed to have discovered.

The second approach analyzed by the author is that of producing biographies of individual cities for the purpose of understanding how they grew, changed and faced problems. Those engaged in writing biographies of cities come from diverse backgrounds; historians, journalists, anthropologists, city planners and some other social scientists, as well as such specialists as engineers, have followed this method. The biographical study is the most popular form of writing on Middle Eastern cities, but Abu-Lughod laments the lack of social science contributions. Social scientists, she says, "recognize that cities are living entities—shaped by the social life within them and in turn modifying and influencing that life." On the other hand, nonsocial scientists "tend to suffer from myopia" because they study a single case too closely and ignore outside influence on the life of a city. A social scientist, for example, should understand how political or economic events a continent away could influence life in the city while an engineer may not. Abu-Lughod sees this myopia as a serious fault because it is impossible to understand urban problems—both current and historical—without fully understanding the interaction of the Arab system with the world system.

The third group of studies tends to be done mainly by demographers and focuses on two themes: the over-urbanization of Arab states compared to Western countries, and hypercephaly—when the main city in a state has a disproportionate percentage of the urban population. Findings indicate that Arab states are over-urbanized in relation to the level of agriculture and industrialization and suffer from hypercephaly. Abu-Lughod's reservation about the studies is that they are purely quantitative and descriptive and fail to analyze, classify, explain or understand. She calls them "mindless statistical manipulations."

Despite the criticisms she levels at the field of urban studies, Abu-Lughod sees some potentially major developments that could increase its importance and move the field forward. Improvements include more attempts to explain as well as describe; to relate studies to social science theories; to place urban events in larger political and economic contexts; to study a wider range of cases, with emphasis on comparative data, in order to understand the variations which exist and explore the functions Arab cities have for their inhabitants. The author believes that if these steps are followed, the study of Middle East cities will catch up to that of urban areas in other regions of the world.

Just as increased urbanization in the Arab World makes the study of cities more important, the growing recognition of the importance of women's roles as well as the addition of new roles in public life for women means that the study of women deserves more and better attention than it has received in the past. Cynthia Nelson's "Old Wine, New Bottles: Reflections and Projections Concerning Research on Women in Middle Eastern Studies" is a detailed and critical examination of the contemporary scholarship, from a broad range of the social sciences, on women, especially Arab women, and "how women scholars try to integrate women into an understanding of social reality." Her purpose is to find the themes which dominate the study of Middle Eastern women in the 1970s and early 1980s and to suggest directions that the field may take in the future.

Nelson identifies four main periods in the study of Middle Eastern women. The first she calls "The Awakening," when there was little interest in the study of women in the region. After World War II and into the 1950s, interest in the study of Middle East women grew rapidly and tended to focus on how socio-political change affected the status of women in society. "This scholarship uncritically assumed the link between a woman's status and the modernizing society," the result being that men were considered as the shapers and keepers of tradition while women were "the vanguard of change." Additional scholarship emphasized the development of the "New Woman" in the Middle East and the field in general analyzed women through western perceptions of modern, civilized or progressive in contrast to what was considered traditional, Islamic and conservative.

The second era Nelson calls "the empirical gaze" which ran into the 1960s. During this period, many of the old ways of studying Middle Eastern women continued as they were "more visible but primarily through the 'gaze' of Western theoretical (and thus androcentric) paradigms." Nelson criticizes the scholarship of this period for being both Western and dominated by males, i.e., Middle Eastern women were being studied by scholars of a different sex as well as different culture and historical traditions. Most articles published in the period were concerned with the changing status, position and role of women and concluded that tradition must be broken to make the advancement of women possible.

In the third period, "the critical response," the study of Middle Eastern women began to reflect the crisis that engulfed Western social science. The issue of "the construction of knowledge about women in the Middle East and who controls the process" led scholars, especially women to ask two important questions: why were so few women studying Middle Eastern women and why did men dominate the field? In addition, in joining the general self-examination underway in the social sciences and buoyed by the strength of the feminist movement, women began to criticize both Western androcentrism and the patriarchy of the Islamic Middle East and conclude that the old paradigms could no longer explain the realities of Middle Eastern women. Moreover, the previous assumption that women were apolitical and parochial simply because politics was a male domain was abandoned, as were the old stereotypes regarding role, status and position. There were largely replaced with newer conceptions of power, patriarchy and production.

Nelson believes this was a time of great growth in the quantity and quality of studies about Middle Eastern women. Researchers began to find that women were important—both politically and economically—and should no longer be considered, as some earlier academics had assumed, as mere pawns in a game.

The final era identified by Nelson is the period of "the indigenous quest" which has seen an increase in both scholarship on women and scholarship on women by Middle Eastern women. More than ever, Middle Eastern women have turned to their own societies and this has lent a new and vibrant legitimacy to their work. This is not to say, however, that Western women stopped studying Middle Eastern women; on the contrary, some excellent studies were undertaken by women and demonstrate that "a greater empirical validity is being accorded to indigenous cultural perspectives than to the conventional western social science models, and one's gender has more significance than one's nationality in gaining access to women's subjective experience." This seems to raise the issue of "possessive exclusivism" discussed by Edward Said, but it cannot be denied that, in the study of women, female researchers have a comparative advantage over males.

Nelson's essay concludes with a discussion of some future courses that the field may take. The current emphasis on indigenous studies and the prior shift in paradigms greatly altered the study of Middle Eastern women, yet the field still suffers from methodological and interpretive problems that "can be resolved with the emergence of new paradigms at many levels of discourse and analysis." Perhaps the greatest difficulty, though, is that no single framework could possibly hope to explain "the entire spectrum of female realities across cultures, let alone the human condition." The future promise of studies on women in Middle Eastern societies rests on the continuous attempt by researchers to be sensitive to the complexities of women's lives across diverse histories, cultures and classes. This will not only add continually to the field but hopefully lead to more relevant and authentic perspectives by which to understand Middle Eastern women.

Following these chapters on cities and women, Part Three shifts to essays which address specific public policy issues. In "Science, Ideology and Authoritarianism in Middle East Economics," Nadia Farah examines the dominance of ideology over science in regard to economics in the Middle East and explains the ideological polarization currently seen in the Middle East. It is clear from the context that, by Middle East she means the Arab World. Farah disagrees with economists who believe the field is purely scientific and, therefore, devoid of any political influence. Instead, she argues that the field is "heavily influenced by political, social and ideological perceptions" and that the form of analysis used by economists is a reflection of their political and social values. In addition, Middle East economics is characterized by a dichotomy between nationalists and internationalists. This, and the very nature of the Middle East economic system, which is explained in this chapter, helps to constrain economics from being a force for development. Rather, "it is in essence the economics of regime survival."

Farah sees the polarization between nationalists and internationalists best reflected in the debate on development strategy which emerged in the 1950s and 1960s. At that time, nationalists argued that industrialization through import substitution was the way to achieve development and end dependency on the West. Heavy state involvement was necessary and a number of radical states such as Egypt, Syria, Iraq and Algeria adopted nationalist economic policies. Initially, import substitution was also favored by liberal economists, but the situation changed in the 1970s when the strategy began to be questioned from all sides of the ideological spectrum. Farah argues that criticism actually began in earnest directly after the defeat of the Arab armies in 1967. Import substitution required heavy state involvement in the economy and the building of a strong state, but that did not prevent the Israeli victory. After the war, literature supporting liberalization of the economy began to appear calling for Middle Eastern states to follow the examples of such economic miracles as Hong Kong, Taiwan and South Korea. In addition, the oil boom of the 1970s resulted in a huge inflow of capital to the oil producers which benefitted nonproducers as well. Farah sees these events as polarizing Arab states. The radical minority of states turned inward to a more "self-reliant" economic policy while the majority adopted open door policies which stressed exports. This shift also reflected the ideological dichotomy between nationalist and internationalist economics.

Farah explains that the economic system in the Middle East is subject to the same kind of ideological debate that the political system is. Western capitalist economists, labelled as internationalists, believe that the only economic problem facing the Middle East is that they are not "more like us." The argument is that all economics are more or less the same and that market forces, if left unhindered by government interference, will drive Middle East economies towards development. But, there are the nationalists who tend to disregard the traditional analytical approaches used by internationalists and instead rely on divergent and often unique methods to explain economic realities in the region. Farah sees the debate between these two positions as setting "the tone for the study of Middle East economics."

What both positions lack, Farah believes, is knowledge of the true nature of the regional economic system. Without such understanding, any attempt to apply a model to the area will fail miserably. It is, therefore, Farah's purpose to accurately and coherently describe the nature of the system and show it to be unique in that economics in the Middle East is not influenced as much by market forces as it is by demands by governments to secure and maintain their existence. Farah labels this "authoritarian economics" and sees it as a logical result of the political forces at work in the area.

Farah argues that economics, whether capitalist or socialist, has both ideological and scientific roots which can be identified by studying economic history. While today's most popular economic models—Marxism and liberalism—have "managed to create a rational economic policy largely separate if not divorced from the ideological and political sphere in which context they evolve," Arab economics is "still at the stage of political and ideological formulations." Those who espouse a particular economic theory in the Middle East are, therefore, doing so in an ideological manner.

Farah's essay contains a stinging attack on both nationalists and internationalists for failing to understand the nature of the economy and the non-economic constraints on economic policy. The problem is especially severe with internationalists who, she says, see the Middle East economic system as an extension of the capitalist economy. For example, the social costs of programs are, she states, never calculated by internationalist economists from such agencies as the IMF and World Bank. While nationalist and radical economists and dependency theorists have tended to produce analysis more in tune with reality in the region, they too have not been able to grasp the nature of the system. This can be seen in the number of their theories which, as she shows, have recently fallen into disfavor.

Farah sees authoritarian economics as the defining characteristic of the Middle East economic system as it affects both market oriented and socialist states. The state has become the dominant economic force regardless of ideology and its main function is redistribution. But it is not redistribution for the sake of increased wealth or justice as much as it is in the interest of securing the stability of the regime. This necessarily produces economic policies which have little positive and sometimes even harmful effects on the economy. Farah criticizes this as "irresponsible" as it is based on the pursuit of a short term object, the security of the regime, rather than the long-term goal of development.

A related by somewhat different line of thought is taken up by Basil al Bustany in his essay, "The Dilemma of Modern Arab Economic Thought" in which the discussion centers around one of the dreams of many Arab nationalists, the economic integration of Arab states. In much the way that Farah has argued that "authoritarian economics" has impeded the development of both the discipline and the area, one could conclude that the pursuit of the chimera of integration has had a similar effect. Al-Bustany outlines the history of the integration argument and attempts to explain the factors which have worked against the realization of economic integration.

The ideal of economic integration necessarily accompanied calls for political union between Arab states that came shortly after those states gained their independence. This was the case for four reasons: Arabs are one nation; survival as an independent nation can be achieved only by larger economic units; no single Arab state can develop independently because of limited resources; and the debatable belief that integration was widely supported by the Arab people.

In much the same way that political union between Arab states failed, economic integration has been an unobtainable objective, although significant economic cooperation exists. Al-Bustany identifies the formation of the Arab League and the creation of the Economic Unity Council as "all embracing framework(s) for mutual economic cooperation." All in all, al-Bustany identifies twenty pan-Arab institutions and organizations which exist today but, for a number of interrelated structural, legal, planning and institutional reasons, are unable to achieve integration.

Despite the resources (human, financial and natural) the Arab World possesses, the economic status quo has not changed. The structural imbalance, the gap between rich and poor Arab states, remains as great today as it was in the past and this has led to a dependency on external resources. The result has been that the poor Arab states have turned to external agents rather than the richer Arab states for help and this too has undermined efforts aimed at integration.

Other constraints are the structural and institutional problems which surround the workings of pan-Arab institutions. The institutions that do exist are often unwieldy and bureaucratic, which has resulted in gross inefficiency in their decision-making apparatus. There is also a widespread lack of commitment on the part of the individual nations to work practically towards integration, although there is certainly a verbal commitment to the concept. Integrationists see this as "representing the most critical element preventing the realization of the economic integration objective." Hence, the belief among integrationists that the political element in the issue must be "neutralized."

Al-Bustany traces the increase in economic interaction between Arab states that took place in the 1970s. This increase largely took the form of financial exchanges from the newly wealth oil producers to the oil poor nations. Throughout the 1970s, a number of economic and political shocks at both the regional and international level had serious economic implications for Middle Eastern states. Economically, the decline in oil revenues hurt oil producers as well as those that had received aid from them. At the political level, wars, conflict and deepened political divisions within the region had the effect of sowing economic as well as political disunity.

Instead of integration, the reality in the Middle East was one of wide economic disparities and disunity; this has been a large blow to integrationist thinking. Having to account for the difference between theory and reality, integrationists were reduced to talking about ways to keep the income gap at present levels and prevent it from getting worse. Al-Bustany explains how the difficulties forced integrationists into one of three trends that have risen since the 1970s: Pragmatism—integrationists who accept whatever comes in the future; Utopianism—integrationists who have totally overemphasized the good qualities of integration; Realism—the label given by al-Bustany to those who still believe that integration is the only means of achieving development.

The dilemma to which al-Bustany refers in the title of his essay is a fundamental failure of Arab integrationists to realize the uniqueness of the Arab economic situation. In their arguments, Arab integrationists often pointed to successful efforts at integration elsewhere in the world to support their claim that integration was a good thing for the Arab World. Al-Bustany sees comparison as a tenuous strategy in light of the Arab situation. Uniqueness has revealed itself in the two ways Arab face the dilemma as individuals. Arabs are members of specific nation states and pride themselves on their independence, while at the same time it is the dream of most Arabs to live united in one state. This is a unique situation which has resulted in a major contradiction within the individual which he believes exists in no other area of the world. A second and related problem is that, for many people in the Arab World unity is not simply an ordinary objective: it is an end in itself.

Arab economists cannot escape from the dilemma that individual Arabs face. Those Arabs who are integrationists have responded to the contradiction within themselves by blaming the lack of political will on the part of the individual states and have called for a neutralizing of the political aspects of integration. Al-Bustany correctly points out that this is an absurd desire because the political element cannot be neutralized in such an important consideration; the political element is a key factor in the integrationist question and their failure to realize this has weakened their cause. Al-Bustany agrees that economic development would be facilitated by integration. However, he realizes the possibility of achieving integration is remote because of the lack of political commitment in the Arab World as well as the lack of resolution in the ongoing dilemma faced by Arabs as individuals. He believes, however, that the political issue would be settled if the identity crisis were to be resolved by the vast majority in favor of the Arab nation. Then, al-Bustany believes, integration could be realized.

Both Farah and al-Bustany raise the issue of the current primacy of existing states as a key determinant of the limits of what social science can achieve. In a similar vein, but with a somewhat different point in mind, the centrality of existing territorial states in the Arab World is a basic assumption of the authors of the last three chapters in this book.

Bahgat Korany's "Biased Science or Dismal Art? A Critical Evaluation of the State of the Art of Arab Foreign Policies' Analysis," is both a survey of literature concerning a number of Arab League states and a critical analysis of how Arab foreign policies are studied. What emerges is the depiction of a field which has concentrated attention on a few states while almost ignoring others. In addition, the field of comparative foreign policy, to which the study of Arab foreign policies belongs, is currently devoid of a dominant paradigm. This had led to considerable methodological diversity but has not yielded a particularly rich body of literature on the subject of the foreign policies of Arab states.

Korany surveys the literature published between 1965 and 1985 concerning the foreign policies of eight Arab League countries, all located in Africa. He found a mere 143 studies for that 20-year period, constituting an average of less than one study per entity per year. These results show that, in general, the foreign policies of these states (Algeria, Egypt, Libya, Mauritania, Morocco, Somalia, The Sudan and Tunisia) are underexamined. However, when the distribution of these studies is analysed, it is obvious that certain countries have been—at least at the quantitative level—relatively over-researched while others have hardly been examined at all. Egypt's foreign policy was the subject of 60 pieces of research. This was followed by Algeria with 35 studies and Libya with 27, a marked contrast with Mauritania and Somalia, which were the subjects of only one article each in the 20-year period with which Korany was concerned.

There are two pressing issues which Korany says need to be addressed. The first question is to discover why so little research has been conducted on the foreign policies of these eight states. The answer, Korany states, is related to the difficulties and constraints faced by field researchers in these locations.

The difficulty in obtaining data heads the list of problems. In the states studied, as well as most other Third World states, foreign policy data are often shrouded in secrecy—a not uncommon practice and hardly unique to the Third World—and also is not preserved in the same fashion as in many countries in the West. Archives, for instance, are rare. The result is that researchers cannot study documents readily and instead must interview informed actors in order to obtain data. Although this is a valuable and important method, it has serious drawbacks, as cultural, nationalistic, and linguistic barriers may limit the information the researcher can get. In addition, to conduct an interview it is necessary to gain the trust of someone at a high enough level to be directly involved in decision-making. This is not always possible, and when it is, it can sometimes take an inordinate amount of time. The result is that obtaining information about these states' foreign policies is often very difficult, so much so that it may influence researchers to study other subjects.

The second constraint is a set of conceptual problems in studying the foreign policies of states. Different periods of time have seen the emergence of contrasting dominant paradigms that dictate what is studied and how it is to be approached. This results in comparative foreign policy being a muddled field; no one theory of state or personal behavior has yet been found that is capable of explaining the actions of all states at all times in all circumstances. Instead, the field has seen a number of theories come and go while others have withstood the test of time but have never really come to dominate the field. Those that have been analyzed and criticized and still remain are often isolated from each other and difficult to integrate. The result, as Korany sees it, is that there are "islands of theory" which seek to explain foreign policy behavior. The lack of an integrated field has, therefore, contributed to the lack of work on the foreign policies of these states in particular and Third World States in general.

The second issue which Korany raises is the question of why certain states seems to be overstudied while others are virtually ignored. Korany suggests that when the pattern of research is analysed one must conclude that a determining factor in making the most frequently examined states interesting to researchers has been their degree of being newsworthy. As Korany says, the number of publications "seem to be correlated with an active pattern of behavior in the world system or in the region." This conclusion is supported by the finding that more works have been published on Egyptian foreign policy than on any other Arab state. This means, therefore, that the number of studies on foreign policies of states is closely connected to "current affairs" and "market demand" forces, which raises interesting questions as to the quality of research undertaken and the motives which have produced it.

In order to illustrate his argument, Korany gives a detailed analysis of one of the "islands of theory" which have been employed in this field. He chooses political psychology, which has had as its dominant form, the "great man" approach to politics, and which reasons that by researching and understanding the man at the top, it is possible to explain state behavior. Korany believes this approach has been "reasonably consistent and industrious in both data collection and concept-application." This is one of the most common forms of Third World foreign policy analysis, as social science researchers, like many Orientalists, have believed that the leader in Third World societies has a greater effect on the state's foreign policy than the leader of a developed society would have.

While Korany states that political psychology has contributed to our understanding of foreign policies in certain states, he does not conclude that state behavior can be explained fully by utilizing this approach. The main difficulties with political psychology are that the acceptance of the leader as the sole motivating force behind foreign policy necessarily causes researchers to ignore all other factors, thus imposing artificial limits on what is important. Furthermore, it is impossible to know what is going on in someone's mind and, therefore, we cannot know with certainty why a leader has made a particular decision. Political psychology is, therefore, flawed in some very important ways and is "guilty of functionalist logic which engages in a form of tautology instead of full-fledged explanation."

The "islands of theory" problem, Korany believes, can be dealt with by integrating the more relevant aspects of each body of theory into a coherent whole. International political economy is considered by him to be the tool which can integrate the field and make it better able to explain state behavior. This is because it is interdisciplinary and avoids the mistake common to most theories of third world foreign policies of excluding internal or external factors for the sake of the other. Because international political economy is certainly not a new theory, Korany speaks not of the birth, but of the "rebirth—(of political economy) with some fundamental adaption in mind." This adaptation requires taking into account local cultural and historical forces in order to mix traditional political economy with indigenous sensitivity. This will make it possible for researchers to combine relevant data collection with observation of social life to give us an "inside" look at the black box, both the structure and culture of Arab society. It is only by doing this that the field of comparative foreign policy can move out of its present muddled state and move toward some kind of understanding of foreign policy. It will thus cease to be either a biased science or primitive art. Having updated his survey to November 1987, Korany finds that considerable progress has been made in this direction by a younger generation. He thus ends his chapter optimistic that this progress will continue to gather greater momentum.

The chief substantive problem with which most foreign policy decision makers must deal is that of national security. This is the preoccupation of scholars and practioners who focus on what is known as "strategic studies." The final two essays in this book deal with aspects of this crucial subject. Edward Haley's "Strategic Studies and the Middle East: Periodical Literature in the United States, 1980–1990," is a survey of periodical literature published in the U.S. dealing with strategic matters relating to the Middle East. Haley's thorough work concludes that certain aspects of strategic studies are overemphasized at the expense of other, potentially crucial, issues and that this overemphasis has resulted in presenting a false vision of reality to those who read the periodicals concerned.

Haley begins with the assertion that strategic studies, in the Western sense, is important and it is vital for Middle Eastern governments to understand the field if they are to survive. Haley recognizes that strategic studies, in the Western sense, is criticized in much of the Third World because it is perceived to be "manipulative, biased toward the West and intellectually incomplete." The result is that Arabs typically shun strategic studies for other fields. This has meant government officials have little indigenous strategic studies expertise. Decision makers, Haley states, are incapable of accurately engaging in strategic studies because they are biased towards satisfying their constituencies and soldiers are also biased towards military solutions. Haley believes there is, therefore, a compelling need for independent, objective academic strategic studies. Haley says that had policymakers and soldiers given more consideration to expert opinion, the Iran-Iraq war and the sending of US marines to Beirut could have been avoided. In a statement reminiscent of that of Nadia Farah, Haley asserts that: "The calculations and proposals of diplomats and soldiers may ignore the interests of their peoples and advance only those of their governments."

In his initial survey and analysis of periodical literature concerning strategic studies in the Middle East, published in the United States and one journal from the United Kingdom from 1980 to 1985, 152 articles were studied. It was found that only six periodicals published ten or more relevant articles. Sixty-five articles dealt with strategic analysis but over half of that number were concerned with Israel, the United States and the Iran-Iraq War. Israel accounted for more than one third of the 65 articles meaning that there has been an uneven distribution of material. Forty-five of the 65 articles dealt with grand strategy and less than one third dealt with operational strategy, tactics or weapons.

Haley's follow-up study, conducted during the summer of 1990, on the literature from 1986 to 1990, found 116 articles on strategic matters, with only five journals publishing ten or more articles. As before, articles on grand strategy and strategy were most numerous and articles on Israel and the United States made up a major portion of published materials. One change Haley noted was that there was more attention given to the PLO and strategic affairs during this period.

Haley's review of the literature is both qualitative and quantitative. On substantive grounds, he faults most of what he read for being ideologically biased and too focused on current, headline grabbing topics. In addition, he has found that little attention has been given to changing military capabilities of states in the region and virtually nothing appears on the relation between military capability and diplomatic behavior. The emphasis on Israel also ignores many issues concerning states with which Israel has little contact and essays concerning grand strategy are also more frequent than warranted by the quality of what has been produced.

Haley's conclusion, therefore, is that the study of strategic issues in the Middle East has serious shortcomings. In addition to the problems mentioned, the bias of journals and the tendency to advocate policy solutions means that journals seldom treat issues objectively or comprehensively— issues are merely skimmed over and the journal then proposes the "correct way of looking at Middle Eastern conflicts." The problem with this, of course, is that in order to fully understand the nature of a conflict, it is necessary to understand how the government views it. The approach used by most journals does not really attempt to explore this dimension of the problem. The deficiencies in the publications, all emanating from the United States, are crucial because these articles are being read by US analysts, academics and policymakers and these key people are likely to be poorly informed about strategic questions related to the Middle East and the Arab World.

As is clear, Haley does not have a high opinion of the overall quality of strategic studies work on the Middle East done in the United States. He did not survey strategic literature in either Arabic or Hebrew, but his estimate is that most material in Arabic would be similarly limited. As for strategic studies research in Hebrew, Haley says:

My guess is that most of the research on strategic matters [pertaining to this area] is conducted in Israel in Hebrew. A related hunch is that a strategic studies community exists only in Israel—a group of concerned and informed individuals which is wider than official military, intelligence, and diplomatic establishments, whose members regularly exchange views with one another on Middle Eastern strategic matters in ways that are cummulative.

Many informed observers of the region would probably agree with Haley's "hunch" regarding the quality of strategic studies in Israel and the presence there of a viable strategic studies community. It could also be argued that strategic studies on the Middle East and Arab World done in either the United States (or Israel) seem to typify all that is wrong with the Orientalist mentality criticized by Edward Said. What, then, is the nature of the indigenous response to this foreign challenge, and what are the prospects for dialogue and discourse between foreign and indigenous experts? The issue, raised but not addressed by Haley, of the quantity and quality of strategic studies in the Arab World is taken up by Kamel Abu Jaber's passionate chapter entitled "Strategic Studies and Middle East: A View From the Region." This essay is an analysis and description of the state of the art in strategic studies in the Arab World and, more importantly, the atmosphere in which Arab academics operate. This ambience has stifled independent academic thought as well as contributed to the creation of a gulf between decision makers and academics that is growing instead of shrinking.

Abu Jaber believes government leaders have a special need for academics in the field of strategic studies, where the constraints on the policymaker are such as to make detailed knowledge and understanding of the concept of strategy impossible. He makes it clear, however, that Arab leaders, for cultural and traditional reasons, are seldom aware of the importance of academics in any field let alone in this vital one.

The Arab World is not unique in this regard, but Arab government leaders seem to have a special distrust of intellectuals because many of them tend, in official eyes, to be too critical, too independent and too prone to dissent. In the traditional culture, dissent is frowned upon and viewed as a shameful act. This view began in the home: the father is considered the head of the family and his decisions are not allowed to be questioned. In much the same manner, citizens of many Arab states are not permitted to criticize the leader. This subservience is reinforced by an educational system which places more emphasis on rote learning than on independent thought and creativity.

Every aspect of life, the public, the private, the social, and the political are subject to constraints which have stunted the growth of Arab research centers and the social production of creative thinking. Abu Jaber says there is a desperate need in the Arab World to modernize, but without independent, creative, visionary thought it will be impossible to do so. To Abu Jaber, traditional authority patterns prevent the Arab World from achieving this goal.

It is obvious that the academic climate in the Arab World is drastically different from that in the West. This helps to create and reinforce certain conceptual problems and has often led Arabs to think about issues in ways different from, but not necessarily superior to, thought patterns in the west. The concept "strategy," for example, is thought of very differently by Arabs than it is by Westerners. To begin with, strategy implies something that will be done in the future. The West has found it relatively easy to look into and plan for the future but the tension—from both internal and external sources—in the Arab World has made it difficult for Arabs to think far into the future. This applies to academic and decision makers alike, who both operate in the short to medium term while ignoring the long term.

The authoritarian nature of Arab society alluded to earlier makes it virtually impossible to plan for the future and has made it difficult for new knowledge and technology to produce much innovation or change. It is precisely that—innovation and change—which the Arab World needs to break its pattern of underdevelopment, dependency and a crisis of identity. The future of Arab society is, therefore, intrinsically linked with the concepts of development, independence and identity. This necessarily means that "strategy" in the Arab World means much more than simply the relationship between political objectives and military capabilities. Yet the question remains of how effectively Arab academia has dealt with the innovation necessary to end the triple crisis threatening the Arab World. To escape constraints is rare. When escape is undertaken it is usually done by individuals. What is needed are for whole institutions to be freed from the limits imposed by tradition in order to meet the challenges of specialized research. This would facilitate the development of the type of strategic studies community mentioned by Haley.

Academic activities are constantly directed or redirected toward the "proper" channels by government officials, who see independent thought as a challenge to the favorable status quo. Creativity is constantly suppressed. These factors continue to keep the quantity and quality of Arab academic output low. Despite its relatively small population, Israel constantly outproduces the entire Arab World in scholarly work.

The Arab concept of strategic studies differs markedly from the Western definition. Even so, research is being done on strategic studies. Abu Jaber sees this research as encompassing four main themes: Pan-Arab national security; the effects the effects of the international system on the Middle East; the military in the Middle East; and the Arab World. However, it remains true that the vast majority of "strategic" studies in the Arab World often deal less with military questions than with socio-economic and developmental issues, for the future is perceived as being much more complex then merely the product of military relationships. Therefore, he says, strategic studies centers, the few of which exist in the area, tend to stress sociological, economic, educational, scientific and developmental issues, sometimes even to the exclusion of military issues. This generalization, perhaps valid when Abu Jaber made it in 1986, seems less true a few years later, especially in Egypt, where the type of strategic studies community referred to by Haley is beginning to function. The problem remains serious as far as the general area is concerned.

This has led to a very interesting situation in which the Arab definition of strategy has been molded to fit the realities of Arab existence almost to spite the Western definition. While this may be necessary, Abu Jaber makes the important observation that it is dangerous to almost totally ignore military issues, as the Arabs have done, because, like it or not, the military plays and will continue to play a great role in the future of the area. By focusing almost entirely on nonmilitary aspects of strategy, the Arabs are ignoring very crucial issues that will ultimately decide the structure of the system.

The field of strategic studies clearly presents both opportunities and problems as a subfield within Arab studies. The latent development of Arab scholarship in this area can perhaps be overcome by, among other things, increased dialogue with western specialists, as part of the discourse called for by several of the authors in this book. However, part of the problem with Arab strategic studies is endemic to the constricted role of intellectuals in the Arab World, and, as Abu Jaber implies, that does not lend itself to an easy solution.

Our Introduction can only suggest the highlights of the chapters of this book. Taken together these papers are representative of some of the most interesting and thought provoking trends in the study of the contemporary Arab World. These essays are not intended to be considered as the final word on any particular topic. Rather, they are intended to convey an impression of the state of the art of Arab studies in the 1980s and to encourage others to contribute to the future of the field by criticism as well as by following the leads of the authors included here.

Terms like the Near East and the Middle East are essentially geopolitical concepts by which a particular area of the world is defined, in this case from the outside, according to a set of criteria which suit those who have done the naming. It is defined by what it is close to, namely Europe, or what it is between, that is, Europe and Africa, or Europe and the "Far East." It may be overdoing it to call such labeling intellectual imperialism, but the effort to deal with the problem of such representation has been part of the motivation for this volume. *The Contemporary Study of the Arab World* focuses primarily on part of what is commonly called the Near or Middle East, namely the Arab World. In this case, we have used a title given to the area by its residents rather than by its conquerors.

The substance of the book suggests that the burgeoning field of Arab studies has enough meat to it to justify its existence, but that it also has some formidable obstacles to overcome if it is to progress further. One of the principal barriers to advancement is the atmosphere of suspicion regarding the motives of researchers, whether indigenous or foreign, in which research on the Arab World is often conducted. The same type of apprehension also applies to the motives of the various possible sources of funding for research, which means that potentially important work is often not done. The atmosphere of distrust is often made worse by a lack of agreement among those in the field regarding a research agenda or even a strategy for devising one. Perhaps some of this anxiety can be dissipated if attention can be directed to the creation of a consensus around a program of research. Hopefully this book will contribute in some small way to that effort.

The authors whose work is presented here are themselves personally sensitive, to varying degrees of course, to the problems mentioned above. Some are foreigners who have travelled to the Arab World in order to do research in the area. Most, however, are either indigenous to the Arab World or have resided in it by choice for prolonged periods of time.

The essays presented here contain a great deal of food for thought. In particular, certain ideas are expressed several times which future scholarship on this part of the world should take into consideration. If Edward Said's *Orientalism* means the death of the consensus produced by the old

Orientalism, it is clear that it is too soon to say that a new consensus has been reached. Nevertheless, some issues seem to have been clarified in the essays which this book contains and it may be possible to mention a few elements which could form the kernel of agreement. It would be presumptuous to try to organize those points in any rank order of importance, but the following issues seem worth mentioning here as a contribution to the debate and discussion regarding an agenda for future research. They are put forward as items for discourse, not as revealed truth. The first set of issues has to do with the problem of values and the role of the intellectual. The second relates to traditional methodological concerns pertaining to interdisciplinary and comparative research on change.

VALUES AND THE ROLE OF THE INTELLECTUAL

Research is not value free.

One point made by several authors in this book is that it is not legitimate for scholarship to be used to attempt to exert power or control over the subjects of the research. This may be especially true if those doing the research, or those paying for it and defining its terms, are not indigenous to the area. This results, however, in an essentially negative position: we know what is not acceptable but it is not entirely clear what type of research is legitimate, for merely to substitute an indigenous elite attempting to impose its will for a foreign one is small progress if any. Scholars, regardless of nationality, must be attuned to the moral and ideological consequences of the research they do. The issue should not be merely who pays for research but also, and more important, who defines its terms, and what those terms are. The strong implication here is that scholars must, in order to avoid the sins of Orientalism, strive for independence. They must also, according to some of the writers in this book, be committed in their research to such concepts as justice, and undertake the task of representing the interests and aspirations of the disenfranchised in the Arab World. This, of course is easier to say than to accomplish but at least three related sets of ideas may help make these ideas operational.

1) RESEARCH MUST BE TRUE TO ITS SUBJECTS.   One possible strategy for dealing with the problem of legitimacy would be to try to insure that

scholarship becomes more understandable and meaningful to the subjects of the study. Research which is not true to its subjects is of questionable validity. One way to move in that direction is to consider the subjects as at least part of the intended audience for the final results of the research. In some cases this may involve oral presentations to them while in others it suggests more frequent translation of work done in foreign languages into an indigenous one. If scholars know they will have to face the subjects of research with the results of the endeavor, they may be more honest in their work. This proposal may be difficult, even impossible, to operationalize in all cases, but it might improve the quality of research in those cases where some form of it is possible. The problem of "representation" may be unavoidable; scholars in this field do "represent" subjects of research to an audience other than those subjects. Even if nationality is shared, representation takes place. When an Egyptian anthropologist studies an Egyptian village, for example, and presents the results to the Egyptian government, he or she has "represented" them to outsiders. If, however, research is tested against the litmus of the reaction of the subjects themselves, and if the policy objective of the research is on behalf of goals acceptable to those subjects, many if not all of the potentially morally questionable aspects of the research relationship can be eliminated. At least an effort should be made to put an end to the "hit and run" research often conducted for governments and other agencies, as well as for doctoral dissertations and other work, in which the researcher has a pre-prepared research framework into which data is forced and out of which a preordained result is extruded after the researcher has left the subjects of study, never to return.

2) DIALOGUE BETWEEN THE HOLDERS OF POWER AND SCHOLARS IS ESSENTIAL UNLESS SCHOLARSHIP IS TO BE IRRELEVANT.   One major problem facing researchers is how to deal with power, privilege, and tradition as they pertain to the Arab World. A related issue is the problem of demands for ideological conformity and what Said labelled "possessive exclusivism." It may be that certain types of research are not being conducted and perhaps cannot be done in the face of tradition, entrenched patriarchic or bureaucratic elites, or opposition by government leaders, whether those leaders are royal, military, or nominally democratic. Ideological mind guards can similarly constrain and proscribe research. To merely exhort against the holders of power may be emotionally comforting, but it seldom achieves anything practical. But to serve a particular

government or power holder at any particular time may be to become part of the problem rather than part of the solution. As if this were not enough, many social scientists feel that not serving the government may condemn them to irrelevance. These statements would seem to hold true regardless of whether the power holders or ideological purists in question are indigenous or are foreign groups trying to secure influence or markets in the area. Clearly, people in this field face a multi-sided and major conundrum. One possible solution may be to establish and maintain a discourse, based as much on solid empirical research as possible, between independent scholars and the holders of political and ideological power. This dialogue could and should include foreign as well as indigenous participants, as the authors of the essay on indigenization have reminded us that such a dialogue is likely to be intellectually fruitful for all concerned. For a variety of political and social reasons, foreign scholars may not be as constrained as indigenous ones by the impediments, discussed by Farah and Abu Jaber, which are presented by the prevailing political order in the area. They may, however, be blocked by nationality barriers from doing certain types of important work, a block which would obviously not apply to indigenous scholars. One possible strategy for overcoming this in some instances would be to employ multinational research teams to investigate topics of mutual interest within a framework which also facilitates the type of discourse referred to above.

3) PART OF THE ROLE OF INTELLECTUALS IS TO REPRESENT THE UN-REPRESENTED.   The Arab World is not unique in having large numbers of governments which are not fully representative of the interests, aspirations and opinions of major segments of the people over whom they rule. Whether the problem this pattern raises is unique is not the point, however. When it exists, intellectuals face a choice. Many elect to cater to the expressed needs of those who hold power. Others are driven by conscience or circumstance to become part of the opposition, while still others take on the role of something akin to a self-appointed public conscience. It is not for us to say which of these choices is best. We do suggest, however, that whichever option one picks, the problem of somehow representing the unrepresented remains. One tactic for dealing with this issue, even for foreign scholars, is to try to "give voice" to the weak, powerless and unrepresented by extensive and verbatim quotations as well as by rigorously and systematically polling such groups. In this way, their feelings, attitudes

and beliefs can become part of the debate and heard by some who otherwise would not want to listen to such views but who will now at least have the opportunity to do so.

COMPARATIVE AND INTERDISCIPLINARY RESEARCH ON CHANGE

Interdisciplinary and comparative research are imperative.

In books such as this it is almost customary to pay tribute to the value of interdisciplinary work. The authors of several of the essays in this book have done so, yet it must be recognized that this principle is honored more in the breach than in the doing. Several scholars have also called for more research which is explicitly and rigorously comparative, but this too is seldom done. Future volumes of this type should not merely call for more interdisciplinary and comparative work; they should contain specific examples of it so that progress can be made along this important front. One dimension of this problem is the "islands of theory" issue, in which progress is made in one area but not integrated or related to progress in another. In this case, better analysis of existing data could produce interesting and vital results if a conscious effort were made to bridge these islands. The Arab World is too diverse and complicated to lend itself to a single etiology theory of causation. Integration and synthesis of existing theoretical frameworks can become an important step in the creation of new paradigms. This too is a case where team research, interdisciplinary and cross-national if possible, would be especially useful.

Research cannot be truly comparative unless and until currently neglected topics and areas are covered more adequately.

One problem in Middle East studies in general and Arab studies in particular is that too much research covers the same countries and topics, to the relative neglect of other countries and topics. Some questions may not be addressed for political reasons, but that does not explain or justify the neglect of all of the important issues which could and should be studied in greater depth. This may be a bigger problem in some disciplines than in others, but it is likely to be true to some degree in all fields currently devoted to the study of the Arab World. We need to not only do a better job of analysing the data now available, especially by spanning the gaps between islands of theory, we need to collect and collate more data, especially regarding neglected areas and topics.

Economic, social and political change can provide an interesting and important focus for future research.

Korany, in his essay on foreign policy, suggests that the presence of controversy has been an important determinant of research topics. However, this begs the question as to who defines what is controversial and what is not. In the case of research on women, the field has attracted attention due more to the personal interest of a large number of women researchers than to a generally high profile regarding controversy over women per se, but the topic is also interesting simply because it involves manifestly important social change. This concern for change should be generalized to form part of a comprehensive research strategy. A few leading questions are obvious. Are different countries experiencing the same types of changes at roughly the same time? Are changes—social, economic or political—taking place because of local pressures, regional ones or are the sources global, affecting most of the world in a particular period? This is not the place to develop a full-blown research program directed at the phenomenon of change. For now, it is enough to raise the question: rather than plowing the same fields over and over again, why not try to identify arenas within which change is taking place, and devote more serious, cross-disciplinary and comparative research to them?

Several scholars now devote all or most of their research attention to the Arab World. This volume is a small contribution to what can become a more self-conscious community of scholars in the field of Arab studies and more broadly in Middle East studies.

Self-consciousness is important for a variety of reasons. Specialists should be aware of the advantages of concentrated knowledge but also must be aware that specialization carries the risk of parochialism. One word which is used perhaps more often than it should be in this book is "unique." It is probable that academics in Arab studies are too quick to ascribe uniqueness to several of the features of the Arab World. In striving to understand particularity it is necessary to avoid the myopia of seeing only Arab things, and failing to see how Arab social, economic and political life is part of and linked to the broader human drama.

Community is also vital, for it implies the sharing of aspirations and a general approach to scholarship. Even if people do not share nationality, ideology or academic discipline, such sharing is possible if there is a commonly accepted set of principles which define, in general terms, how they are to proceed. If scholars are part of such a community they may more easily build on each other's work and contribute to knowledge in a way which is cummulative.

The points made above suggest that such a community could and indeed should be built around certain shared notions. For example, scholars should be aware that research is not value free, and that humanists and social scientists alike must be true to their subjects and make some meaningful effort to give voice to the unrepresented. It should also be realized that an extended discourse between indigenous and foreign scholars, as well as with holders of power, is necessary if research is to be both relevant and intellectually enriched by all possible currents of thought. None of this will be easy and much of it will be resisted by many, but the effort should be worthwhile because it will contribute to the growth and development of a more productive scholarly community. Additionally, comparative and interdisciplinary work focused on change, and on relatively neglected topics, groups, and countries, is mandatory if we are to reach a stage where more scientifically valid and socially useful generalizations about the Arab World can be made.

One final point is worth making. Scholars should be aware that the audience for their work is not a disembodied, apolitical group of like-minded academics in which everyone shares all of the most important values and beliefs. Scholarly work has a variety of audiences, both within the academy and outside it, and its uses are not always clear to its producers or even subject to their control. Debate, discussion, and dissension are the norm, but, if they occur within the type of community mentioned, these potentially fractious activities will contribute more to its growth than its dissolution. It is in that spirit that this book has been written.

NOTES
1. Edward Said, *Orientalism* (New York: Pantheon Books, 1978), p. 202.
2. Ibid., p. 94.
3. Ibid., p. 92.
4. Ibid., p. 106.
5. Wilfred Cantwell Smith, *On Understanding Islam: Selected Studies* (The Hague: Mouton, 1981), p. 10.

PART ONE: NEO-ORIENTALISM

1   Orientalism Reconsidered

EDWARD W. SAID

THE PROBLEMS THAT I would like to take up each derive from the general issues addressed in *Orientalism*. The most important of these are: the representation of other cultures, societies, histories; the relationship between power and knowledge; the role of the intellectual; the methodological questions that have to do with the relationships between different kinds of texts, between text and context, between text and history.

I should clarify a couple of things at the outset. First, I use the word "Orientalism" less to refer to my book than to the problems to which my book is related; I shall be dealing with the intellectual and political territory covered both by *Orientalism* (the book) as well as the work I have done since. Second, I would not want it to be thought that this is an attempt to answer my critics. *Orientalism* elicited a great deal of comment, much of its positive and instructive; a fair amount of it was hostile and in some cases abusive. But the fact is that I have not digested and understood everything that was written or said. Instead, I have grasped those questions raised by my critics which strike me as useful in focussing an argument. Other observations—like my exclusion of German Orientalism, which no one has given any reason for me to have *included*—have frankly struck me as superficial, and there seems no point in responding to them. Similarly, the claim made by some, that I am ahistorical and inconsistent, would have more interest if the virtues of consistency, whatever may be intended by the term, were subjected to rigorous analysis; as for my ahistoricity, that too is a charge weightier in assertion than in proof.

As a department of thought and expertise, Orientalism of course involves several overlapping aspects: first, the changing historical and cultural relationship between Europe and Asia, a relationship with a 4,000-year-old history; second, the scientific discipline in the West according to which, beginning in the early nineteenth century, one specialised in the study of various Oriental cultures and traditions; and third, the ideological suppositions, images and fantasies about a region of the world called the Orient. The common denominator between these three aspects of Orientalism is the line separating Occident from Orient, and this, I have argued, is less a fact of nature than it is a fact of human production, which I have called imaginative geography. This, however, does not mean that the division between Orient and Occident is unchanging, nor that it is simply fictional. It is to say—emphatically—that, as with all aspects of what Vico calls the world of nations, the Orient and the Occident are facts produced by human beings, and as such must be studied as integral components of the social, and not the divine or natural, world. And because the social world includes the person or subject doing the studying as well as the object or realm being studied, it is imperative to include them both in any consideration of Orientalism. Obviously enough, there could be no Orientalism without, on the one hand, the Orientalists, and on the other, the Orientals.

This is, in reality, a fact basic to any theory of interpretation, or hermeneutics. Yet there is still a remarkable unwillingness to discuss the problems of Orientalism in the political or ethical or even epistemological contexts proper to it. This is as true of professional literary critics who have written about my book, as it is of the Orientalists themselves. Since it seems to me patently impossible to dismiss the truth of Orientalism's political origin and its continuing political actuality, we are obliged on intellectual as well as political grounds to investigate the resistance to the politics of Orientalism, a resistance symptomatic precisely of what is denied.

If the first set of questions is concerned with the problems of Orientalism reconsidered from the standpoint of local issues like who writes or studies the Orient, in what institutional or discursive setting, for what audience, and with what ends in mind, the second set of questions takes us to a wider circle of issues. These are the issues raised initially by methodology. They are considerably sharpened by questions as to how the production of knowledge best serves communal, as opposed to sectarian, ends; how knowledge that is nondominative and noncoercive can be produced in a setting that is deeply inscribed with the politics, the considerations, the positions and the strategies of power. In these methodological and moral reconsiderations of Orientalism, I shall quite consciously allude to similar issues raised by the experiences of feminism or women's studies, black or ethnic studies, socialist and anti-imperialist studies, all of which take for their point of departure the right of formerly un- or mis-represented human groups to speak for and represent themselves in domains defined, politically and intellectually, as normally excluding them, usurping their signifying and representing functions, overriding their historical reality. In short, Orientalism reconsidered in this wider and libertarian optic entails nothing less than the creation of objects for a new kind of knowledge.

I should return to the local problems I mentioned first. The hindsight of authors not only stimulates in them a sense of regret at what they could or ought to have done but did not; it also gives them a wider perspective in which to comprehend what they did. In my own case, I have been helped to achieve this broader understanding by nearly everyone who wrote about my book, and who saw it—for better or worse—as being part of current debates, contested interpretations and actual conflicts in the Arab-Islamic world, as that world interacts with the United States and Europe. In my own rather limited case, the consciousness of being an Oriental goes back to my youth in colonial Palestine and Egypt, although the impulse to resist its accompanying impingements was nurtured in the post-Second World War environment of independence when Arab nationalism, Nasserism, the 1967 War, the rise of the Palestine national movement, the 1973 War, the Lebanese Civil War, the Iranian Revolution and its horrific aftermath, produced that extraordinary series of highs and lows which has neither ended nor allowed us a full understanding of its remarkable revolutionary impact. It is difficult to try to understand a region of the world whose principal features seem to be that it is in perpetual flux, and that no one trying to comprehend it can, by an act of pure will or of sovereign understanding, stand at some Archimedean point outside the flux. That is, the very reason for understanding the Orient generally, and the Arab World in particular, was first, that it prevailed upon one, beseeched one's attention urgently, whether for economic, political, cultural or religious reasons, and second, that is defied neutral, disinterested or stable definition.

Similar problems are commonplace in the interpretation of literary texts. Each age, for instance, reinterprets Shakespeare, not because Shakespeare changes, but because, despite the existence of numerous and reliable editions of Shakespeare, there is no such fixed and nontrivial object as Shakespeare independent of his editors, the actors who played his roles, the translators who put him in other languages, the hundreds of millions of readers who have read him or watched performances of his plays since the late sixteenth century. On the other hand, it is too much to say that Shakespeare has no independent existence at all, and that he is completely reconstituted every time someone reads, acts or writes about him. In fact, Shakespeare leads an institutional or cultural life that among other things has guaranteed his eminence as a great poet, his authorship of thirty-odd plays, his extraordinary canonical powers in the West. The point I am making here is a rudimentary one: that even so relatively inert an object as a literary text is commonly supposed to gain some of its identity from its historical moment interacting with the attentions, judgements, scholarship and performances of its readers. But this privilege was rarely allowed the Orient, the Arabs or Islam, which separately or together were supposed by mainstream academic thought to be confined to the fixed status of an object frozen once and for all in time by the gaze of western percipients.

Far from being a defence either of the Arabs or Islam—as my book was taken by many to be—my argument was that neither existed except as "communities of interpretation," and that, like the Orient itself, each designation represented interests, claims, projects, ambitions and rhetorics that were not only in violent disagreement, but were in a situation of open warfare. So saturated with meanings, so overdetermined by history, religion and politics are labels like "Arab" or "Muslim" as subdivisions of "The Orient" that no one today can use them without some attention to the formidable polemical mediations that screen the objects, if they exist at all, that the labels designate.

The more such observations are made by one party, the more routinely they are denied by the other. Anyone who tries to suggest that nothing, not even a simple descriptive label, is beyond or outside the realm of interpretation is almost certain to find an opponent saying that science and learning are designed to transcend the vagaries of interpretation, and that objective truth is, in fact, attainable. This claim was more than a little political when used against Orientals who disputed the authority and objectivity of an Orientalism intimately allied with the great mass of European settlements in the Orient. At bottom, what I said in *Orientalism* has been said before me by A.L. Tibawi, by Abdullah Laroui, by Anwar Abdel Malek, by Talal Asad, by S.H. Alatas, by Frantz Fanon and Aimé Césaire, by Sardar K.M. Pannikar and Romila Thapar, all of whom had suffered the ravages of imperialism and colonialism, and who, in challenging the authority, provenance, and institutions of the science that represented them to

Europe, were also understanding themselves as something more than what this science said they were.

The challenge to Orientalism, and the colonial era of which it is so organically a part, was a challenge to the muteness imposed upon the Orient as object. Insofar as it was a science of incorporation and inclusion by virtue of which the Orient was constituted and then introduced into Europe, Orientalism was a scientific movement whose analogue in the world of politics was the Orient's colonial accumulation and acquisition by Europe. The Orient was, therefore, not Europe's interlocutor, but its silent Other. From roughly the end of the eighteenth century, when the Orient was rediscovered by Europe, its history had been a paradigm of antiquity and originality, functions that drew Europe's interests in acts of recognition or acknowledgement but *from* which Europe moved as its own industrial, economic and cultural development seemed to leave the Orient far behind. Oriental history—for Hegel, for Marx, later for Burkhardt, Nietzsche, Spengler and other major philosophers of history—was useful in portraying a region of great age, and what had to be left behind. Literary historians have further noted in all sorts of aesthetic writing and figurative portrayals that a trajectory of "Westering," found for example in Keats and Holderlin, customarily saw the Orient as ceding its historical preeminence and importance to the world spirit moving eastwards away from Asia and towards Europe.

As primitivity, as the age-old antetype of Europe, as a fecund night out of which European rationality developed, the Orient's actuality receded inexorably into a kind of paradigmatic fossilisation. The origins of European anthropology and ethnography were constituted out of its radical difference, and, to my knowledge, as a discipline, anthropology has not yet dealt with this inherent political limitation upon its supposedly disinterested universality. This is one reason Johannes Fabian's book, *Time and the Other: How Anthropology Constitutes Its Object,* is both unique and important. Compared, say, with the standard disciplinary rationalisations and self-congratulatory clichés about hermeneutic circles offered by Clifford Geertz, Fabian's serious effort to redirect anthropologists' attention back to the discrepancies in time, power and development between the ethnographer and his/her constituted object is all the more remarkable. In any event, what for the most part got left out of the discipline of Orientalism was the very history that resisted its ideological as well as political encroachments. That repressed or resistant history has now returned in the various critiques and attacks upon Orientalism, as a science of imperialism.

The divergences between the numerous critiques of Orientalism as ideology and praxis are very wide nonetheless. Some attack Orientalism as a prelude to assertions about the virtues of one or another native culture: these are the natives. Others criticise Orientalism as a defence against attacks on one or another political creed: these are the nationalists. Still others criticise Orientalism for falsifying the nature of Islam: these are, grosso modo, the believers. I will not adjudicate between these claims, except to say that I have avoided taking stands on such matters as the real, true or authentic Islamic or Arab World. But, in common with all the recent critics of Orientalism, I think that two things are especially important—one, a methodological vigilance that construes Orientalism less as a positive than as a critical discipline and therefore makes it subject to intense scrutiny, and two, a determination not to allow the segregation and confinement of the Orient to go on without challenge. My understanding of this second point has led me entirely to refuse designations like "Orient" and "Occident."

Depending on how they construed their roles as Orientalists, critics of the critics of Orientalism have either reinforced the affirmations of positive power in Orientalism's discourse or, much less frequently alas, they have engaged Orientalism's critics in a genuine intellectual exchange. The reasons for this split are self-evident: some have to do with power and age, as well as institutional or guild defensiveness; others have to do with religious or ideological convictions. All are political—something that not everyone has found easy to acknowledge. If I may use my own example, when some of my critics agreed with the main premises of my argument, they still tended to fall back on encomia to the achievements of what Maxime Rodinson called "la science orientaliste." This self-serving view lent itself to attacks on an alleged Lysenkism lurking inside the polemics of Muslims or Arabs who lodged a protest with "western" orientalism. This preposterous charge was made despite the fact that all the recent critics of Orientalism have been quite explicit about using such "western" critiques as marxism or structuralism in an effort to override invidious distinctions between East and West, between Arab and western truth, and the like.

Sensitised to the outrageous attacks upon an august and formerly invulnerable science, many certified professionals whose division of study is the Arabs and Islam have disclaimed any politics at all, while vigorously pressing an ideologically intended counter-attack. I should mention a few of the more typical imputations made against me so that you can see Orientalism extending its nineteenth-century arguments to cover an incommensurate

set of late twentieth-century eventualities. All of these derive from what to
the nineteenth-century mind is the preposterous situation of an Oriental
responding to Orientalism's asseverations. For unrestrained anti-
intellectualism, unencumbered by critical self-consciousness, no one has
quite achieved the sublime confidence of Bernard Lewis. His almost
purely political exploits require more time to mention than they are worth.
In a series of articles and one particularly weak book—*The Muslim Discovery of Europe*—Lewis has been busy responding to my argument, insisting
that the western quest for knowledge about other societies is unique, that
it is motivated by pure curiosity, and that, in contrast, Muslims were neither able nor interested in getting knowledge about Europe, as if knowledge about Europe was the only acceptable criterion for true knowledge.
Lewis's arguments are presented as emanating exclusively from the
scholar's apolitical impartiality, whereas he has become a widely rated authority for anti-Islamic, anti-Arab, Zionist and Cold War crusades, all of
them underwritten by a zealotry covered with a veneer of urbanity that has
very little in common with the "science" and learning Lewis purports to be
upholding.

Not quite as hypocritical, but no less uncritical, are younger ideologues
and Orientalists like Daniel Pipes. His arguments, as demonstrated in his
book *In the Path of God: Islam and Political Power*, would appear to be at
the service not of knowledge but of an aggressive and interventionary
state—the US—whose interests Pipes helps to define. Pipes speaks of Islam's anomie, its sense of inferiority, its defensiveness, as if Islam were one
simple thing, and as if the quality of his either absent or impressionistic evidence were of the most secondary importance. His book testifies to
Orientalism's unique resilience, its insulation from intellectual developments everywhere else in the culture, and its antediluvian imperiousness as
it makes its assertions and affirmations with little regard for logic or argument. I doubt that any expert anywhere in the world would speak today of
Judaism or Christianity with quite that combination of force and freedom
that Pipes allows himself about Islam. One would also have thought that a
book about Islamic revival would allude to parallel and related developments in styles of religious insurgence in, for example, Lebanon, Israel and
the US. Nor is it likely that anyone anywhere, writing about material for
which, in his own words, "rumor, hearsay, and other wisps of evidence"
are the only proof, will in the very same paragraph alchemically transmute
rumour and hearsay into "facts," on whose "multitude" he relies in order
"to reduce the importance of each." This is magic quite unworthy even of

high Orientalism, and although Pipes pays his obeisance to imperialist Orientalism, he masters neither its genuine learning nor its pretence at disinterestedness. For Pipes, Islam is a volatile and dangerous business, a political movement intervening in and disrupting the West, stirring up insurrection and fanaticism everywhere else.

The core of Pipes's book is not simply its highly expedient sense of its own political relevance to Reagan's America, where terrorism and communism merge into the media's image of Muslim gunners, fanatics and rebels, but its thesis that Muslims themselves are the worst source for their own history. The pages of *In the Path of God* are dotted with references to Islam's incapacity for self-representation, self-understanding, self-consciousness, and with praise for witnesses like V.S. Naipaul who are so much more useful and clever in understanding Islam. Here, of course, is the most familiar of Orientalism's themes; or: they cannot represent themselves, they must therefore be represented by others who know more about Islam than Islam knows about itself. Now, it is often the case that you can be known by others in different ways than you know yourself, and that valuable insights might be generated accordingly. But that is quite a different thing that pronouncing it as immutable law that outsiders ipso facto have a better sense of you as an insider than you do of yourself. Not that there is no question of an *exchange* between Islam's views and an outsider's: no dialogue, no discussion, no mutual recognition. There is a flat assertion of quality, which the western policymaker, or his faithful servant, possesses by virtue of his being western, white, non-Muslim.

Now this, I submit, is neither science, nor knowledge, nor understanding: it is a statement of power and a claim for absolute authority. It is constituted out of racism, and it is made comparatively acceptable to an audience prepared in advance to listen to its muscular truths. Pipes speaks to and for a large clientele for whom Islam is not a culture, but a nuisance; most of Pipes's readers will, in their minds, associate what he says about Islam with the other nuisances of the 1960s and 1970s—blacks, women, post-colonial Third World nations that have tipped the balance against the US in such places as UNESCO and the UN, and for their pains have drawn forth the rebuke of Senator Moynihan and Mrs. Kirkpatrick. In addition, Pipes—and the rows of like-minded Orientalists and experts he represents as their common denominator—stands for programmatic ignorance. Far from trying to understand Muslims in the context of imperialism and the revolt of an abused, but internally very diverse, segment of humanity, far from availing himself of the impressive recent works on Islam in different histories and societies, far from paying some attention to the immense advances in critical theory, in social science, in humanistic research and in the philosophy of interpretation, far from making some slight effort to acquaint himself with the vast imaginative literature in the Islamic world, Pipes obdurately and explicitly aligns himself with colonial Orientalists like Snouck Hurgronje and shamelessly pro-colonial renegades like V.S. Naipaul.

I have talked about Pipes only because he serves to make some points about Orientalism's large political setting, which is routinely denied and suppressed in the sort of claim proposed by its main spokesman, Bernard Lewis, who has the effrontery to disassociate Orientalism from its 200-year old partnership with European imperialism and associate it instead with modern classical philology and the study of ancient Greek and Roman culture. It is worth mentioning that this larger setting comprises two other elements, namely, the recent prominence of the Palestinian movement and the demonstrated resistance of Arabs in the United States and elsewhere against their portrayal in the public realm.

The question of Palestine and its fateful encounter with Zionism, on the one hand, and the guild of Orientalism, its professional caste-consciousness as a corporation of experts protecting their terrain and their credentials from outside scrutiny, on the other hand, together account for much of the animus against my critique of Orientalism. The ironies here are rich. Consider the case of one Orientalist who publicly attacked my book, he told me in a private letter, not because he disagreed with it—on the contrary, he felt that what I said was just—but because he had to defend the honour of his profession! Or, take the connection—explicitly made by two of the authors I cite in Orientalism, Renan and Proust—between Islamophobia and anti-Semitism. Here, one would have expected many scholars and critics to have seen the conjuncture, that hostility to Islam in the modern Christian West has historically gone hand in hand with, has stemmed from the same source, has been nourished at the same stream as anti-Semitism, and that a critique of the orthodoxies, dogmas and disciplinary procedures of Orientalism contributes to an enlargement of our understanding of the cultural mechanisms of anti-Semitism. No such connection has ever been made by critics, who have seen in the critique of Orientalism an opportunity for them to defend Zionism, support Israel and launch attacks on Palestinian nationalism. The reasons for this confirm the history of Orientalism, for, as the Israeli commentator Dani Rubenstein has remarked, the Israeli occupation of the West Bank and Gaza, the destruction of Palestinian society and the sustained Zionist assault upon Palestinian nationalism have quite literally been led and staffed by Orientalists. Whereas in the past, it was European Christian Orientalists who supplied European culture with arguments for colonising and suppressing Islam, as well as for despising Jews, it is not the Jewish national movement that produces a cadre of colonial functionaries whose ideological theses about the Islamic or Arab mind are implemented in the administration of the Palestinian Arabs, an oppressed minority within the white-European-democracy that is Israel. Rubenstein notes with some sorrow that the Hebrew University's Islamic studies department has produced every one of the colonial officials and Arab experts who run the Occupied Territories.

Another irony should be mentioned in this regard: just as some Zionists have construed it as their duty to defend Orientalism against its critics, there has been a comic effort by some Arab nationalists to see the Orientalist controversy as an imperialist plot to enhance American control over the Arab World. According to this implausible scenario, the critics of Orientalism are not anti-imperialists at all, but covert agents of imperialism. The logical conclusion from this is that the best way to attack imperialism is not to say anything critical about it. At this point, I concede that we have left reality for a world of illogic and derangement.

Underlying much of the discussion of Orientalism is a disquieting realisation that the relationship between cultures is both uneven and irremediably secular. This brings us to the point I alluded to a moment ago, about recent Arab and Islamic efforts, well-intentioned for the most part, but sometimes motivated by unpopular regimes, who, in drawing attention to the shoddiness of the western media in representing the Arabs or Islam, divert scrutiny from the abuses of their rule. Parallel developments have been occurring in UNESCO, where the controversy surrounding the world information order—and proposals for its reform by various Third World and socialist governments—has taken on the dimensions of a major international issues. Most of these disputes testify first to the fact that the production of knowledge, or information, of media images, is unevenly distributed: its main centres are located in what, on both sides of the divide, has been polemically called the metropolitan West. Second, this unhappy realisation, on the part of weaker parties and cultures, has reinforced their grasp of the fact that, although there are many divisions within it, there is only one secular and historical world, and that neither nativism, nor divine intervention, nor regionalism, nor ideological smokescreens can hide societies, cultures and peoples from each other, especially not from those with the force and will to penetrate others for political as well as economic ends. But, third, many of these disadvantaged post-colonial states and their loyalist intellectuals have, in my opinion, drawn the wrong conclusions, which are that one must either attempt to impose control upon the production of knowledge at the source, or, in the worldwide media market, attempt to improve, enhance, ameliorate the images currently in circulation without doing anything to change the political situation from which they emanate and by which they are sustained.

The failings of these approaches are obvious: one need not belabour such matters as the squandering of immense amounts of petro-dollars for short-lived public relations scams, or the increasing repression, human rights abuses, outright gangsterism that has taken place in many Third World countries, all of them occurring in the name of national security, and occasionally of fighting neo-imperialism. What I do want to talk about is the much larger question of what is to be done, and how we can speak of intellectual work that is not merely reactive or negative.

One of the legacies of Orientalism, and indeed one of its epistemological foundations, is historicism, that is, the view propounded by Vico, Hegel, Marx, Ranke, Dilthey and others, that if humankind has a history, it is produced by men and women, and can be understood historically, at given epochs or moments, as possessing a complex, but coherent unity. So far as Orientalism in particular and the European knowledge of other societies in general have been concerned, historicism meant that the one human history uniting humanity either culminated in or was observed from the vantage point of Europe, or the West. What was neither observed by Europe nor documented by it was, therefore, "lost" until, at some later date, it too could be incorporated by the new sciences of anthropology, political economics and linguistics. It is out of this later recuperation of what Eric Wolf has called people without history, that a still later disciplinary step was taken: the founding of the science of world history, whose major practitioners include Barudel, Wallerstein, Perry Anderson and Wolf himself.

But along with the greater capacity for dealing with—in Ernst Bloch's phrase—the nonsynchronous experiences of Europe's Other, has gone a fairly uniform avoidance of the relationship between European imperialism and these variously constituted and articulated knowledges. What has never taken place is an epistemological critique of the connection between the development of a historicism which has expanded and developed enough to include antithetical attitudes such as ideologies of western imperialism and critiques of imperialism, on the one hand, and, on the other, the actual practice of imperialism by which the accumulation of territories and population, the control of economies and the incorporation and homogenisation of histories are maintained. If we keep this in mind, we will remark, for example, that in the methological assumptions and practice of world history—which is ideologically anti-imperalist—little or no attention is given to those cultural practices, like Orientalism or ethnography, affiliated with imperialism, which in genealogical fact fathered world history itself. Hence, the emphasis in world history as a discipline has been on economic and political practices, defined by the processes of world historical writing, as in a sense separate and different from, as well as unaffected by, the knowledge of them which world history produces. The curious result is that the theories of accumulation on a world scale, or the capitalist world system, or lineages of absolutism a) depend on the same percipient and historicist observer who had been an Orientalist or colonial traveller three generations ago; b) they depend also on a homogenising and incorporating world historical scheme that assimilated nonsynchronous developments, histories, cultures and peoples to it; and c) they block and suppress latent epistemological critiques of the institutional, cultural and disciplinary instruments linking the incorporative practice of world history with, on one hand, partial knowledges like Orientalism, and on the other, with continued "western" hegemony of the non-European, "peripheral" world.

The problem is once again historicism and the universalising and self-validating that has been endemic to it. Bryan Turner's important little book, *Marx and The End of Orientalism,* went a great distance towards fragmenting, dissociating, dislocating and decentring the experiential terrain covered at present by universalising historicism. What he suggests, in discussing the epistemological dilemma, is the need to go beyond the polarities and binary oppositions of marxist-historicist thought (voluntarisms v. determinism, Asiatic v. western society, change v. stasis) in order to create a new type of analysis of plural, as opposed to single, objects. Similarly, in a series of studies produced in interrelated and frequently unrelated fields, there has been a general advance in the process of breaking up, dissolving and methdologically as well as critically reconceiving the unitary field ruled hitherto by Orientalism, historicism and what could be called essentialist univeralism.

I shall give examples of this dissolving and decentring process in a moment. What needs to be said about it immediately is that it is neither purely methodological nor purely reactive in intent. You do not respond, for example, to the tyrannical conjuncture of colonial power with scholarly Orientalism simply by proposing an alliance between nativist sentiment buttressed by some variety of native ideology to combat them. This, for example, has been the trap into which many Third World and anti-imperialist activists fell in supporting the Iranian and Palestinian struggles, and who found themselves either with nothing to say about the abominations of Khomeini's regime or resorting, in the Palestine case, to the time-worn cliches of revolutionism and rejectionary armed-strugglism after the Lebanese debacle. Nor can it be a matter simply of recycling the old marxist or world historical rhetoric, whose dubious accomplishment is merely the reestablishment of the intellectual and theoretical ascendancy of the old, by now impertinent and genealogically flawed, conceptual modes. No: we must, I believe, think both in political and theoretical terms, locating the main problems in what the Frankfurt theory identified as domination and division of labour. We must confront also the problem of the absence of a theoretical, utopian and libertarian dimension in analysis. We cannot proceed unless we dissipate and redispose the material of historicism into radically different pursuits of knowledge, and we cannot do that until we are aware that no new projects of knowledge can be constituted unless they resist the dominance and professionalised particularism of historicist systems and reductive, pragmatic or functionalist theories.

These goals are less difficult than my description sounds. For the reconsideration of Orientalism has been intimately concerned with many other activities of the sort I referred to earlier, and what it now becomes imperative to articulate in more detail. Thus, we can now see that Orientalism is a praxis of the same sort as male gender dominance, or patriarchy, in metropolitan societies: the Orient was routinely described as feminine, its riches as fertile, its main symbols the sensual woman, the harem and the despotic—but curiously attractive—ruler. Moreover, Orientals, like housewives, were confined to silence and to unlimited enriching production. Much of this material is manifestly connected to the configurations of sexual, racial and political asymmetry underlying mainstream modern western culture, as illuminated respectively by feminists, by black studies critics and by anti-imperialist activists. To read, for example, Sandra Gilbert's brilliant recent study of H. Rider Haggard's *She* is to perceive the narrow correspondence between suppressed Victorian sexuality at home, its fantasies abroad and the tightening hold on the nineteenth-century male imagination of imperialist ideology. Similarly, a work like Abdul Jan Mohammed's *Manichean Aesthetics* investigates the parallel, but unremittingly separate artistic worlds of white and black fictions of the same place, Africa, suggesting that even in imaginative literature a rigid ideological system operates beneath a freer surface. Or in a study like Peter Gran's *The Islamic Roots of Capitalism,* which is written out of an anti-imperialist and anti-Orientalist, meticulously researched and scrupulously concrete historical stance, one can begin to sense what a vast invisible terrain of human effort and ingenuity lies beneath the frozen Orientalist surface formerly carpeted by the discourse of Islamic or Oriental economic history.

There are many more examples of analysis and theoretical projects undertaken out of similar impulses as those fuelling the anti-Orientalist critique. All of them are interventionary in nature, that is, they self-consciously situate themselves at vulnerable conjunctural nodes of ongoing disciplinary discourses where each of them posits nothing less than new objects of knowledge, new praxes of humanist activity, new theoretical models that upset or, at the very least, radically alter the prevailing paradigmatic norms. One might list here such disparate efforts as Linda Nochlin's explorations or nineteenth-century Orientalist ideology as working within major art-historical contexts; Hanna Batatu's immense restructuring of the terrain of the modern Arab state's political behaviour; Raymond Williams's sustained examination of structures of feeling, communities of knowledge, emergent of alternative cultures, patterns of geographical thought (as in his remarkable *The Country and The City*); Talal Asad's account of anthropological self-capture in the work of major theorists, and his own studies in the field; Eric Hobsbawm's new formulation of "the invention of tradition" or invented practices studied by historians as a crucial index both of the historian's craft and, more important, of the invention of new emergent nations; the work produced in reexamination of Japanese, Indian and Chinese culture by scholars like Masao Miyoshi, Eqbal Ahmad, Tariq Ali, A. Sivanandan, Romila Thapar, the group around Ranajit Guha *(Subaltern Studies),* Gayati Spivak, and younger scholars like Homi Bhabha and Partha Mitter; the freshly imaginative reconsideration by Arab literary critics—the *Fusoul* and *Mawakif* groups, Elias Khouri, Kamal Abu Deeb, Mohammad Bannis, and others—seeking to redefine and invigorate the reified classical structures of Arabic literary tradition, and, as a parallel to that, the imaginative works of Juan Goytisolo and Salman Rushdie, whose fictions and criticism are self-consciously written against the cultural stereotypes and representations commanding the field. It is worth mentioning here, too, the pioneering efforts of the *Bulletin of Concerned Asian Scholars,* and the fact that twice recently, in their presidential addresses, an American Sinologist (Benjamin Schwartz) and Indologist (Ainslee Embree) have reflected seriously upon what the critique of Orientalism means for their fields, a public reflection as yet denied Middle Eastern scholars. Perennially, there is the work carried out by Noam Chomsky in political and historical fields, an example of independent radicalism and uncompromising severity unequalled by anyone else today; or in literary theory, the powerful theoretical articulations of a social, in the widest and deepest sense, model for narrative put forward by Fredric Jameson; Richard Ohmann's empirically arrived-at definitions of canon privilege and institution in his recent work; revisionary Emersonian perspectives formulated in the critique of contemporary technological and imaginative, as well as cultural ideologies by Richard Poirier; and the decentring, redistributive ratios of intensity and drive studied by Leo Bersani.

In conclusion, I should try to draw them together into a common endeavour which can inform the larger enterprise of which the critique of Orientalism is part. First, we note a plurality of audiences and constituencies; none of the works and workers I have cited claims to be working on behalf of one audience which is the only one that counts, or for one supervening, overcoming Truth, a truth allied to western (or for that matter eastern) reason, objectivity, science. On the contrary, we note here a plurality of terrains, multiple experiences and different constituencies, each with its admitted (as opposed to denied) interest, political desiderata, disciplinary goals. All these efforts work out of what might be called a decentred consciousness, not less reflective and critical for being decentred, for the most part non- and in some cases anti-totalising and anti-systematic. The result is that instead of seeking common unity by appeals to a centre of sovereign authority, methodological consistency, canonicity and science, they offer the possibility of common grounds of assembly between them. They are, therefore, planes of activity and praxis, rather than one topography commanded by a geographical and historical vision locatable in a known centre of metropolitan power. Second, these activities and praxes are consciously secular, marginal and oppositional with reference to the mainstream, generally authoritarian systems against which they now agitate. Third, they are political and practical inasmuch as they intend—without necessarily succeeding—the end of dominating, coercive systems of knowledge. I do not think it too much to say that the political meaning of analysis, as carried out in all these fields, is uniformly and programmatically libertarian by virtue of the fact that, unlike Orientalism, it is not based on the finality and closure of antiquarian or curatorial knowledge, but on investigative open analysis, even though it might seem that analyses of this sort—frequently difficult and abstruse—are in the final count paradoxically quietistic. We must remember the lesson provided by Adorno's negative dialectics, and regard analysis as in the fullest sense being *against* the grain, deconstructive, utopian.

But there remains the one problem haunting all intense, self-convicted and local intellectual work, the problem of the division of labour, which is a necessary consequence of that reification and commodification first and most powerfully analysed in this century by Georg Lukacs. This is the problem, sensitively and intelligently put by Myra Jehlen for women's studies, whether, in identifying and working through anti-dominant critiques, subaltern groups—women, blacks, and so on—can resolve the dilemma of autonomous fields of experience and knowledge that are created as a consequence. A double kind of possessive exclusivism could set in: the sense of being an excluding insider by virtue of experience (only women can write for and about women, and only literature that treats women or Orientals well is good literature), and second, being an excluding insider by virtue of method (only marxists, anti-orientalists, feminists can write about economics, Orientalism, women's literature).

This is where we are at now, at the threshold of fragmentation and specialisation, which impose their own parochial dominations and fussy defensiveness, or on the verge of some grand synthesis which I, for one, believe could very easily wipe out both the gains and the oppositional consciousness provided by these counter-knowledges hitherto. Several possibilities propose themselves; I shall conclude simply by listing them. A need for greater crossing of boundaries, for greater interventionalism in cross-disciplinary activity, a concentrated awareness of the situation—political, methodological, social, historical—in which intellectual and cultural work is carried out. A clarified political and methodological commitment to the dismantling of systems of domination which since they are collectively maintained must, to adopt and transform some of Gramsci's phrases, be collectively fought, by mutual siege, war of manoeuvre and war of position. Lastly, a much sharpened sense of the intellectual's role both in the defining of a context and in changing it, for without that, I believe, the critique of Orientalism is simply an ephemeral pastime.

Reprinted with permission from *Race and Class* XXVII, no. 2 (Autumn 1985), pp. 1–15.

2 Hermeneutics of the Old and New Orientalism

Antonio Roberto Gualtieri

ORIENTALISM AND THE HERMENEUTIC OF DOMINATION

As EDWARD SAID has asserted, Orientalism is not a transcendental access to objective knowledge of the peoples and civilizations of the East, and especially the Islamic world, but is rather an historical product. He says, "Orient and Occident are manmade."[1] Further, "'The Orient' is itself a constituted entity."[2] "Orientalism is a 'system of ideological fictions.'"[3] More specifically, Orientalism is a cultural product of European and, latterly, American provenance. In this respect Said says, "the Orient was almost a European invention."[4]

But Orientalism is not a pure product of the imagination. Rather, it is an expression and means of Western power and domination over the Orient. Said writes:

I myself believe that Orientalism is more particularly valuable as a sign of European-Atlantic power over the Orient than it is a veridical discourse about the Orient (which is what, in its academic or scholarly form, it claims to be). In Foucault's language, Orientalism is a 'discourse of power.'

In sum, Orientalism is a complex, western, cultural product with three interdependent factors: 1) Orientalism is an academic tradition or scholarly enterprise; 2) Orientalism is an affair of the imagination, a style of thought about the other, construed in this instance as the mysterious and somewhat degenerate easterner; 3) Orientalism is a western

51

institution for "dominating, restructuring, and having authority over the Orient." [5]

This interpretation of Orientalism as a human cultural product serving the imperial compulsions of the West does not mean that Orientalism may be dismissed as a phantasmagoric mist that evaporates the moment the bright morning sun of truth is turned upon it. It is closely intertwined with "enabling socio-economic and political institutions" which lie at its base and bestow "redoubtable durability." In other words, Orientalism is a cultural super-structure whose material base is the West's imperialist relation to the Orient.

Since one ingredient of the complex Orientalist structure of domination is the academic enterprise, certain epistemological and hermeneutical questions come to the fore. What is the nature and status of scholary statements? Can they claim to be true in some objective sense?

Said feels obliged to disclose his own assumptions on these questions under the rubric of "the distinction between pure and political knowledge." Said is a literary critic and his concerns reflect the ongoing debate in that field between the positions represented by Hans-Georg Gadamer and E.D. Hirsch.[6] On the one side, there is the allocratic view epitomized by Hirsch (at least during one period) asserting that interpretations of texts (and by extension, other cultural products) are objectively cognitive in important degrees. Our interpretations are capable of grasping, in significant measure, the object as it is, that is, the meaning intended by historical authors and creators or classical interpreters.

On the other side is the autocratic view represented by Gadamer contending that our interpretations are "political" acts, that is, projections or applications of subjective needs and purposes upon the text or thing to be grasped. Said adopts, on the whole, the autocratic or subjectivist option. He writes:

No one has ever devised a method for detaching the scholar from the circumstances of life, from the fact of his involvement (conscious or unconscious) with a class, a set of beliefs, a social position, or from the mere activity of being a member of a society. These continue to bear on what he does professionally. . . . [7]

Granted, there are ambiguities in Said's elaboration of his hermeneutical position. The very phrase which follows the citation above goes on to say that "naturally enough his research and its fruits do attempt to reach a level of relative freedom from the inhibitions and the restrictions of brute everyday reality." The next sentence continues: "For there is such a thing as knowledge that is less, rather than more, partial than the individual (with his entangling and distracting life circumstances) who produces it." Perplexity deepens when this assertion (which appears to support a dialectical view of the observer's subjective role in the production of knowledge) is immediately followed by the claim: "Yet this knowledge is not therefore automatically nonpolitical." We are left uncertain as to just where Said stands on the question of interpretation.

Further evidence of Said's hermeneutical ambivalence is to be seen in his confession:

> I would not have undertaken a book of this sort if I did not also believe that there is a scholarship that is not as corrupt, or at least as blind to human reality, as the kind I have been mainly depicting. An excellent recent instance is the anthropology of Clifford Geertz.[8]

There are traces in *Orientalism* that Said wishes to maintain a dialectical view which recognizes that subjective, culturally specific factors exercise a scholarly influence on a spectrum ranging from propaganda to a relative grasp of the objective nature of the expressions under investigation. Nevertheless, the residual effect of the sustained and repetitive argument of his book is to emphasize the subjectivist and relativist dimensions of scholarship.

Said evinces, as do many contemporary literary critics, a substantial indebtedness to Nietzsche's dictum that, "Truths are illusions about which one has forgotten that this is what they are." Although Said employs Nietzsche's term "perspectivism" only in a footnote, it is clear that this is the orientation that guides much of Said's analysis of Orientalism, as it does his hermeneutical approach in general. According to perspectivism, all human achievements, even such intellectual ones as science and philosophy that masquerade as knowledge, or artistic ones such as music and poetry, are in fact only subjective perspectives on the world and not a cognitive grasp of the world of objects as they really are. Such perspectives function to enhance the will to power of the observers and creators. It is one of the paradoxes of the will to power that allegations of objective truth serve to enhance the self-expression and domination of those who make such claims.

Temperamentally and philosophically I am much attracted by such sub-jectivist hermeneutical perspectives. I recall vividly reading Abraham Hes-chel's book *Israel: An Echo Of Eternity,* which I had been asked to review. Heschel, in my personal hagiography was numbered amongst the saints; I resonated both to his concerns with morality and with mysticism. I appre-ciated the peace-seeking initiatives which he took during America's Viet-nam war. Nevertheless, it was his book as much as anything else that caused me to despair about the scholar's vocation. That book is an aston-ishing assembly of the stereotypes and charades that have plagued the Pal-estinian question. I was astounded that shop-worn calumnies and propa-gandistic justifications could be advanced by so prominent and moral a scholar in defence of Israel's actions, particularly during the 1967 war to which the book was a response. It struck me that scholarly claims to seek objective truth and to formulate statements about things that approximate to the way they are in reality was one monstrous illusion, and that scholars, like all lesser mortals, were the victims of subjective historical and cultural forces that predetermine what could be seen and how it would be valued. Said also generalizes from a specific instance of ideological scholarship to a general critique of intellectual pretension: "A powerful series of political and ultimately ideological realities inform scholarship today... Contem-porary Orientalism teaches us a great deal about the intellectual dishonesty of dissembling on that score. . . . "[9] Accordingly, I have an initial disposi-tion to concur in Said's hermeneutic that descries in the history of western encounter with the East, including its academic tradition, an expression of cultural deformation and domination that employs the presumptive truth claims of scholarship to further the purposes of imperial control. "Orien-talism calls in question the possibility of nonpolitical scholarship" says Said, and I am inclined to agree.

Yet, I have to conclude that Said's thesis is the victim of overkill. Its condemnation of the tradition of western scholarship about the Muslim world is unrelieved. In fact, it strikes me as so strange as to almost ap-proach dishonesty that he would publish in 1978 a book sweepingly in-dicting western scholarship about the Muslim world without so much as mentioning in a footnote the work of Wilfred Cantwell Smith, which by this time had already attained a place of considerable prominence in schol-arship on Islam. The proper assessment of Said's thesis on Orientalism is not that it is wrong, but that it is monolithic and undialectical. There can be little doubt that his portrayal of the western tradition of scholarship about Islam does, in fact, accord in important measure with the way things have been. However, though his criticisms extend into the modern period to include the work of Bernard Lewis and H.A.R. Gibb, he does not have a word to say about Marshall Hodgson and Cantwell Smith. Moreover, in light of Smith's testimony to the value and percipience of his teacher Gibb's work, I am inclined to question Said's numbering of Gibb amongst the gallery of culprits. I myself gratefully acknowledge the usefulness, at an early stage of my understanding of Islam, of Gibb's survey—unfortunately entitled *Mohammedanism*.

WILFRED CANTWELL SMITH'S PERSONALIST HERMENEUTIC

The "new Orientalism" largely ignored by Said is evinced in the work of Wilfred Cantwell Smith. Smith's studies in Islam are carried out on the basis of a personalist hermeneutic that allows him an important and valuable degree to transcend the prevailing western outlook on Islam and to see it from the participant's point of view. This is exemplified in his treatment of Islamic law where he contrasts the western view of *shari'ah* as an historical product, with the Muslim understanding of it as an eternal pattern deriving from the mind of God. Smith explains that:

> The term *Islam* in the Qur'an itself has been the object of considerable study both by Muslims and recently by western scholars. The two groups differ in that the latter, regarding the text as expressive of the mind of Muhammad, aim at reconstructing the historical meaning of the seventh century A.D. whereas Muslims, regarding it as expressive, if we may say so of the mind of God, may legitimately interpret it in the light of a continuingly contemporary understanding of its timeless validity.[10]

A succinct summary of the personalist methodology that animates Smith's study of Islam and the history of religions in general is to be found in the preface to his 1961 CBC (Canadian Broadcasting Corporation) radio talk on "The Shaha-dah as Symbolic Representation of Muslims' Faith" where he says:

> Rather than proffering as expected a brief outline of the various "systems." I tried instead to convey a sense of what it might be like to be a

human being living in the light of one or other of them. . . This approach was in line with my general position that "the study of religion is the study of persons," and that one should think not of an abstraction called "Hinduism," "Buddhism," or the like but of the way that the various elements constituting these are seen by participants. The various "religions" as concepts are potentially misleading abstractions, I had come to feel, and the task of the student of religion is not to focus on them nor on their data except as a step towards understanding how those data are perceived by persons of faith; and even more, how the world is perceived, and life in their light.[11]

This conviction that the primary role of the scholar of religion is to ferret out the way in which the rich symbolic life of participants in a cumulative religious tradition mediates the sense of reality and the authoritative values by which they ought to live, runs through all of Smith's work. The primary object of study is not an abstract, reified system typically expressed in intellectual terms, nor some objectified history, but rather, the intersection of the tradition with the faith of the participants. What the sensitive observer grasps is the participants' transcending vision of reality that their tradition mediates and by which they seek to live. The adoption of a personalist outlook in religious studies provides a theoretical bulwark against that academic manipulation of data which results in the falsification of religious persons and cultures. In commenting upon his article entitled, "Some Similarities and Some Differences Between Christianity and Islam" Smith says, "In line with my general personalist orientation, it shifted the focus of attention from the data of any given religious 'system' to the role of those data in the lives of the persons concerned."[12]

Smith demonstrates a critical spirit that makes him question prevailing western assumptions with regard to other religions and other cultures and, at the same time, makes him capable of respecting the autonomy of Islam. He writes, for example, in "Islamic History as a Concept":

For it is a fallacy growing out of the particularities of the modern West to think of religion as one of the factors in human life, one among others. To impose this Western-cultural aberration on one's understanding of other civilizations is to distort.[13]

Considerable criticism has been levied against Smith for his claim that to proceed, as has most western secular scholarship, in total disregard of the transcendent element in human life and history, is to fail to understand the Islamic vision and Muslim history. In this respect he says, "The work [on Islamic law] constituted for me an important step in my discernment of the transcendent element in the conceptualizing by Muslims of their world."[14]

An important feature of Smith's style of Orientalism is its confirmatory procedure. Smith argues that it should be the goal of scholars of comparative religion to make statements about the faith of others that are recognizable as relatively accurate representations by the very persons about whom they are made. Thus Smith, as a western Christian scholar, seeks to formulate descriptions and interpretations of Islam that are intelligible not only to the community of western academics, but also to educated Muslims. In commenting upon his lecture, "Is the Qur'an the Word of God?" he demonstrates that he practices what he preaches. He says, "As usual, I did not publish this piece until I had tried it out also on a Muslim audience, which I had had an opportunity to do in India the following year." In generalizing his procedures Smith writes:

> The arguments of a student of religion, or of a particular religious or indeed any human community, should in principle be persuasive to other intellectuals, not only, but in addition also to intelligent and alert members of the group[s] about which he and she writes.[15]

Implicit in Smith's personalist hermeneutic is a genuine humility which functions as a safeguard against presumptuous and dominating judgments about the other. In his Iqbal Memorial lectures delivered at the University of Punjab in 1974 he says:

> Although it would be awkward for me actually to write the entire lecture in this form, nonetheless, especially this evening with the Islamic material, I am quite genuinely, and firmly, in effect prefacing every sentence of my talk, and certainly the total presentation of it, with the question: "Is it the case that... ?" I hope that each of you will accept this question as directed to him; and will be kind enough to let me know your answer. I sincerely hope that you will tell me how far I have understood, and how far I have misunderstood, the Islamic position.[16]

It was precisely Smith's attempt to understand Islam in a way that would win the consent of Muslims that propelled him upon a thorough-going revision of the customary ways of thinking about religion and conducting religious study in the western, secular-dominated university. A reductionist secularism pervading the academy had resulted in a methodological inability to come to terms with Islam and, as Smith was subsequently to generalize, with the whole of humankind's classical religious history. He contrasted the conventional orientation of secular Orientalism with the novel and respectful categories that would be necessary in this way:

> The standard Western orientalist has tended to look at Islam as a mundane phenomenon, an historical actuality that he objectively studies. For him it is not an idea in the mind of God, but a purely human construction on the stage of history. I personally do not share this; and indeed part of my present study in trying to wrestle with the problem of an outsider attempting to understand a religion not his own is pushing me to the conclusion that such understanding requires a fairly serious revision of many of our terms and concepts.[17]

An unexpected stress in Edward Said is his insistence that one of the consequences of Western Orientalism has been to characterize Muslims as creatures apart; that is to say, as persons with a tradition and orientation that distinguishes them radically from others, especially Westerners. I say that this is unexpected because the dominant trend in the contemporary world seems to be the assertion of uniqueness—particularly national and cultural. In the face of cultural and economic imperialism from the West, the instinctive response has been to assert the legitimacy of cultural autonomy and the value of the distinct cultural heritages of colonized peoples. Over against this prevailing pattern, we discern Said berating Orientalism for its failure to recognize the universal humanity of eastern peoples, preferring its exotic pictures of the mysterious, even sinister, Oriental.

Clearly, the preferred solution to this problem is a dialectical one that recognizes in all persons and cultures the interplay of distinctive psychological, cultural and historical forces on the one hand, and a universal, shared human essence on the other. Ironically, an Orientalist of the stripe of Cantwell Smith has been censured by some critics for adopting an interpretation of religion which emphasizes universal human faith, thereby obscuring allegedly the particularities of the history of diverse religious communities. This is yet another instance of Smith in fact doing the very thing which Said claims western Orientalists do not do, i.e., perceive the universal humanness of eastern peoples.

In the prefatory remarks to his paper entitled "Religious Diversity: Muslim-Hindu Relations in India," Smith observes:

> It is obtuse, I have felt, not to recognize both the unitedness and the dividedness of humankind. Given my concern for the former, I have at times perhaps appeared to some to be less than duly sensitive to the latter. This would be delinquent not only as regards India and its history, but for religious and in fact for human diversity at large. It would be superficial to underestimate the persistent and radical nature of our human differences; or to suppose that one may bypass these or may subordinate them to some glib generalized thesis. Rather, and this I had come to see as near the heart of comparative religious study, and of human-history study: one must recognize diversity in its full starkness, wrestle with it in its full recalcitrance, and come out with synthesis, if at all, only very clearly on the other side.[18]

In other words, although Smith is dedicated to the discernment of the common human essence which is so important to Said, he feels it would be equally insulting and dehumanizing towards people of other faiths to assimilate them too readily into common categories in such a way as would deprive them of the value of their unique histories and careers.

CONCLUSION

I believe sufficient evidence has been marshalled to support the point that Said's critique of western Orientalism is vitiated by its selective purview that excludes representatives of a "new Orientalism" exemplified in my discussion on Wilfred Cantwell Smith. No doubt there are others in addition to Hodgson and Geertz. The case of Smith is particularily useful because of his hermeneutical self-consciousness; the title of his book is deliberately chosen for its multivalence. His intention is not only to set out certain scholarly conclusions about the history and quality of *Islam,* but also to delineate certain methodological procedures for the *study* of Islam.

In a sense, Said's program resembles Smith's; Said's purpose is not only to record the content of Orientalism's enquiry into Islam, but also, and mainly, to analyse the hermeneutic of domination that was (and still is) at work.

How should Said's argument be assessed? I have said little about specific scholars identified by Said as instances of Orientalism in its pejorative falsifying and imperialistic sense; he has been excoriated by some critics on the grounds of misrepresentation. My own judgement is that however mistaken he might be in particular instances advanced as evidence, Said has correctly discerned and analysed a general tendency in western scholarship respecting Islam. The chief stricture to be levelled against Said is that his work lends itself to the interpretation that "Orientialism," as he depicts it, exhausts the whole (or nearly so) of the western academic study of Islam. To criticize Said for partiality of judgement, however, is not to deny that he had an important point. Wilfred Cantwell Smith expresses, in effect, a degree of agreement with Said's condemnation of the western Orientalist enterprise. Smith draws attention to the way in which much western scholarship of the past has demeaned Islam in Muslim eyes by detranscendentalizing it. Whereas Muslims, for the most part, have understood Islam as either faith, that is, an active personal involvement with God or, alternatively, as the ideal pattern for life revealed by God to Muhammad, the western Orientalist has reduced it to a human, historical manifestation.

My focus has been on the contrasting hermeneutical approaches of the old and new Orientalism. Accuracy demands that we acknowledge, beside the target of Said's attack, another possibility within western scholarship about Islam which I have designated the "new Orientalism." This alternative approach to the religious faith of others—so fruitfully pursued by Cantwell Smith—is animated by a personalist hermeneutic in place of the objectifying hermeneutic of domination.

NOTES

1. Edward Said, *Orientalism,* (New York: Pantheon Books, 1978), p. 5.
2. Ibid., p. 322.
3. Ibid., p. 321.
4. Ibid., p. 1.
5. Ibid., p. 328.
6. Gadamer approaches hermeneutics as a philosopher; Hirsch as a professor of English. The issues entailed in this debate concerning allocratic and autocratic theories of interpretation may be discerned in E.D. Hirsch Jr., "The Politics of Theories of Interpretation," *Critical Inquiry* (9 September 1982).
7. Said, p. 10.

8. Ibid., p. 326.
9. Ibid., p. 327.
10. Wilfred Cantwell Smith, *On Understanding Islam: Selected Studies* (The Hague: Mouton, 1981), p. 46. In this chapter I have restricted my citations to this single book of Smiths. Because the book is a sort of reprise of Smith's entire career in the study of Islam and the hermeneutical implications of such study, it serves to focus the issue discussed in the chapter.
11. Ibid., p. 26.
12. Ibid., p. 223.
13. Ibid., pp. 15–16.
14. Ibid., p. 87.
15. Ibid., p. 282.
16. Ibid., p. 115.
17. Ibid., p. 59.
18. Ibid., pp. 217–18.

PART TWO: METHODOLOGICAL PERSPECTIVES ON THE STUDY OF THE ARAB WORLD

3 Dilemmas in Middle Eastern Social Sciences
*Contours of the Problem of the Relevance of Western
Paradigms as Guides to Research, Policy and Practice*

MARK C. KENNEDY

THE INROADS OF COLONIALISM into the Middle East followed the decline of the Ottoman Empire. These inroads were subsequently traversed by European social scientists representing every discipline, and those vanguards of western progressive thought brought with
them a variety of theories as paradigms for the understanding of societies
and cultures that were already under colonial rule.[1] Thus entered the functionalism of Durkheim, the historico-cultural relativism of Weber, and the
historical materialism of Marx—all of which were nineteenth century in
European creations.

Despite the remarkable differences between these theoretical models,
their modern protagonists were convinced that their common intellectual
foes were the social and political philosophers of the eighteenth century
and their intellectual counterparts of today. Equally convinced they were
that their own training and methods would enable them to understand
Middle Eastern societies, their evolutionary dynamics and enable them
also to articulate their findings in the language of science. As early as 1940,
for example, E.E. Evans-Pritchard and Meyer Fortes declared:

> We have not found that the theories of political philosphers have
> helped us to understand the societies we have studied, and we consider
> them of little scientific value.[2]

Functionalism lent to social anthropology a certain geometry and co-
herence, facts fitted into this view of society-as-organism and gave "society" the appearance of an articulated whole, changing only by functional

differentiation along a lineal continuum, from simple and sacred to heterogeneous and rational. Beginning in the early 1960s, as other paradigms were introduced in the study of the Middle East, functionalism as a model for research and understanding languished. Its near demise was not due so much to the "success" of other paradigms as to a critical rethinking of this model as a guide to understanding. Anthropologists *in situ,* and not solely their detractors, became quite aware of the limitations of functionalism as a tool for scientific understanding.

By the 1960s then, functional theorists enjoyed no higher a prestige as a science than they had earlier attributed to the speculative philosophers of the eighteenth century. Functionalism had "ceased to carry conviction."[3] Worsley, five years later, spelled out the conditions of this demise in his treatise, *The End of Anthropology.* By 1970, social anthropology could not be viewed as a coherent, rigorious body of knowledge.[4] Obviously, something had to be done to rescue anthropological credibility. What could be done to explain this quick transition from conviction to disenchantment?

Swartz, Turner and Tuden[5] averred that anthropology had become too ingrown, too out of touch with other disciplines. Being out of touch seemed to explain their plight. The solution proposed was to establish "a dialogue, if not a marriage, between anthropology and the other disciplines concerned with comparative politics."[6] This seemingly sensible idea was based, however, on a false premise.

Given the fact that each discipline is itself fragmented by highly divergent, theoretical perspectives, such a "marriage" of social anthropology to other disciplines is a house of subdued intellectual conflict. To argue that interdisciplinary dialogue would resolve any of those disputes is a claim based on misplaced concreteness. The dialogue that should take place is not so much between the disciplines as it is within them in an effort to resolve the divisive issues that stem from conflicting theoretical models. Such dialogue however is scarcely to be heard.

Nevertheless, anthropology has flirted with every conceivable discipline and associated ideologies—political science, demography, political economy, epistimology, economics, statistics, ecology, psychology, phenomenology—a flirtation which lent to this discipline the same configurations of internal chaos as now exists in its sibling disciplines. Gone, as a predominant feature, is the grand tradition of functionalism which once conferred to anthropology its assured and coherent style. What exists within it, exists also in other social sciences, namely discord without dialogue, bureaucratically arranged.

The remaining, prominent paradigms in the Middle East (aside from neo-classical economic theory) are varieties of Marxist and Weberian theoretical models. These too are currently under critical scrutiny in the Maghreb, in Egypt and even in Turkey, the one-time heartland of the Ottoman Empire. Far less inclined to question the applicability of any Western model, ostensibly, are the literary products issuing from Kuwait and Saudi Arabia.

THE PROBLEM OF RELEVANCE

When the critical literature of Turkey and the Maghreb is compared, what stands out is that scholars in each area confront this problem of relevance but come up with different solutions. Turkish scholars tend to accept Weberian sociological categories as highly useful for analysis of Turkish bureaucracy and in comprehending the maintenance of political legitimacy;[7] whereas, the reverse tends to be true of Maghrebi scholarship. One is tempted to infer that the issue of the relevance of Western paradigms of analysis is defined differently in each area due to the differences in the nature and duration of the colonial encounter therein.

What then are the facets, the nuances, of this problem of relevance? What solutions, if any, are proposed? For some, no Western model is relevant, and an indigenous paradigm, per region, is proposed. For others, indigenization of social science is a repugnant notion; these scholars are either eclectic or else seem rather uncertain protagonists either of a Marxist model or some variation of Weberian relativism. Still others, either Marxists or Weberian, do question their own categories and priorities of observation and analysis, use them cautiously, and find certain shortcomings regarding what valuable information is necessarily excluded due to the nature of the model itself. Still other scholars seem quite unaware that there is any problem here at all, and they continue, as it were, to hoe in their own garden, talking mostly to each other and denying that their procedures rest on ideological foundations.

In Egypt, the problem of relevance takes a different tone. With some exceptions, it is not a problem so much of questioning the adequacy of western paradigms as it is a problem of how to have one's own views, one's own studies and knowledge be effective, not merely to countervail existing government policies and development plans, but also to have a hand in the development planning process itself—if only to reverse the growing dependency of Egypt on global corporations and the world banking system. In this regard, the official paradigm is neo-classical economic theory, as espoused by the regime and its foreign partners, and which Egyptian social scientists propose to countervail.

Until the summer of 1986, Maghrebi scholars, especially in Tunis, had reason to be optimistic about having a hand with the government in the development planning process. Today, however, this optimism pales as sociological inputs into this process are remarkably decreased. As in Egypt's plight, the marginalization of universities has become what Egyptian scholars call "the crisis of intellectuals."

WESTERN PARADIGMS IN THE MAGHREB: SYNTHESIS OR INDIGENIZATION?

Attempts to construct any synthesis of discrete paradigms are as rare in the Maghreb as they are anywhere in the world. To go beyond the contradictory premises of Western paradigms which first emerged in Europe's nineteenth century, is rarely a priority task. Resolving the issues between these competing paradigms is far less inviting than hoeing in one's own garden of intellectual delicacies. It would be a singularly ambitious undertaking, perhaps a futile one.

Nevertheless, such a task was recently undertaken. Nicholas Hopkins[8] identified three models used at different times by Maghrebi scholars in their social research and interpretive thoughts; he sought, by critical review of the literature of each of them, to sort out what valuable information was excluded by the nature of the paradigms themselves in order to develop, he said, "an appropriate language and model for talking about the society of the Maghreb." These models bore these names: the heartland-hinterland model, the segmentary-factional model, and the political economy model. The first, stressed the study of the Maghreb state in its formal relation to its peripheral political, economic, and social institutions. The second focussed on the balanced opposition between structural groups, and the ability of individuals to make alliances favourable to their own interests (a pluralist, partly instrumentalist approach). The third, a structuralist global approach, is the familiar global theory of the dependency of peripherial nations on the central, global powers.

The heartland-hinterland model, like functionalism, was abandoned soon upon its emergence. By the end of the colonial rule, it became defunct when situations to which it had been relevant were profoundly changed after independence, and as a new dependency was forming. Hopkins concluded his astute analysis in this manner:

> The needed model should combine the goal perspective of political economy and its focus on change and the reasons for change, with the richness in local detail of the segmentary and factional approaches.[9]

This is good advice. Fortunately it is not a model which lays down rigid categories for data classification, and it does leave room for individual and group inter-relations in influencing social outcomes at the macro level. As new models emerge, he said, the older ones should be "kept handy." The approach advocated by Hopkins was actually utilized, independently, in El Haj Bilal Omer's study of the transformation of villages in the Dongola province of Sudan (1982)—villages that due to micro-relations between town merchants and village traders and peasants ultimately transformed the mode of production, mechanizing it, and locking local society into the global economic system, thus transforming its social formations. And all this, without government intervention! Not all dependency is planned dependency in some areas like Sudan where traders rather than statesmen, are key persons in social change.

There is too great a preoccupation with models and model-building. It is refreshing, therefore, to come across works such as Saad Ibrahim's study of Moroccan urbanization, not to mention his more recent study of an emerging new Arab social order. In both studies, the guiding methodological idea is to get involved in the social issues of our time; get immersed in the situation and then attempt to see what sense, what order, can be discovered in the facts observed, and without necessarily being mentally structured, first to last, by any particular model.[10] This is not to say that there was no conceptual orientation in mind when these studies were underway, even though the published outcomes bear the earmarks of a political-economy model. Rather, in getting involved in social issues in making careful on-site observations, one is not dominated by a single theoretical scheme.

What any paradigm does, of course, is to set up for the user the particular types of questions about the "basic problems" of existence in particular social and historical contexts. It also sets up a range of allowable answers to these questions—thereby excluding the questions and permissible answers which characterize other paradigms. Thus, historical materialists who research the precolonial, colonial, and post-colonial Maghreb are "pretuned" by such concepts as "essence," "inner logic," "feudal mode of production," "neo-colonialism," "petty bourgeousie," "ruling elite," "proletariat," "Asiatic mode of production," and "class struggle." When this paradigm is expanded to include extra-regional forces of change, other modular terms are used that are consistent with "capitalist imperialism," and "peripheral dependency" to serve as guides to observation, description and analysis.

This does not imply that Marxists in the Maghreb are uncritical of the paradigms they consciously use. Gallisot, for example, an Algerian historical materialist, is quite aware that the theoretical model of "feudalism," as applied to precolonial Algeria, "presents an irritating case for Marxist analysis." What led to comparing the precolonial situation to countries characterized feudalism were conditions of societal complexity and the productive capacity of precolonial Algeria. Gallisot went on to say:

> Unfortunately here, the conception of feudalism established on the basis of data borrowed from the European economy... is found being put to poor use when applied to Algerian society.[11]

What did Gallisot do about this? He created a sub-category of feudalism and called it "command feudalism." This seemed justifiable to him because the social hierarchy gave "an Asiatic aspect" to precolonial Algeria. "But other factors," he said, "run counter to this Asiaticness and follow contrary to the lines paralleling European feudal evolution."[12] Thus, and against empirical findings, Euro-centrism in a Marxist modality, becomes the bed of Procrustes.

Another Marxist historian, Driss Ben Ali, had the same difficulty with precolonial Morocco—i.e. with its nonfeudal institutions. Yet instead of examining these institutions closely, in terms of their role in society, he pushed them aside saying in effect that the resemblances to feudalism were greater than the differences, that in making "significant and wide ranging comparisons," regarding the mode of production, one "must deal with the essence of it and not with several scattered aspects."[13] Again, the paradigm dictates what will and will not be included as data for analytical purposes.

There are Marxist scholars, however, who reject such notions of "feudalism," "hydraulic" society and "Asiatic mode of production." Samir Amin's antipathy to Euro-centrism in Marxist thought, as well as his observations about the failure of such concepts in the Maghreb to be descriptive, led him to replace those terms with the more general concept of "tributary mode of production" of which feudalism is but one sub-type. This concept, would describe a stage of *economic* development of productive forces (without machines) which would yield surplus production; and *politically,* it would apply to a complete state (city, kingdom, empire), that would supercede village political controls—rendering them subject to a broader politicality.[14]

Marxist paradigms are continually undergoing critical revision through more regional research into the history and present situations of the Maghreb. Rigidity is slowly giving place to flexibility and inventiveness. There are times even when Marxists step way out of their paradigmatic framework and seem to become cultural anthropologists or symbolic interactionists. Amin's treatment of ideology as behavior, for example, eradicates the strict dichotomy between "sub-structure" and "super-structure" that is so typical of orthodox Marxism. Here, ideas and actions merge as one and, therefore, have interpretive significance—such as social and personal identity significance of abandoning traditional clothing as an acquired consciousness.[15]

Weberian paradigms utilize a different language, a different set of basic questions and permissible answers. Socialist questions about the "inner logic" of precolonial social structures do not appear and have no significance for social research. The issue of whether Middle Eastern countries at the periphery will become socialist more quickly than the capitalist center is a matter of indifference for contemporary Weberians in the Maghreb. Moreover, this Marxist prediction is not borne out in the growing dependency of peripheral countries today. Zghal observes that while Weberian scholars use and defend their ideal types in principle, the reality is that there are no new ideal types and few modifications of old ones which could be geared to the reality of Maghrebi society.

Typically, historical relativism as a model demands first a study of indigeneous values, beliefs, ideologies that comprise culture and would engage researchers in constructing ideal types more suited to Maghrebi reality. It would demand a study of political institutions, the state and its laws as related, or unrelated, to these values and ideologies. Weberian scholars in the Maghreb are not doing this, but instead, are stuffing their findings into preconstructed ideal types that seemed to work for Weber's historical studies of feudal Europe, and for his several forms of "rational" and "irrational" action. In doing so, both Hemassi[16] and Moore[17] admitted to difficulty—e.g., the lack of goodness of fit between the model of feudal patrimonialism for example and the nature of the distribution of Maghrebi authority. That is, authority in the Maghreb did not exert evenly distributed control over the whole territory in any region. The gradations of continuous control ostensibly characteristic of the patrimony of the vassals of Europe was absent. Both authors toyed with a Khaldunian model but in the end resorted to patrimonialism as the guiding beacon for interpretation.[18]

INDIGENIZATION AS AN ALTERNATIVE

Euro-centrism, in theory and methodology, is now a preoccupation of Tunisian scholars among whom there is evident a tendency to abandon or subdue all Western paradigms, and to embark upon a search for an appropriate, indigenious theoretical orientation. The tendency here is to tie this search to the task of "decolonizing" society and social science and to create a viable postcolonial social reality.

"Is it possible," Zghal asks, "for Middle Eastern specialists in the social sciences . . . to study the social structures of their countries within the limits of the Marxist perspective without questioning either the marginal secondary features of this perspective or its central core as well?"

The answer given is no. Marxists and Weberians themselves have seen this. Marina Lazreg, for example, admits that the terminology borrowed from the West is "not entirely adequate," that terms like "bourgeoisie" "do not have the same meaning in the Algerian case."[19] Samir Amin also sees the inadequacy of this term and others as well. Weberians see similar inadequacies with Weberian ideal types. Moreover, the results of applying their models, even when the questionable terms are changed, lead to very different portrayals of Maghrebi societies and their transformations.[20]

Taking a cue from Michel Foucault, Abdelkader Zghal and Frej Stambouli of the University of Tunis, place little value on any theoretical model imported from Europe, rooted as they are in Europe's great societal transformation of the eighteenth and nineteenth centuries. Citing Foucault, they argue that this transformation from feudalism to industrial capitalism was a unique "historical moment" of Western civilization, a moment not replicable beyond the West. Social philosophers and social scientists in that period constructed diverse theories of that unique transformation—theories particular to that transformation, and not to any other. Yet their theories, historically particular as they were, claimed to have unlimited generality—a fallacy owing to the fact that they did not pause to examine the institutional foundations of their own thoughts.[21]

Zghal and Stambouli[22] are agreed that the difference between the theories of Marx, Durkheim and Weber are less important than their similarities. It is their similarities which, in Zghal's words, place them in the same, culture-bound "epistemological field" of nineteenth century Europe. While neither Stambouli nor Zghal succeeded in connecting these similarities to their institutional underpinnings, it is true, all the same, that all are in some sense continuum theories which in different words claim an inevitable transformation from sacred to secular social organization, from irrational to rational; from emotional to rational; or else, as for Marx, religious concepts linger on in capitalist society as an opiate, an inconsequential part of the super-structure and insignificant for explaining industrial capitalism. The institutional roots of these theories lay, in part, in Christendom's centuries-old separation of Church and State—a condition which for other centuries did not exist in Islamic civilization.

It is argued in effect that what industrial capitalism was to Europe, colonialism was to the Middle East—a truncation of Arabo-Muslim civilization in its various forms in the Maghreb and the Mashreq. Just as Western theorists reached back to understand what went before their transformation, so must Middle Eastern scholars rediscover what society was like before colonialism, and, without conceptions of feudalism and patrimonialism which were spawned in the studies of Europe's transformation. The social formations which colonialism produced, and which the politics of dependence sustained, must be changed in such a way as to bridge between the present realities of the Maghreb and what remains of traditional society. Zghal writes:

> Since Ibn Khaldun's work attempted to comprehend one of the great historical moments of Middle Eastern culture, the transition of his own time in the 14th century, I suggest that we get away from the usual practice of treating Ibn Khaldun as merely a native informant and that we consider him as the author of a scholarly conception of a method for grasping what we include under the notions of "hierarchy" and "social stratification" . . . I am neither thinking of substituting Ibn Khaldun for Marx and Weber, or suggesting a retreat inside. . . the Arabo-Muslim tradition. My goal is to release debate over the notions of "hier-

archy" and "social stratification" from the narrow framework of the Western intellectual tradition of the 19th century.[23]

At the same time, he and Stambouli both feel that the growing economic and political dependency on the Western institutions and global corporations must be reversed, if the Maghreb is to find itself, rediscover its identity and determine its own development.

Stambouli agrees and points to the successive changes in sociological thought in the Maghreb. The 1960s were a turning point from a bourgeois Durkheimian functionalism which dominated in the colonial period to the *sociology of decolonization* which became pragmatic in the universities of Morocco, Algeria and Tunisia. It was a period when, for the first time, young Maghrebi scholars took control, and this generation set themselves a twofold task:

> To start processes of *general* decolonization in order to recover the historical identity of their peoples, and to define the most efficient modalities of a balanced social development which alone could give way to progressive technology and modernity in their countries.[24]

Stambouli's program for building a new Maghreb includes an emphasis on regionalism, not nationalism, "giving priority to social actors who are carriers of radical change (youth, women, poor peasantry, new urban masses, working classes), and to political factors which seek to block change (neocolonialism, dependence, parasitic classes)."[25]

He calls for cultural and political involvement of social scientists to struggle against "theological and theocratic aspects of Islamic ideology to free social thought from dogmatic assumptions." Scholars must avoid the cloistered, servile posture so typical of academics. Such a posture stands in contradiction, he said, with scientific goals. What Stambouli advocates is *action research* which involves scholars and young people in different walks of life in projects designed to decolonize and reshape society. Thus, sociology becomes a political entity and catalyst to societal development.

Both Stambouli and Zghal wrote with confidence and enthusiasm. They, and others, appeared to be influential in terms of shaping development plans. There was no sense in being alienated from those in power. Thus, their optimism and enthusiasm to get on with the job. This was a mood remarkably different, however, from what is being felt in Egypt as "the crisis of intellectuals." Moreover, since 1986, this same crisis became manifest also in Tunisia.

THE PROBLEM OF RELEVANCE IN EGYPT: SOME OBSERVATIONS

Action research as it appeared in the Maghreb seems hardly possible in Egypt. Development planning is regime-bound and tied to the interests of the foreign agencies of dependency—i.e., the IMF, USAID, and indirectly to the global corporations that have penetrated Egypt as they have penetrated the Maghreb. Generally too, but not exclusively, the Egyptian government exercises a virtual monopoly over certain forms of social research. The probability of a significant, continuous input of social scientists (other than those who espouse neo-classical economic theory) is miniscule.

The problem of relevance in Egypt, therefore is remarkably different from what the situation was in the Maghreb. It is not so much a question of constructing an indigenous theoretical model, as it is a question of how to make relevant ideas effective in national development planning. And this would involve a demystification of the ideology, or propaganda, which is publicized as the rationale behind the country's present "Productive Open Door Economic Policy," and its offspring—the five-year plan (1982–1987). This is the ideology of "free enterprise," the rhetoric of supply and demand, and the "trickle down" notions espoused both by the agencies of dependency and the governmental advocates of the present open door economic policy—a post-Nasser transition which has moved Egypt's most notable intellectuals off-stage.

Waiting in the Wings: Political Economy after Nasser—A Case of Extroverted Development

Nasser's policy is now well known. Sadat's open door policy, now continued under President Hosni Mubarak, is a reversal of the policy of Arab Socialism and Arab Nationalism. It has a legal structure, described and critiqued by Abdel-Khalek (1979; 1981). It has a political structure representing a new, post-Nasser elite class as carefully described by Hinnebusch (1981). It has produced a great deal of discontent among Islamic fundamentalists and the poor, as well as among political economists who occupy a political position of being off-stage, waiting in the wings. This general discontent climaxed first in the food riots of 1977. It emerged in 1986 in the recent riots of the conscripted security police. These conditions of discontent have been described and interpreted by several scholars, including Raymond Baker who hinted at the possible assassination of Anwar Sadat as early as 1981.

What is the crux of the matter are the negative effects of this policy which have moved Egypt from introverted to extroverted development. In breaking up the remains of the government's former control over development, this policy put the control largely, not exclusively, in the hands of the outside agencies of dependency. The new policy opened investment to outsiders in every field—industry, mining, energy, tourism, transport, land reclamation, cultivation, housing, urban development, banking, insurance, contracting. As Abdel Khalek put it, "There is no sanctuary for genuine national investment."[26]

Critiques from the Left—A Crucial Choice

In 1977, Samir Radwan concluded his analysis of the failure of Nasser's socialism with these words:

> It appears that the failure of the transition to socialism has put Egypt at the crossroads; either there must be more radical policies to continue this transition to socialism or there will be capitulation and a return to an open door policy reminiscent of the post-Muhammed Ali era when Egypt was integrated into the world capitalist system with all that implies—neo-dependency and persistent underdevelopment.[27]

Radwan's was not exactly a prophecy because the return to the open door policy had already begun. But the "more radical policies" he alluded to have not emerged, and the once-predicted transition to socialism is nowhere visible. The choice for an Open Door Policy was made.

The Present Debate

Is this choice good or bad for Egypt? The planning establishment's neoclassical economists feel it is good. They argue that the further penetration of Egypt by global corporations in the long run will benefit everyone because what comes in at the top will trickle to the bottom, provided that all subsidies on survival goods are abolished so that "free enterprise" is allowed to operate unchecked.[28]

This argument has been disputed rigorously on all sides in an effort to prove that the stated goals of this policy are not being achieved, and that the reverse is happening. These critiques are empirically based and indicate a decapitalization of Egypt as a direct consequence of applying the five year plans based on this policy. Karima Korayem[29] demonstrated an increasing gap between rural and urban incomes. Later, she demonstrated a negative impact on the distribution of disposable income of the elimination of food subsidies (1982). The negative and positive consequences of economic assistance to Egypt have been aired and debated at the American University in Cairo.[30] The migration of villagers into the cities, partly consequential to the introduction of capital intensive farm technology, has assured a supersaturation of people in the informal employment sector in urban Egypt.[31] There are studies which indicate the failure of the economy to meet ever-expanding basic needs and which document a growing condition of malnutrition in urban areas.[32]

This brief portrayal of the current situation brings out several vital issues: decapitalization, unemployment and the growing gap between the rich and poor against a rising GNP, with all the social problems these entail.

Some social scientists feel that the greater evil in the open door policy is not the failure of its goals so much as it is bureacratic inefficiency, corruption, apathy, elite cynicism, consumerism, and the need for more democratization and indigenous participation in policy-making.[33] Galal Amin would agree, but while recognizing the failure of the open door policy, he points to a deeper problem—a general abandonment of Egyptian culture and Egyptian creativity based in that culture. He chides his Marxist colleagues who accept the western model for development but who then complain about the gross inequity in the distribution of the national income. The one cannot be had without the other.[34]

INTERPRETIVE SUMMARY

The problem of relevance has many facets. First, Marxist and Weberian scholars alike, in the Maghreb and elsewhere in the Middle East, have noted the inadequacies of the paradigms they use as guides to observation, description, analysis and theoretical interpretation of precolonial, colonial and postcolonial conditions of development. Their experiences of the differences between their theoretical models and actual conditions have in some cases made for a modification of these models, while in other cases, these crucial differences have been glossed over. In still other cases, some of the key categories of these Western models have been rejected, and other concepts more suitable to the region and more useful generally have emerged. What seems to be happening then, is a gradual, albeit piecemeal, correction of the models imported from Europe. Two models have all but vanished—functionalism and the "heartland-hinterland" approach.

Second, at least one scholar[35] has attempted to construct a synthetic model out of those that have been utilized already; and the question naturally arises, if all such models hark back to a historically unique period of transformation, why bother to engage in resolving the present differences between them?

Third is the issue involved in attempts to construct an indigeneous model. Aside from Euro-centrism inherent in current approaches to the understanding of Middle Eastern societies in transition, the essential problem is to create a paradigm which squares with a region's own historic moment. This is being attempted now, especially in the Maghreb by releasing debate about hierarcy and social stratification from its narrow Western confines or else by action research engaged in decolonizing society and social science to discover one's own regional identity, one's own mode of development and to break away from the political and economic bondages of dependency.

Fourth there is a tendency simply to become involved personally in the crucial issues of the Arab Middle East and in a nonprogrammatic, critical way to become immersed in the data in an effort not only to make a modicum of difference in development, but also to see what new order there may be emerging out of the chaos of very complex situations.

Fifth, for those who are quite satisfied with their own way of understanding, the problem is how to countervail a given regime's own development model—in particular how to countervail the ideology, the fact, and the negative consequences of the open door policy—how, in short, to participate in the planning process in order to reverse the negative consequences of that policy.

Sixth, and most crucial, is the problem of the alienation of certain scholars from participation in policy-making and its implementation. This has been construed time and again as the problem of democratization. For as long as any regime remains hermetically sealed, except to foreign influence, and as long as it maintains a monopoly with its foreign donors over development planning, and as long as it maintains certain control over what shall and what shall not be investigated, there seems little probability that a nonservile social science can endure or flourish—except in isolation, waiting in the wings.

NOTES

1. See, for example, Talal Asad, *Anthropology and the Colonial Encounter* (London: Ithaca Press, 1973); and Victor Turner, *Colonialism in Africa 1870–1960*, Vol. 3 (Cambridge: Cambridge University Press, 1971).

2. Edward Evans-Pritchard and Meyer Fortes, eds., *African Political Systems* (London: Oxford University Press, 1955), p. 4.

3. Edmund Ronald Leach, *Rethinking Anthropology* (London: The Athlone Press, 1961).

4. For examples see Rodney Needham, "The Future of Anthropology: Disintegration or Metamorphosis?" in *Anniversary Contributions to Anthropology: Twelve Essays* (Leiden: E.J. Brill, 1970); Edwin Ardner, "The New Anthropology and It's Critics," *Man* 6, no. 3 (1971); and Asad.

5. M.I. Swartz, V.W. Turner and A. Tuden, eds., *Political Anthropology* (Chicago: University of Chicago Press, 1968).

6. Cited by Asad.

7. See the works of Metin Heper as an example.

8. Nicholas Hopkins, "Tunisia. An Open and Shut Case," *Social Problems* 28, no. 4 (April 1981).

9. Hopkins, p. 69.

10. Saad Eddin Ibrahim, *Population and Urbanization in Morocco*. Cairo Papers in Social Science, Vol. 3, Monograph 5 (Cairo: American University in Cairo, 1980) and Saad Eddin Ibrahim, "Images of the New Arab Social Order," in *International Review of Modern Sociology* 12, no. 2 (Jan.–June 1982), special issue.

11. Abdelkader Zghal, "Marxist and Weberian Traditions and the Social Structures of the Middle East," *International Review of Modern Sociology* 12, no. 1 (Jan–June, 1982), special issue, p. 23.

12. Ibid.

13. Ibid.

14. Ibid.

15. Ibid., p. 31.

16. Elbaki Hermassi, *Leadership and National Development in North Africa* (Berkeley: University of California Press, 1972).

17. Clement Henry Moore, *Politics in North Africa* (Boston: Little-Brown and Company, 1976).

18. Zghal, p. 25.

19. Ibid., p. 30.

20. Ibid., pp. 26–28.
21. Mark C. Kennedy, *Division of Labour and the Culture of Capitalism: A Critique of the Institutional Foundations of Western Theories*, Ph.D. Thesis, State University of New York at Buffalo, 1968.
22. Frej Stambouli, "Sociology, Methodology and Action Research: The Case of the Arab Maghreb," *International Review of Modern Sociology* 12, no. 2 (1982), special issue, edited by Mark C. Kennedy.
23. Zghal, p.18.
24. Stambouli, p. 43.
25. Ibid., p. 48.
26. Gouda Abdel-Khalek, "The Open Door Economic Policy in Egypt: A Search for Meaning, Interpretation, and Implication," in *Studies in Egyptian Political Economy*, edited by H.M. Thompson, Cairo Papers, Vol. 2, Monograph 3, first edition March 1979, second edition July 1983, p. 86.
27. Samir Radwan, *Agrarian Reform and Rural Poverty, Egypt 1952–1975* (Geneva: International Labor Office, 1977), p. 99.
28. M. Field Haviland, "Whither Social-Political Development in the Emerging Nations," *Social Problems* 28, no. 4 (April 1981).
29. Karima Korayem, "The Rural Urban Income Gap in Egypt and Based Agricultural Pricing Policy," *Social Problems* 28, no. 4 (April 1981).
30. Earl Sullivan, ed., *Impact of Development Assistance in Egypt*. Cairo Papers, Vol. 7, Monograph 3 (Cairo: American University in Cairo Press, 1984).
31. Mahmoud Abdel-Fadil, "Internal Sector Employment in Egypt," in Richard Lobban, ed. *Urban Research Strategies for Egypt*. Cairo Papers in Social Science, Vol. 6, Monograph 2 (June) (Cairo: American University in Cairo Press, 1983).
32. Amr Mohie-Eldin, *Income Distribution and Basic Needs in Urban Egypt*, Cairo Papers, Vol. 5, Monograph 3 (Cairo: American University in Cairo Press, 1982).
33. Ali E. Hillal Dessouki, "A Case Study of Policy Making in Egypt." *Social Problems* 28, no. 4 (April, 1982), pp. 415–16.
34. Ibid., p. 440.
35. Nicholas Hopkins, "Models in the Maghreb: Notes from Political Anthropology," *International Review of Modern Sociology* 12, no. 1 (Jan–June 1982) special edition.

4 Anthropology and the Call for Indigenization of Social Science in the Arab World

Soheir Morsy, Cynthia Nelson, Reem Saad and Hania Sholkamy

THE STRUGGLE AGAINST political hegemony left its imprint on social science discourse among expatriate and indigenous scholars alike. In the West, movements of national liberation that erupted in the 1950s and 1960s in the so-called Third World, created a fundamental crisis within social science. This crisis led to the emergence of a "critical" perspective among western social scientists, particularly anthropologists, who began to question the very epistemological premises of their discipline.[1] Among indigenous researchers the intellectual expression of the political struggle was symbolized by the call for "decolonizing anthropology."[2] Beyond the politically-inspired rejection of anthropology's distinctive-other tradition, and the related restriction on access by outside investigators, some indigenous social researchers asserted that studies carried out by nationals would produce more authentic knowledge.[3]

As people who had never been a significant enough part of social science, professional communities began to challenge the values on which western researchers' selective analytical criteria were premised,[4] anthropologists proceeded to "reinvent" their discipline.[5] Critical anthropology extended "towards an anthropology of women"; a feminist critique of western scholarship on women emerged.[6] Similarly, as the "distinctive-other" began to "talk back at the social scientist,"[7] reassessment of modernist interpretations of international development prompted the consideration of "new opportunities in applied anthropology."[8] Within a framework of participatory action research, the focus on "indigenous knowledge systems,"[9] and "partisan participation"[10] replaced the idea of "trading new lives for old."[11]

81

In anthropology's traditional "research settings" of the periphery, the internal crisis of the social sciences became the focus of debate.[12] Among anthropologists, for whom the cultural construction of knowledge is axiomatic, a derivative proposition linking researchers' national identity and scientific production appeared as "indigenous" or "native" anthropology. Affected by the calling for a reflexive anthropology, some researchers discussed the incorporation of the "insider" anthropological perspective in terms of "advantages/disadvantages" or "complementarity."[13] Among scholars who extend primary consideration to the social production of knowledge, intellectual developments in the periphery began to be addressed in the context of historically-specific political economic transformations affecting the "world order of anthropology."[14]

Regarding the Arab World, rejection of Orientalist scholarship has taken various forms.[15] These have ranged from the call for "Islamization of knowledge"[16] to analysis of underdevelopment of scholarship in the context of center-periphery articulation,[17] and in relation to the state.[18] In terms of development-oriented research, the international pattern of division of scientific labor and the role of foreign researchers have also come under scrutiny.[19] Discourse on development raised the question "whose knowledge counts?",[20] exposed the fundamental political economic basis of "joint venture" development assistance research,[21] and pointed to state-imposed restriction on grass roots development projects.[22]

As consideration of specific strategies for indigenization of the social sciences followed the relatively facile call for their decolonization, attention has turned to analysis of "the shaping" of national social science scholarship.[23] Focusing on the Arab World, this chapter contributes to this effort by drawing on current debates surrounding proposed regional strategies of indigenization of the social sciences.[24] Attention extends to a proposed "Arab anthropological orientation" as an elaboration of the idea of "indigenous" anthropology.[25]

Following this introductory section, the chapter addresses the social/historical context of the quest for indigenization, and the related identification of epistemological/methodological limitations of Western social science paradigms applied to the study of the Arab World. Major trends of indigenization are then examined; critical review extends to the idea of an "Arab anthropological orientation." Beyond discussion of the limitations of the epistemological stance on which such a call is based, the next major section addresses the idea of indigenous anthropology through a critical examination of anthropological studies of women in the Arab World.

Drawing on case studies of Participatory Action Research in the Third World, we then proceed to examine the extent to which this body of thought can enable those who follow it to produce indigenous knowledge which would enhance the development of the Arab World.

Finally, the concluding section summarizes its major arguments. It is argued that while Arab social scientists have begun to question the epistemological foundations of social inquiry, they have not, at least so far, produced a distinctive "indigenous" alternative.

MAJOR TRENDS OF INDIGENIZATION

The debate concerning the indigenization of the social sciences in the Arab World should be viewed within the political and intellectual context in which it originated, namely the national liberation movements, the accompanying anti-imperialist ideology in the Third World, and the crisis in Western social science respectively. This call for indigenizing the social sciences possesses two very closely related components which are the epistemological/methodological and the political/ideological. With regard to methodology, it is argued that the existing body of social science is abstracted only from one part of the world, namely European American Society. Western social "science," of presumably universal relevance and applicability, when addressing non-Western societies has chosen to compromise social realities in these societies rather than admit a limitation in its generalizing capacity.

The political component of the problem is the persistence for a long time of this idea and the context in which it began to be criticized. The realization of the Western bias in social theory came along with the rejection of Western economic and political hegemony, and the call for indigenizing the social sciences reflected an anti-imperialist stance.

The politicized context of the debate on indigenization had the merit of uncovering the epistemological/methodological problem of Western social science, by seriously questioning its claim to universality. However, more often than not those undertaking "indigenization" attempts in the Arab World have substituted the epistemological by the political. Thus their main objective was to be "intellectually independent" rather than to assert their role in reformulating the existing body of social scientific theory. This is the main problem of indigenization now; the rejection of Western political and economic hegemony carried with it a rejection of Western social science almost entirely, and hence the call for going back to Arab/Islamic sources and the preference to use them exclusively. Therefore, the indigenization trend again commits an epistemological blunder by trying to create a local "theory," which is derived from and can only deal with Arab reality. It also has the serious defect of classifying social science according to nationality of the scholar thereby obscuring political and ideological differentiation among social scientists in the Arab World as well as the West.

This problem is further complicated by the fact that the two components of the issue are hardly separable. It is important to differentiate between an ideological reaction to Imperialism and the desire not to be identified with it on the one hand and the researcher's right to have a political and ideological choice on the other, i.e., between the political dimension of the epistemological issue (non value-free social science) and the political context of the indigenization quest (anti-West).

INDIGENIZATION TRENDS IN THE ARAB WORLD

In the Arab World there has been an increasing awareness and interest in the issue of indigenization. A number of related conferences and debates were held all over the Arab World. The issue of indigenization is addressed in terms of a recognition of the existence of a crisis of Arab World intellectuals in general, and a crisis of social science in the Arab World in particular. Two major trends can be identified in terms of the definition of this crisis and their implications for "indigenization." These may be grouped into two broad orientations: the "radical," and the so-called "neo-traditionalist." The "radical" perspective stresses the socio-economic roots and causes of the crisis and its relation to economic dependency. Proponents of this orientation do not reject the contribution of Western social thought, and consider it an important or, rather, inevitable component of Arab social science. But they acknowledge the existence of specificities in Arab society, and the need for some kind of indigenization of Arab social science. The task of indigenization according to this group should be undertaken as part of the struggle against the actual dependency relations.

Advocates of the alternative neo-traditionalist perspective, although acknowledging the dependent context in which the intellectual crisis takes place, address this crisis only in terms of an ideological confrontation between the Arabs and the West. By virtue of this view, they tend to reject the contributions of Western social thought *en toto*. They stress an inherent specificity of Arab social reality and the impossibility of comprehending it except in terms of concepts derived from this specificity.

The view of the "radicals" on the crisis of social science in the Arab World is that this crisis (both its causes and ways of transcending it) is inseparable from the general socio-economic and political situation. The basic premise adopted by this group is summarized by Higazy:

> The present state of sociology in the Arab World . . . is the result of a number of objective social, economic and political conditions and at the same time participates in perpetuating those conditions. That is to say that the relationship between the crisis of social science and that of society is dialectical and should be analysed, diagnosed and tackled on this basis.[26]

The causes and manifestations of the crisis of social science in the Arab World from the radicals' point of view can be summarized as follows:

1) The missing link between societal problems and intellectual production, led to the intellectuals' alienation and powerlessness. Although not a typical representative of this group, Galal Amin succinctly describes this situation: "If the intellectual is to be really honest with himself, he is bound to admit how very insignificant has become the power of his written or spoken word vis-a-vis the power of the modern state, the modern corporation and the modern technocrat."[27]

2) The absence of democratic and political institutions led to the emergence of a group of social scientists tied to the government establishment which justify and perpetuate.[28]

3) Cultural and intellectual dependency on the West which led to the existence of a body of social science of little relevance to Arab society. Higazy sees the problem as resulting from unselective importation of Western theories coupled with a lack of "indigenous" alternatives. He says: "We do not produce real science, but import and consume without consideration, confusing useful and useless."[29] Both argue that the Arab World was mainly penetrated by conservative theories (especially functionalism and positivism) which were congenial to the role played by many Arab social scientists as justifiers of the status quo.

This group's call for an "Arab social science" is tied to their particular definition of the intellectual crisis in the Arab World. Most importantly, they stress the role that social science should play in bringing about change in Arab society. Although they contend that the crisis of society and of social science are both products of a situation of dependency, and that the ultimate solution of the social science crisis is bound by the solution of the crisis of society, they argue that Arab social science should not await this "ultimate" solution but should itself play an active role in the struggle against dependency. They stress that intellectual work should be accompanied by political action,[30] and many of the members of this group are in fact politically active in some way. The bearing of this position on the task of creating an "Arab social science," as they envision it, is that it should concern itself with identifying specific challenges facing the society and constructing *relevant* paradigms to meet them. Thus for this group, "toward an Arab social science" could be taken to mean "toward a relevant social science."

An important issue in this respect is the position of this group regarding Western social theory. This group acknowledges the need for indigenization of social science in the Arab World. However, this should not be done in isolation from the existing body of knowledge, though it may be mainly Western in origin. This is because they do not view Western social thought as a homogeneous body of knowledge that should be accepted or rejected as a whole. Arab Marxists especially have recently believed the need to stress the differences between trends of Western social thought, since the initial "indigenous" assault on "modernization" theory and Western development models has become vulgarized into an indiscriminate assault on "Western ideas."

This group can be credited for a rather accurate *description* of the crisis. However, beyond that little has been done to illustrate HOW this characterization of the crisis, though accurate, can lead to its transcendence. Also, their vision of "indigenization" addresses more the political aspect of the crisis without addressing the methodological elements involved in creating this "Arab social science."

The other trend is represented by the "neo-traditionalists," a label bestowed upon them by the radicals during a debate between the two groups held in Cairo in January 1983 with the title: "Tradition and the Incoming Thought." Members of this group do acknowledge both the existence of political and economic dependency and the existence of a crisis in social science in the Arab World. However, they see these as parallel phenomena, whose relationship to one another is undialectical. The vision of this group is best articulated by Adel Hussein, who seeks "a methodoloy for creating an independent theoretical structure."[31] The basic premise of this "methodology" is "acknowledging the central conception of the dominant ideology, the ideology of the Islamic civilization. This central conception for us is the belief in God, the Creator."[32] This, to him, is the basic determinant of Arab Islamic social thought which interacted with the "historical environment" producing traditions and institutions. This interaction should, in turn, be the basis for creating independent sociological schools. But, the central conception of the West is secularism, which also conditioned its institutions and social thought. Hussein sees that Arab Islamic theories should not be against the use of some theoretical constructs discovered in the West as long as they are not a direct outcome of the secular ideology.[33]

Hence the call for indigenization here means constructing a *specific* theory built on the *essence* of Arab civilization and rejecting the *essence* of Western civilization. This definition of the problem implies that Western and Arab social thought are ultimately irreconcilable because the essences of the two civilizations are *anyway* incompatible, and not because the encounter happened in the context of Western economic and political hegemony within historically defined conditions.

An attempt to address the methodological aspect of "indigenization" is presented by Zghal. He tries to break away from the Western intellectual tradition when dealing with Middle Eastern structures. He situates this attempt in the context of questioning the relevance to the Middle East of Marxist and Weberian traditions, being products of the nineteenth century industrial transformation in Europe. His main point is that Middle Eastern scholars are not obliged to choose between either Marx or Weber, and that they should free themselves from this by turning to indigenous alternatives. Taking Ibn Khaldun as such an alternative proposes that:

> . . . a contemporary and faithful interpretation of Ibn Khaldun's method requires us to phrase his sense of problem or analytical framework in terms having a level of abstraction higher than that of the notions of social class (in the economic sense) or even of societies (in the sense of a politically, economically and culturally homogeneous state). Only at this level of abstraction can we appreciate a general and comparative theory of different forms of social structuring which are not informed by a single historical experience.[34]

Zghal implies the necessity of generating nomothetic propositions and not just a theory relevant to the Middle East. The case being so however, it is not clear how this attempt would be different had we been using Marx or Weber rather than Ibn Khaldun, for after all Ibn Khaldun is no less a product of his time than either Marx or Weber. In other words, raising the level of abstraction or broadening Khaldunian concepts to be more encompassing of various empirical situations has got nothing to do with Ibn Khaldun being an indigenous scholar. Raising the level of abstraction in a sense implies doing away with the quest of a methodology of specific relevance. Thus the use of Ibn Khaldun here would only provide a contribution of *content,* of another empirical situation (albeit embedded in a particular methodological perspective) to be taken account of while constructing categories of global relevance.

AN ARAB ANTHROPOLOGICAL ORIENTATION

The indigenization trend just described extends to anthropology. Beyond the proliferation of studies carried out by indigenous researchers, documentation of Arab researchers' experiences of "studying (their) own society,"[35] and the evaluation of such studies in terms of "advantages and disadvantages,"[36] reference has been made to an aspired "Arab anthropological stance."[37] This idea of an "Arab" anthropological orientation is clearly an extension of the notion of "indigenous" anthropology, defined as "the practice of social and cultural anthropology in one's own national setting."[38] Contrary to our interpretation, advocates of such labelling suggest that it "should not imply an intellectual separation."[39] A similar cautionary note follows the related suggestion of an "Arab" anthropological stance. In addressing the question "do we want an Arab anthropology or an Islamic anthropology?" Fahim goes on to state:

> My position in relation to these questions... is that choice must be made within the framework of supporting the scientific character of anthropology, not its (national) identity. It is not useful, in my opinion, epistemologically, or even practically, to differentiate between what may be described as western anthropology versus another non-western (anthropology), or to call for the development of separate national anthropologies, each independent and isolated from the other. What needs to be done is to continue the process of discussion and debate.[40]

He then explains:

> Based on my conviction of not (resorting to) compartmentalization of science or its formulation on the basis of nationality, race, or religion, I still find it difficult to overlook completely or minimize the influence of the national orientation or class affiliation or intellectual orientation on the theoretical foundation of the researcher's framework and belief (system).[41]

While we agree with the utility of comparing different anthropologists' culturally-mediated rendering of social reality, we disagree with the lumping of our no doubt different and possibly contradictory theoretical/methodological evaluations, under the blanket label "indigenous" or "Arab" anthropology. This homogenizes some of the very differences which are said to "hold the promise of contributing to a more profound cross-cultural study of humanity."[42] Adoption of the idea of "indigenous" anthropology, and the derivative "Arab" form, is related to the current trend in *"Western," "nonindigenous"* anthropology of calling for a reflexive anthropology. But such a call "remains trivial (unless) Self and Other are illuminated alike."[43] "Indigenous anthropology" as a label does not in and of itself illuminate either and therefore does not deserve any claim of contributing to epistemological development. Contrary to the above-noted assertion, this label leaves one with the impression that the "practice of. . . anthropology in one's own national setting" is different enough from other anthropological practices to deserve a separate typological category.

While differences between non-Western and Western as well as non-Arab and Arab anthropologists no doubt exist; it is not realistic to assume that "we" are *uniformly* different from "them" as implied by the designation which sets "our" anthropology apart from "theirs." If one agrees with the proposition of nonuniformity of "our" theoretical/methodological productions, then one is confronted with the question of the utility of the designation "indigenous" or "Arab" to begin with. If one is committed to the use of the label, then one must also be ready to disclose, or at least research, the meaning, theoretical, methodological, political economic, or otherwise of the "practice of social and cultural anthropology in one's own national setting."

Rejection of the idea of "indigenous" or "Arab" anthropology is an extension of our renunciation of anthropology's selective recognition of selected dimensions of researchers' social identity and their relation to theoretical formulation. The "indigenous" label, intended to differentiate the work of local scholars, is itself not far from the logic which defines anthropology as the study of "others." It also bears resemblance to the Orientalist intellectual differentiation between "us," the West and "them," the non-West.[44] Illustrative of the homogenization of "our" stance (through the juxtaposing of "Arab" and "Orientalist" outlooks) is Fahim's suggestion that

> ... an important task for Arab anthropologists... (is)... directing part of their studies to reviewing the anthropological writings of western anthropologists which is nothing but orientalism."[45]

Implicit in this suggestion is the assumption that Arab anthropologists have been insulated from Orientalism. The suggestion also runs counter to Fahim's above noted declaration that "[I]t is not useful... to differentiate between what may be described as Western anthropology versus another non-Western (anthropology)."[46] Indigenous anthropologists' accounts of their own societies, reveal that, not unlike nonindigenous anthropologists, we too are affected by "universal" professional disciplinary theoretical standards and definitions of "appropriate" research topics,[47] as well as Orientalism.[48]

Arab anthropologists have, and will no doubt continue to provide new insights and critiques of mainstream anthropological theory and methodology. But to assume that this will lead to the development of an "indigenous" form of the discipline overlooks, not only variation among indigenous anthropologists, but the more fundamental global influences to which we are all subjected.

ARAB SOCIETY AND THE WORLD ORDER OF SOCIAL SCIENCE

The idea of indigenization of the social sciences has been useful in bringing to our attention the false claim to universalism implicit in social science models which are based on the experiences of Western society. Thus historical and cultural specificity has been forced into the spotlight. But aside from such contributions of indigenization trends, "[t]here is considerable fuzziness in the explication of its objectives; the intellectual content of the alternative it seeks is not clearly spelled out."[49] Indeed, as S.C. Dube has remarked regarding the proponents of "Indian" sociology, the proponents of "Arab" social science have "never proceeded to demonstrate convincingly what that approach might be and how it could be applied in actual practice."[50] While local scholars' concern with relevance and commitment in social research is at the very least implicit in the demand for indigenization, it is not clear how the practice of social science ". . . in one's native country, society, and/or ethnic group"[51] insures such relevance and commitment.

More fundamental are the global influences to which Arab scholars are subjected, and the related "patron-client relationship" between Arab social scientists of peripheral social formations and their more powerful counterparts in the center. Indigenous status forms but one dimension among others linked to general and specific ideological orientations and influenced by historically and individually specific experiences. While we cannot determine the exact relationship between knowledge and social status, we do know that knowledge enhances the exercise of power and control. The crucial question for us is the locus of social science professional control. In class and patriarchal societies (of "our own national settings") which are integrated into a global political economy characterized by power asymmetries, nationality is not equivalent to support of the interest of the masses, the "objects" of our social scientific inquiries. Indigenous researchers' own descriptions of their "indigenous" experience indicate that, not unlike our nonindigenous counterparts, we too are affected by "universal" professional disciplinary theoretical standards, definitions of "appropriate" research topics, and the "publish or perish" commandment.[52]

With regard to the idea of an "Arab" anthropological orientation, it is worth noting that more and more anthropologists now recognize that the problems confronting "our people" cannot be adequately understood through studies of single cultures, nations, or even continents.[53] The limitations of such narrow research foci hold true regardless of whether studies are carried out by indigenous or nonindigenous anthropologists. For so long as we continue to uphold the discipline's dominant tradition which fails to take into account the fact that people, including indigenous researchers, construct their cultures in interaction with one another and not in isolation,[54] we will only contribute to the mystification of the causes of "our people's" sufferings and underdevelopment, thereby undermining the declared commitment to "relevance" in social research.

It is worth noting that science production, social and otherwise, in addition to being historically and situationally specific, is the output of people whose thought patterns reflect the "truths" of their social milieux.[55] To the extent that indigenous anthropologists' social milieux are not simply and purely "indigenous," neither are our thought patterns nor the "truths" of our scientific productions. As a result of colonial domination, and in the post colonial period, when local scholars continued to be trained by Western mentors, theoretical orientations were transferred to "indigenous" social science disciplines virtually in toto. As the US and the European countries emerged as centers of economic domination their importance in the scientific field rose in consequence.[56]

"Indigenous" interpretations of local social phenomena have not been insulated from the influence of this domination. Thus, in addition to such influence as the researcher's gender, theoretical orientation and cultural values and nationality, knowledge among Third World social scientists, including Arabs, is to a large extent affected by the political economic agendas of the global centers of power.[57] Within the framework of a global political economy, political economic hegemony has its counterpart in intellectual circles. The idea of "Arab" or "Islamic" science may well give an impression of distinctiveness of local anthropological knowledge thereby detracting from the reality of the "satellite" nature of local scientific output, and more generally intellectual dependency. Contrary to such an impression, Western intellectual hegemony no doubt leaves its imprint on "indigenous" scholarship, social scientific and otherwise. Local scholars are in many cases influenced by the globally dominant Western intellectual culture, not simply through their training in the West but through the propagation of Western intellectual standards which reach them in their own backyard.[58] Moreover, they "... have to work... under difficult conditions... their leadership has a definite tilt towards the West... funds are far from adequate... It is understandable that many Third World scholars should pick up crumbs, thrown by the affluent countries... Financial dependence breeds academic subordination."[59]

Within the framework of dependent intellectual relations the major scientific paradigms continue to develop in the West and are imported into the dependent countries. In general only minor variations are introduced locally. Even when the major theoretical developments are produced in the periphery (as in the case of dependency theory), they are legitimated in the center. As a Third World scholar has explained:

The diffusion model of knowledge that operates between the center and the periphery really leads to a colonial division of labour in the academic world, paralleling divisions in the economic and political worlds. Most of the important works, the major issue and paradigms in the sciences are developed and undertaken in the center while mostly only minor professional issues and sub-problems are tackled by scientists in the dependent country... in the periphery the dependent structures give rise to mimicked knowledge. In addition (dependency) acts as a suppressor of creativity.[60]

Research priorities, important theoretical issues, as well as applied research topics and even indigenous social research (forced upon Western anthropologists by new political realities in the Third World and shortage of research funds at home) are thus determined in the centre and exported to dependent countries as the "most recent scientific fashions of the Western World."[61] By working on the specifics of the local permutations of general social "laws," Third World social scientists are not creating "indigenous" generalizations but providing "raw materials" which contribute to theoretical developments in the centre. Our "indigenous" contributions of specificity do not necessarily contrast with "nonindigenous" generalizations.[62]

While indigenous peoples' struggle against colonial domination no doubt contributed to the development of liberal social science, it should be noted that within the framework of intellectual dependency critical perspectives adopted in countries of the periphery may not necessarily be "indigenous" in origin but a reproduction of counter-orthodox orientations in the centre. In fact, indigenous scholars may adopt such novel approaches, not because they are necessarily compatible with local realities, but because they think that these scientific paradigms represent "aims and methods of universal validity."[63]

As is the case for other parts of the Third World, the Arab countries' independence from colonial rule did not by any means terminate intellectual dependence on the West. The underdevelopment of the Arab World and its economic dependency continued to be reflected in "indigenous" social science. Accordingly,

... the Arab pseudo bourgeoisie (continued) to import social science from the West as if it were importing automobile spare parts... we were missing the critical perspective... Our analysis proceeded according to the "scientific" standards dictated by the western paradigm-in-crisis... [our Arab crisis of the social sciences reflects] the social nature of the class structure which "imports" the paradigms of social science and "translates" them into academic and research programs.[64]

In the context of the power asymmetry which characterizes the relationship between the Arab World and the West, the latter is the source of social scientific paradigms and the Arab World continues to be the object of scientific analysis.[65] The priorities of such scientific analysis themselves are part of the agenda of integration of the Arab economy into the global market structure. As some Arab scholars have recently explained,

> The integration of the Arab economy into the capitalist market is impossible without attention. . . to the study of the economic, social and political situation in order to determine [appropriate] means of penetration of Western economic interests. It was inevitable that science fulfill this function. Thus the modern research sector pioneered the study of the problems and issue which foreign investors should understand before, and during the administration of their [local] projects. . . [consequently], the modern sector of scientific research was developed by the fine elements of [wo/]men of science, to the detriment of the national sector of scientific research.[66]

In short, it may be argued that intellectual dependency is but a manifestation of the political economy of underdevelopment of the Arab World. Egypt, the Arab country with the largest community of researchers, provides a good illustration of the relationship between intellectual dependency and political economic dependency. In this regard it has been suggested that:

> no matter how much we try to explain and rationalize, the balance of intellectual development without doubt suffers from a deficit. . . Thus deficit in Egypt has become a generalized phenomenon which is inflicted upon the balance of trade, the balance of payments, and the state treasury. It affects the intellectual balance also. Even if other countries import more of our intellectual products than we do of theirs, this will remain only a superficial remedy because they import ours to benefit from it while we import theirs to show off.[67]

Arab social scientists may proudly point to past indigenous traditions of social analysis such as Ibn Khaldun's, and identify Arab predecessors of modern day schools of anthropological thought. But under the current sociohistorical conditions of Arab underdevelopment we must also note how often they turn to one Western statement of admiration or another to legitimate the significance of intellectual ancestors' genius.

Legitimation of scholarly worth from without is highly valued in Arab communities of scientists. In the context of intellectual dependency the reputation of scientists is determined by their "international" stature. Such "international" fame ultimately involves scientific production which approximates the standards imposed by the communities of elite scientists of the centre. As is the case of other indigenous social scientists, Arab researchers' scholarship is subject to evaluation according to "international" standards. Thus, when a review of an Arab anthropologist's work brought charges of "absence of new theoretical insights,"[68] the indigenous researcher, a major proponent of the idea of an "Arab anthropological orientation," pointed out that he had noted local researchers' need for "objective neutrality."[69] Evidently "Arab" anthropology has come full circle to the discipline's objectivism. It is also worth noting that Arab scholarship is subject to evaluation in light of *current* standards of "international" scientific development. Thus, a review of an Arab anthropologist's recently published book suggests that "(at) times... (the book)... reads like a pre-1960s ethnography that focuses on kinship and marriage in a community perceived as relatively isolated. Greater attention to the kinds of historical and political economic issues that are *now*-engaging many scholars of the Middle East and elsewhere would have significantly increased the book's impact."[70]

Still another example of how "Arab" scholarship is evaluated according to "non-Arab" standards is the *New Arab Social Order* (1982). In contrast to the praise which this study has received in the Arab World, and the awarding of a prestigious prize to its author, a recent review of the book advises social scientists to "trust the more reliable sociological concepts and methods used by their less adventurous colleagues who circumambulate exotica."[71]

Those who have established reputations based on international standards and related scientific orientations may enjoy recognition in the West while their work continues to be known to only a minority of compatriots and relevant to even fewer. In the absence of independent, well organized local communities of scientists which enjoy appropriate political support of scientific creativity (which fundamentally involves critical thinking), only individual scientists with ties to the advanced centres of science abroad continue to pursue their work and attain standards of "excellence."

The concept of "indigenous Anthropology" provides an illusion of local creativity in relation to anthropological knowledge thereby detracting from the reality of the "satellite" nature of local scientific output. Glamourous labels aside, recognition of the continued flourishing of dependent knowledge and subsequent analysis of the complex politico-economic linkages which perpetuate this form of scientific production are essential steps in the direction of developing indigenous creativity in social research. Since it is a particular social epistemology which prevents the development of a science of Anthropology which is relevant to the Arab World, any ambitions of developing such a science require serious consideration of the necessary social changes.[72]

FEMINIST ANTHROPOLOGY AND THE QUEST FOR INDIGENIZATION

A period of major intellectual crisis among Western as well as Middle Eastern scholars emerged in the late 1960s and early 1970s that had a profound impact on the subsequent scholarship on women in the Middle East. This crisis involved unprecedented self-criticism and radical rethinking in the social and human sciences in response to the political turmoil abroad as well as in the United States including the feminist challenge. Conventional scholarship on the Middle East prior to the 1960s tended to exclude women and feminist issues from theory and method. Even Edward Said's masterful critique of "Orientalism" was silent on the problem of women as Other except for a few lines about Kuchuk Hanem.[73]

It is particularly from the early 1970s onward that scholarship on women begins to reflect the critical trends occuring in both the Third World and the West, and suggests that the epistemological problem of women as Other began to pose a challenge—ideologically, theoretically and methodologically for those engaged in the construction of knowledge about Arab societies and cultures.

Many women scholars doing research on women in the Middle East have thought they were rectifying the colonial and/or androcentric bias of conventional research by focusing their attention on the "women's situation." Despite this focus the conceptual and methodological approaches they have used have been grounded primarily in positivist epistemology.

The recent scholarship on "women in the Arab Middle East" seems to reflect a much greater awareness that to understand the social experience of Middle Eastern women today in all its variations and permutations, one has to take into account the diversity of that experience within specific modalities of religious ideology, social and economic organization and political rule.[74] This is by no means an easy task but the challenge seems to demand a very different kind of scholarship than that which typified the research of the earlier decades. If "a new wind of cultural decolonization is blowing through the Arab Middle East," which is having a profound impact on the lives of women, then we should expect a new scholarship to emerge in order to grasp and understand it. Those scholars who are attempting to understand and explain this very phenomenon (some are committed to changing it as well), are also confronting their own cultural identities and modes of knowing in ways that never previously were considered to be part of the research "problematique." It is in this context of the challenge of authenticity and relevance of one's own research to the broader political struggle of decolonizing the mind that the scholarship on women in the Arab Middle East of the 1980s must be examined.

To suggest possible directions in answering these questions the reader is referred to Cynthia Nelson's Chapter 9, "Old Wine, New Bottles," in this volume, particularly the discussion on the ethnographic studies by Abu-Lughod (1986) and Altorki (1986). Recent trends in anthropological studies of Arab women accord greater empirical validity to indigenous cultural perspectives than to the conventional western social science models. In the spirit of a reflexive anthropology,[75] more and more researchers are making a concerted effort to allow the analytic models to come from the "mouths of their informants."

While the work of indigenous scholars expresses a greater critical awareness of ethnocentric and androcentric bias in western social science it does not reflect a uniquely indigenous anthropology. The quest for indigenization among feminist anthropologists on Arab women is but an extension of a more general, politically inspired, "paradigmatic-shift" reflected in anthropological work in general.

DEVELOPMENT STUDIES ACTION RESEARCH DEBATES

A growing interest in the social sciences has been in "action" and the "actor." Consequently, the 1970s and 1980s have witnessed a slow maturation of what have come to be called practise oriented approaches.[76] Orlando Fals Borda chose the term Participatory Action Research (PAR) to describe research that necessarily implies participation of both subject and object, even though this very distinction is undermined.[77] The practitioners of PAR focus on the function and relevance of the participant native. This focus comes as a reaction to the academic ethos of standardized knowledge which has historically devalued the actors' point of view. This form of knowledge is also seen to be a child of the positivist tradition in the west and therefore alien to nonwestern scholars. Although as yet not central to the Arab debate concerning the "indigenization" of the social sciences, PAR lays claim to an indigenous nonwestern, if not specifically Arab solution. Using the works of phenomenologists and Neo-Marxists for intellectual guidance, PAR postulates that by positing the conjunction between conscious reflections of the native and the action ensuing which aims at transforming reality as theoretical focus, it has arrived at the threshhold of a truly indigenously inspired mode of investigation.

PAR is then a term that refers to a group of diverse membership. These researchers agree on the fact that it is only the social actor who can define his/her own problems and their solutions. This is because the only real fact is the individual consciousness which is irreducible. Every other thing or fact is a construct of this consciousness. Consequently, the only truth we can derive from a social situation is the knowledge we get from the social actors. We must not distort the quality of peoples' subjective experiences nor isolate consciousness from the world it perceives. Having this theoretical qualification in mind, they try to help the underprivileged.[78]

The more progressive members of the Praxis school of PAR interpret these theoretical qualifications as referring to peoples' right to intervene and make choices concerning their own futures. By enjoining people as planners as well as executioners of revolution, they sidestep the risk of becoming a dominant class by virtue of their advanced progressive consciousness.

Examples of PAR projects can be found in India, Sri Lanka, Tanzania and Bangladesh. Both Africa and Asia have little in common except a very clear claim to having reached indigenous, people-oriented social science.[79]

In critically evaluating these claims and scrutinizing them for methodological and theoretical consistency, it is hoped that a contribution can be made to the debate concerning an Arab or indigenous social science. Besides looking at the state of the art of the Arab debate itself, we believe that it is important to see this debate in a third world context.

The Problems that PAR Solves

On the theoretical and methodological level many social scientists today try to avoid academicism because of its isolation from social reality.[80] In rejecting standardized knowledge the alternative has been to seek out indigenous knowledge, or the wisdom of the poor. PAR is part of this trend. The work of Paulo Freire in Columbia has greatly affected action researchers, especially those who are inclined towards the left. Freire tried to create a "Science of the Proletariat" so as to break the monopolization imposed over knowledge production by the consumer class of intellectuals. By combining the subversive science of the repressed and silent culture with a research technique based on participation, he sought to produce radical and "positive" changes in society.[81] Freire states that the only way we can help and understand the other is by starting a process of conscientization in which "... men, not as recepients [recipients], but as knowing subjects achieve a deepening awareness of the sociological reality which shapes their lives and of their capacity to transform that reality."[82]

Freire, and other scholars, although inspired by Historical Materialism grew apart from left wing political parties and other progressive movements in the Third World because they challenged the Leninist idea of the role of the vanguard. In postulating that social transformation is the task of a vanguard which have a consciousness that surpasses that of the masses, progressive elements are in fact sponsoring another form of domination since they are recommending a paternalistic strategy of development.[83] The alternative is to play a catalytic role in the struggle that the people themselves undertake. The guarantee that the people will undertake such a struggle is based on the premise that the Establishment acts in ways which make the masses angry and militant and uncovers their intrinsic and true class consciousness. That is the reason why the masses need nothing but temporary support which is provided by the action researcher.[84]

In the light of these assumptions we can understand better why action researchers see themselves as mere catalysts. On the ideological level they are breaking the exploitative relationship between the researcher and the researched. They find an ideological bias in subject-object relationships.[85] They refuse to become a detached class of intellectuals and so strive to overcome the separation between mental and manual labor. The basic concept that lies at the heart of their innovative work is, as we have already mentioned, *Praxis*. Here, however, we find that it is taken for granted that the researcher is progressive. Freire's work shows us that the "stimulation" of the masses was clearly unsuccessful. They wound up placing their idea of knowledge at the service of the popular interest and propagating the diffusion of Historical Materialism, or rather a replica of it developed in other contexts and other social formations.[86]

The aim of such attempts is to devise a science of the people, or rather of the "proletariat." The result was the imitation of Marxist postulates or a situation of mimesis. The dilemma of praxis, that is, to establish a relation between social theory and social practice, is complicated when attempted by outsiders. The solution presented by PAR is that the natives themselves bring about this relationship between theory and practice since only they can truly represent the interests of the class involved in the formulation and accumulation of knowledge. The role of the intellectual is to intervene in a "sensitive" way since ". . . it is the height of arrogance for . . . (the nonindigenous) to impose normative choice on the indigenous masses."[87] One cannot deny, however, that it is difficult to estimate qualitatively and quantitatively what is meant by "sensitive" intervention. It is difficult to imagine how the researcher can avoid playing the role of the enlightened stranger. Even in this case of training locals to perform the set catalytic role, they are still set apart from the rest of the natives by virtue of the research situation itself. If the researcher wishes to deny having any particular class interests which he/she is serving, the vested interest in making the project a successful one cannot be ignored.

The premise that conscientization is necessary because the rural poor, by virtue of their material conditions, have a class consciousness which is temporarily shadowed is a contradiction from the point of view of methodology. The wish to develop people's power involves taking for granted people's desire for empowerment. Granted that it is only the social actor who defines his/her own problems and their solutions and that the only truth researchers can arrive at is the social actor's truth; granted all that still PAR does, in certain ways, distort the quality of people's subjective experience. The reason for this is the researcher's initiative that creates a research situation. In the final analysis, the researcher remains a producer in the relations of knowledge production, especially when the question of evolving written reports is raised. The verification of the literature rests with the community of scholars who are its readers. It is the writer's understanding of the situation that is written up. Although the initial process of knowledge production may have been one in which natives actively participated, in writing up, this knowledge is processed by the cognitive structures of the researcher which have been developed in other social formations. The native's point of view, as in other examples of ethnographic literature, is reinterpreted by the researcher. True the problematic of indigenous vs. nonindigenous knowledge is addressed by PAR but it is not successfully solved.

As an alternative development approach PAR may be successful on a small scale. To sustain its own methodological postulates and yet generate alternative macro-level development present two irreconcilable tasks. Abandoning, for obvious reasons, the notion of forcing people's participation, it is difficult to reconcile the process of active participation of natives as individuals, the give and take of collective discussions and reflection, with a macro-level development policy. The very epistemological objectivity of this methodology is considered to be internal to the collectivity concerned.[88] How then can we apply the methodology on a bigger scale without evolving restrictive structures to insure that different groups do not infringe on one another? There also remains the question of whose participation counts. Besides the problem of defining one's unit of analysis, whether it is a nation, a district, a village or a household, what of those who do not participate; people who are marginalized either by choice or by group stigma. If we impose on them the normative choice of participant natives we are foregoing PAR stance *vis a vis* forcing choices on individuals. Moreover, there is an implicit assumption that amongst the poor and the powerless there is no differentiation whether material or otherwise. That is within one group the researcher does make the choice of who he/she ally themselves to and consequently ignore others. These and other problems do undermine PAR as an alternative development scheme.

PAR does not necessarily lead to the socialization of the relations of knowledge production, either. The knowledge derived from the research situation is not necessarily "indigenous" in the sense that it is free of "alien" paradigmatic restriction, especially in the case of progressive PAR researchers. People are enjoined as producers of knowledge but are affected and directed by the advanced progressive consciousness of the researcher.

This school does hold promise for a better path to development from below. In its practice it could achieve some positive results if it was endowed with a lot more than it can sustain, methodologically speaking. Its practitioners could achieve better results if they recognize the possibility of following a course of people-based participatory development by dealing with existing methodologies instead of attempting to invent new ones. While not wishing to be judgemental, it must be said that PAR has as yet not justified its claim to innovation by persisting to describe itself as ". . . the incidental development of an ad-hoc methodology guided by. . . researcher's theoretical basis. . . (which involved) the unconscious assimilation of eclectic and often contradictory ideas."[89]

The lack of theoretical consistency or methodological homogeneity does not detract from the value of PAR as an embodiment of a reaction against the state of the art of the social sciences. In drawing attention to the value of the indigenous knowledge of the powerless, and to the dangers of empiricism and positivism, PAR is in effect pointing the way towards a critical social science. Whether it can accommodate Arab/Third World ambitions of the production of an indigenous social science is another matter. It is our opinion that, methodologically speaking, it cannot.

CONCLUSION

Political freedom was won more than a generation ago; the fight for economic independence is being fought; the battle for the Mind has scarcely begun. Only when the intellectual doors of perception are cleansed will the Third World be able to gamble with the fundamental realities.[90]

The authors of this chapter, representing indigenous (Morsy, Saad and Sholkamy) as well as nonindigenous (Nelson) scholars, have been conducting fieldwork in and on the Arab world for nearly twenty-five years. From these experiences we have become increasingly aware of the political, epistemological and methodological issues raised in the "call for the indigenization of the social sciences." This paper represents our collective effort to render problematic this concept of "indigenization" with specific reference to its use and meaning in the praxis of social science (particularly anthropology) in the Arab world.

We began by locating the point in time at which the "call" appeared and examined the socio-political and academic contexts in which it had particular appeal. This period also coincided with the rise of "the feminist critique" of social science scholarship and its androcentric bias. Hence gender was joined to that of nationality as critical factors in the construction of knowledge in anthropology. We have tried to demonstrate that the facile definition of indigenous anthropology as "the practice of social and cultural anthropology in one's own national setting" obscures a number of critical issues in the production of social science knowledge—rather than illuminating Self and Other alike. Primary among these issues is the recognition that the call for an indigenous social science (based on its *a priori* assumption of homogenity among indigenous scholars) can actually serve to support those very political economic conditions that continue to perpetrate a western domination of the institutions and practices of social science in the Third World, including the Arab World.

Our critique is not directed against the quest for a more relevant and authentic social science both among non-Western as well as Western scholars. Rather it is to suggest that this quest, viewed within the political and intellectual context in which it originated—namely the national liberation movements and the accompanying anti-imperialist ideology in the Third World and the crisis of relevance of Western social science—gave rise to the taken-for-granted assumption that nationals studying their own societies—or women studying their own gender—would cleanse the intellectual doors of perception and produce more authentic and relevant knowledge.

This chapter concludes that this has not been the case. The reasons for this, we suggest, lie in the following themes: 1) Many who claim to be practicing "indigenous anthropology" do so without rendering problematic the context of dependency in which the production of so-called indigenous knowledge is taking place. 2) Those claiming to be practicing indigenous anthropology seem to follow the same logic as the "old" traditional Western social scientists who lumped "us" (The Third World) as distanced from "them" (the Western World) on the assumption that Arab, African, Latin American, Islamic, etc., are "indigenous" similarly. This logic commits a serious epistemological blunder by obscuring the diverse political and ideological stands among social scientists both in the Arab World and the West. Also this logic has a serious flaw in trying to create a local "theory" which is derived from and can only deal with Arab reality. 3) Methodologically many who claim to be practicing "indigenous anthropology" are oblivious to the research relationship with those with whom they engage in research. What is critically overlooked is how we *can* and how we *must* engage others in the act of inquiry. For those who are *not* oblivious to the research relationships, the attempt to construct indigenous knowledge becomes the methodological issue *sine qua non* of indigenous anthropology. In one trend, as exemplified in feminist scholarship, the researcher becomes critically self-conscious of the significance of gender in research thus muting the prior claim of nationality. In another trend reflected in Participatory Action Research or "action research," the indigenous researcher, in the role of "enlightened interventionist," reflects his/her own class or vested intellectual interests and therefore, does not overcome the problem of producing a truly indigenous (people's) knowledge; 4) A final reason that suggests that an indigenous social science has not yet appeared, lies in the realm of pedagogy—a theme we did not specifically address, but which bears directly on the production of indigenous knowledge—that is, what knowledge do you teach? How do you teach this knowledge and to what "ends"? Is there evidence that the institutions of higher learning in the Arab World have developed an "indigenous curriculum" for social science? Are there any attempts to do so? Whose interests would be served by the teaching and praxis of an "indigenous social science"?

Although we have been critical in our examination of the concept of indigenous social science, we do not wish to end this paper on a note of pessimism. For those who truly seek alternatives to the paradigms of Western social science that not only were created during a period of colonization but also flourished by emphasizing the existence of the "distinctive other," the call for indigenization of the social sciences reflects the attempt to transcend these historical limitations by creating a greater linkage between theoretical formulations and socio-historical reality.

Critics of Western (or colonial) social science, for example Mafeje or Asad,[91] have demonstrated how functional theory served the interests of bourgeois Western colonial society both at the center (Europe) and the periphery (The Third World). But very few have consciously attempted to go beyond critique and engage in what Adonis called "a new search of discovery and rebuilding."[92] A recent trend within the Arab World to seek a new Arab social science has produced an increasing number of "cultural critics of Arab society" that is, an indigenous movement of secular criticism by indigenous scholars critiquing contemporary Arab and Western social realities.

As Sharabi states:

The period of the 1970s and 1980s which marks the neopatriarchal society's highest material prosperity and the beginning of its social and political disintegration, coincides with the emergence of an impressive body of scholarly and critical works forming the *first radical critique* [emphasis ours] of neopatriarchal culture and society.[93]

Thus over the last two decades, the new critique has given rise to a *new kind of discourse*—one in which the *appropriation* of Western concepts and approaches—particularly those of the social sciences, Marxism, structuralism, and deconstruction—became possible. The systematic questioning of ideological, religious and fundamentalist thought became possible by the prospect of an independent *rereading* of history and society.[94]

Perhaps the deepest penetration made by the new criticism was in those areas that were most closely guarded by the neopatriarchal discourse— in the domains of the unthought *(impensee)* and the unsaid *(non dit)* of the body of sexuality, of the generally prohibited. For the new mode of discourse, customs, traditions, rituals were no longer truths or values but clues and signs and symbols disclosing meanings and purposes which neopatriarchal discourse sought to hide or distort: For example the sexual question, women, political power, and sexual repression.[95]

But even Sharabi regards these Arab writers and scholars engaged in the new cultural criticism as second degree critics, in the sense that "none of them can be properly regarded as a truly creative or original historian, philosopher, sociologist, etc."[96] It falls short of truly theorizing thought. They are more methodologists than theoreticians "for they have been engaged more in promoting a critical approach than in devising an original theory."[97]

The significance of Sharabi's views to the purposes of our paper is that he points us in a direction as to what might be a fruitful way to think about the "call for indigenization." The difficulties that the new critics confront and seem unable to resolve are: 1) the persistence of the (invisible) Western categories and codes which penetrate their ways of thought and expression; 2) the problem of "translation"—of making the transition from one paradigm to another, of rendering one cognitive system intelligible in terms of another and he raises the very interesting question: "What does it mean to be a cultural and linguistic outsider reading the Western text from the outside?"; and, 3) their didactic mode of discourse, reflected in their rhetorical tone and in their concern to insert borrowed concepts more than to ground the discourse in intelligible "Arab" terms.

However, he suggests one possible strategy for overcoming these difficulties—a strategy that might have some relevance to the process of "indigenization." He suggests:

Perhaps it could be that only radical gestures, similar to one suggested by the traditionalist position but in the opposite direction, i.e., total immersion in the Western discourse, might make it possible to grasp the foreign text from within, and to approach neopatriarchal reality neither as an alien other nor as a defensive Self (i.e., neither from the position of external dependency nor of internal submission), but as a reality in and for itself. And this, I believe is largely the kind of break the new critics concerned with deconstructing the neo-patriarchal discourse seem to aim at.[98]

What this would translate to in our context would be for indigenous and nonindigenous scholars alike to engage in the praxis of demystifying both Western and patriarchal frameworks toward the goal of a unifying synthesis and a creative theory, in which Self and Other could enter a discourse that reflects concern and commitment to human values of freedom, justice and equity rather than abstract "universalism." As self-conscious intellectuals we have the duty and responsibility to illuminate the political nature of social research whether indigenous or otherwise. It is in this spirit that the present critique is offered.

NOTES

1. See Gerald Berreman, "Is Anthropology Alive? Social Responsibility in Social Anthropology," *Current Anthropology* 9 (1968), pp. 391–96; K. Gough, "World Revolution and the Science of Norm," in *The Dissenting Academy*, edited by Theodore Roszak (London: Chatto and Windus Ltd., 1986); Dell Hymes, *Re-Inventing Anthropology* (New York: Random House, 1969); A. Gouldner, *The Coming Crisis in Western Sociology* (New York: Basic Books, 1970); Jean Cepons, ed., *Anthropologie et Imperialism* (Paris: Francois Maspero, 1975); Gerrit Huizer and B. Mannheim, *The Politics of Anthropology* (The Hague: Mouton, 1979); Eleanor Leacock, "Marxism and Anthropology," in *The Left Academy: Scholarship on American Campuses* (New York: McGraw Hill, 1982), pp. 242–76; and Eric Wolf, *Europe and the People Without History* (Los Angeles: The University of California Press, 1982).

2. See J. Banaj, "Crisis in British Anthropology," *The New Left Review*, no. 64 (1970), pp. 71–85; B. Magubane, "A Critical Look on the Indices Used in the Study of Social Change in Modern Africa," *Current Anthropology* 12 (1971), pp. 153–70; R. Stavenhagen, "Decolonizing Applied Anthropology," *Human Organization* 30, no. 4 (1971); and Talal Asad, ed., *Anthropology and the Colonial Encounter* (London: Ithaca Press, 1973).

3. See Ben Jalloun, "Decolonizing Sociology in the Maghreb: The Usefulness and Risks of a Critical Function," *Le Monde Diplomatique*, August 1974, p.

28; and Hussein Fahim, "Anthropology and Contemporary Arab Thought," paper presented at the Symposium "The Arab Intelligensia," Cairo, March 28–31, 1987.

4. June Nash, "Introduction" in *Sex and Class in Latin America: Women's Perspectives on Politics, Economics and the Family in the Third World,* June Nash and Helen Safa, eds. (New York: Bergin, 1980), p. 15.

5. Hymes.

6. See for example, Cynthia Nelson, "Women and Power in Nomadic Societies," in *The Desert and the Sown: Nomads in the Greater Society* (Berkeley: Institute of International Studies, University of California, 1973), pp. 43–59; Leacock; M.Z. Rosaldo and Louis Lamphere, *Women, Culture and Society* (Stanford: Stanford University Press, 1974); Shirley Ardener, ed., *Perceiving Women* (London: Ithaca Press, 1975) and Karen Sacks, "State Bias and Women's Status," *American Anthropologist* 78 (1976), pp. 565–69.

7. B. Scholte, "Cultural Anthropology and the Paradigm Concept: A Brief History of their Recent Convergence," in *Functions and Uses of Disciplinary Histories,* Loren Graham et al., eds., Vol. VII, pp. 229–78 (Dordrecht, Holland: D. Reidel Publishing Co., 1983), p. 235.

8. Leacock, 1974, cf. Andre Gunder Frank, "Anthropology = Ideology; Applied Anthropology = Politics," *Race and Class* 7, no.1 (1975), pp. 57–68.

9. D.N. Brokensha et al., *Indigenous Knowledge Systems and Development* (Landham, Md.: University Press of America, 1980).

10. R. Stavenhagen, "Decolonizing Applied Anthropology," *Human Organization* 30, no. 4 (1971).

11. Margaret Mead, *New Lives for Old* (New York: New American Library, 1961).

12. Ikenna Nzimiro, "The Crisis in the Social Sciences: The Nigerian Situation" Third World Forum Occasional Papers, No. 2, Mexico: Third World Forum Coordinating Secretariat, 1977; S.C. Dube, *On Crisis and Commitment in Social Sciences;* Yogesh Atal, ed., (New Delhi: Abhirov Publications, 1983); and Susantha Goonatilake, *Aborted Discovery: Science and Creativity in the Third World* (London: Zed Press, 1984).

13. Good examples are Hussein Fahim and K. Helmer, "Indigenous Anthropology in Non-Western Countries: A Further Elaboration," *Current Anthropology* 21, no. 5 (1980), pp. 644–50; Soraya Altorki, "The Anthropologist in the Field: A Case of 'Indigenous Anthropology' from Saudi Arabia," in *Indigenous Anthropology in Non-Western Countries,* H. Fahim, ed. (Durham: Carolina Academic Press, 1982) and Emiko Ohnuki-Tierney, "'Native' Anthropologists," *American Ethnologist* 11, no. 3 (1984), pp. 584–86.

14. See Tomas Gerholm and U. Hannerz, "Introduction: The Shaping of National Anthropologies," special issues of *Ethnos,* Stockholm: Etnografiska Museet, 1982; Susantha Goonatilake, *Aborted Discovery: Science and Creativity in the Third World* (London: Zed Press, 1984).

15. Ahmed Khalifa and Soheir Loutfi, eds., *The Problematic of Social Sciences in the Arab Homeland* (Beirut: Dar El-Janweer, 1984) in Arabic.

16. Ismail al-Faruqi, "Meta-Religion: Towards a Critical World Theology,"

American Journal of Islamic Social Sciences 3, no. 1 (1986), pp. 13–58; Sayyid Syeed, "Islamization and Linguistics," *American Journal of Islamic Social Sciences* 3, no. 1 (1986), pp. 77–78; and Muhammed A. Ma'ruf, "Towards an Islamic Critique of Anthropological Evolutionism," *American Journal of Islamic Social Sciences* 3, no. 1 (1986), pp. 89–108.

17. Abdel Ghaffar Ahmed, "The State of Anthropology in the Sudan," Special issue of *Ethnos* (Stockholm: Etnografiska Museet, 1982); Galal Amin, "The Crisis of the Intellectuals in the Third World," *The New Path* (December 1985) (Cairo: American University in Cairo, 1985) and Ali El-Kinz, "The Theoretical and Political Problematic of Arab Social Science." *Al-Mustaqbal al-Arabi* 48, no. 2 (1986), pp. 29–34, in Arabic.

18. Mahmud Abdel Fadil, *Reflections on the Egyptian Economic Question* (Cairo: Dar al-Mustaqbal al-Arabi, 1983) in Arabic; Mohammed Abu Mandur, "Work and the Mysteries of Egyptian Agriculture," *Al-Ahali*, March 14, 1984, in Arabic; and Mohammed El-Sayeed Selim, "The Impact of Egyptian-American Academic Research," The Impact of Egyptian-American Academic Research," The Cairo/Massachusetts Institute of Technology Program, *Cairo Papers in Social Science* 7, no. 1 (1984), pp. 57–67.

19. Soheir Morsy, "US Aid to Egypt: An Illustration and Account of US Foreign Assistance Policy," *Arab Studies Quarterly* 8, no. 4 (1986), pp. 358–89.

20. Cynthia Nelson, "Whose Knowledge Counts: Discourse and Development in an Egyptian Rural Community," in *Impact of Development Assistance on Egypt*, E.L. Sullivan, ed., Cairo Papers in Social Science, Vol. 7, no. 3 (1984), pp. 45–56.

21. Soheir Morsy, "Indigenous Anthropology in the Context of Intellectual Dependency," paper presented at the Annual Central States Meetings of the American Anthropological Association, Chicago, Illinois, March 21–23, 1986.

22. Sayed Yassin, "In Search of a New Identity for the Social Sciences in the Arab World: Discourse, Paradigm and Strategy," unpublished paper, International Middle East Conference on the State of the Art of Middle East Studies, August 1–3, 1986.

23. Gerholm and Hannerz.

24. See El-Kinz; Adel Hussein, *Toward a New Arab Thought: Nasserism, Development and Democracy* (Cairo: Dar al-Mustaqbal al-Arabi, 1985) in Arabic; and M. Sid Ahmed, "The Crisis of the Intellectuals in the Third World," *The New Path* (December 1985) (Cairo: American University in Cairo, 1985).

25. Fahim, *Indigenous Anthropology*; Fahim, "Anthropology and Contemporary Arab Thought."

26. M.E. Higazy,"The Contemporary Crisis of Sociology in the Arab World," *Al-Mustaqbal al-Arab* (1985), pp. 60–61.

27. Amin, p. 12.

28. Higazy; and S. Sary, "Arab Sociologists and the Study of Arab Societal Problems: A Critical Practice," *Al-Mustaqbal al-Arabi*, no. 75 (1985), pp. 85–95, in Arabic.

29. Higazy, p. 62.
30. Ibid., p. 82.
31. Hussein, p. 30.
32. Ibid.
33. Ibid., p. 32.
34. Zghal, p. 35.
35. Altorki and Camillia el-Solh, eds., *Studying Your Own Society: Arab Women in the Field* (Syracuse: Syracuse University Press, 1985).
36. Altorki; Fahim and Helmer; L. Ahmed, "Western Ethnocentrism and Perspectives of the Harem," *Feminist Studies* 8 (1982), pp. 521–34; and Hussein Fahim "Foreign and Indigenous Anthropology: The Perspectives of an Egyptian Anthropologist," *Human Organization* 36, no. 1 (1977), pp. 80–86 and 10.
37. Fahim, "Anthropology and Contemporary Arab Thought," p. 2.
38. Hussein Fahim, The Story of Anthropology (Kuwait: Alam al: Marifa, 1982 and 1986), p. 252, in Arabic.
39. Ibid.
40. Translation of Fahim, "Anthropology and Comtemporary Arab Thought" , p. 5.
41. Ibid., p. 6.
42. Fahim, "Anthropology and Contemporary Arab Thought."
43. J. Kirkpatrick, "Review of Louis Dumont's *Essais Sur L'individualism: Une Perspective Anthropologique sur L'ideologie Modern*" (Paris: Editions Du Senil, 1983), *American Anthropologist* 87 (1985), p. 168.
44. Goonatilake, p. 25; and Edward Said, *Orientalism* (New York: Pantheon, 1978).
45. Fahim, "Anthropology and Contemporary Arab Thought," p. 9.
46. Fahim, "Foreign and Indigenous Anthropology," p. 5.
47. Morsy.
48. Richard Antoun, "On the Modesty of Women in Arab Muslim Villages: A Study in the Accommodation of Tradition," *American Anthropologist* 70 (1968), pp. 671–97; and N. Abu-Zahra, "On the Modesty of Women in Arab Muslim Villages: A Reply," *American Anthropologist* 72 (1970), pp. 1979–89.
49. Dube in Atal, Y., ed., pp. 77–78.
50. Ibid., p. 7.
51. Fahim and Helmer, p. 644.
52. Fahim, "Foreign and Indigenous Anthropology," p. 82.
53. Magabane; and James Faris, "Pax Britannica and the Sudan: S.F. Nadel," in *Anthropology and the Colonial Encounter*, Talal Asad, ed. (London: Ithaca Press, 1973).
54. Magubane; and Faris.
55. Sandra Harding and Merril B. Mintikka, eds., "Introduction" in *Discovering Reality* (Dordrecht: D. Reidel Publishing Company), p. xii.
56. Goonatilake, p. 107.

57. Cf. S. Tiffany, "Paradigms of Power: Feminist Reflections on the Anthropology of Women in Pacific Island Societies," Working Paper No. 79, WID (East Lansing: Michigan State University, 1985), p. 2.

58. M. Sid Ahmed, "The Crisis of the Intellectuals in the Third World," *The New Path* (December, 1985) Cairo: The American University in Cairo.

59. Dube in Atal., p. 89.

60. Goonatilake, pp. 110–11.

61. Ibid., p. 111.

62. Cf. Diweedar in T. Abdel Hakim (moderator), "Development in Egypt and the Homeland: A Theoretical Discussion," *Fikr* 7 (October 1985), p. 33, in Arabic.

63. As quoted in Goonatilake, p.108.

64. Ghali Shukri,"Conceptual Problems on the Arab Road Towards a Sociology of Knowledge," *Al Mustaqbal al-Arabi* 77, no. 7 (1985), pp. 126–36 and 131, in Arabic.

65. As cited in Shukri, p. 132.

66. Murad Wahba et al., "Proceedings of the Conference on Intellectual Dependency" *Al-Tarbiya al-Mucasra* 3 (May 1984): 209–26, (in Arabic) and Badran.

67. M. Faraq, "Intellectual Dependency and Political Dependency," paper presented on the Symposium on the Arab Intelligencia, Cairo, March 28–31, 1987, p. 37.

68. Peter Allen, "Review of Hussein Fahim's *Egyptian Nubian Resettlement and Years of Coping,*" *American Anthropologist* 87 (1985), pp. 462–63.

69. Fahim, "Anthropology and Contemporary Arab Thought," p.152.

70. Lois Beck, "Review of Altorki, *Women in Saudi Arabia: Ideology and Behaviour Among the Elites,*" *American Anthropologist* 89 (1987), p. 163, emphasis added.

71. Theodore Downing, "Review of Saad Eddin Ibrahim's *The New Arab Social Order: A Study of the Social Impact of Oil Wealth,*" *American Anthropologist* 85 (1983), p. 995.

72. Goonatilake, pp. 3 and 143.

73. Said, pp. 186–88 and 207.

74. Lois Beck and Nikki Keddie, eds., *Women in the Muslim World* (London: Harvard University Press, 1978); D. Waines, "Through the Veil Darkly: The Study of Women in Muslim Societies" *Comparative Studies of Society and History* 24, no. 4 (1982):, pp. 642–59; Nikki Keddie, "Problems in the Study of Middle Eastern Women," *International Journal of Middle East Studies* 10 (April 1979). pp. 225–40; and J. Tucker, "The Decline of the Family Economy in Mid-19th Century Egypt," *Arab Studies Quarterly* 1, no. 3 (1979), pp. 245–71.

75. B. Scholte, "Cultural Anthropology and the Paradigm Concept: A Brief History of their Recent Convergence," in *Functions and Uses of Disciplinary Histories,* Loren Graham et al., eds., Vol. VII (Dordrecht: D. Reidel Publishing Co., 1983), pp. 229–78.

76. S. Ortner, "Theory in Anthropology Since the Sixties," *Comparative Studies in Society and History* 26 (1984), pp. 126–66.

77. M.A. Rahman,"The Theory and Practice of Participatory Action Research," unpublished paper, Tenth World Congress of Sociology, Mexico City, 1982.

78. R. Gorman.

79. J. Maeda et al., "Go UJAMAA," *Development: Journal of Society of International Development* 1 (1981), pp. 29–34; Rahman, Md. Anisur, "Concept of an Inquiry" *Development: Journal of Society for International Development* 1 (1981), pp. 3–6; Rahman, "The Theory and Practice of Participatory Action Research"; A.O. Anacleti, *Jipemoyo. Development and Culture Research,* Vol. 2 (Uppsala, Sweden: Scandanavian Institute of African Studies, 1980).

80. F. Stambouli, "Sociology, Methodology and Action Research. The Case of the Arab Meghreb," *International Review of Modern Sociology* 12, no. 1 (1982), pp. 39–50.

81. O. Fals-Borda, "The Challenge of Action Research," *Development: Journal of Society International Development* 1 (1981), pp. 55–63.

82. M. Yron, *Development By People: Citizen Construction of a Just World* (New York: Praeger Publishers, 1983), p. 15.

83. Rahman.

84. Gran.

85. O. Fals Borda.

86. Rahman.

87. Gran, p. 47.

88. Rahman, p. 15.

89. R. Bryceson, "Research Methodology and the Participatory Research Approach," in Anaclete, A.D., *Jipemoyo: Development and Culture Research* 2 (1980), p.13.

90. G. Bell-Villada, "Decolonizing the Mind" *South: The Third World Magazine* 29 (January 1983) , p.19.

91. A. Mafeje, "The Problem of Anthropology in Historical Perspectives: An Inquiry into the Youth of the Social Sciences," *Canadian Journal of African Studies,* no. 22 (1976), pp. 307–22; Talal Asad, ed., *Anthropology and the Colonial Encounter* (London: Ithaca Press, 1973).

92. Adonis quoted in Hisham Sharabi, "Cultural Critics of Arab Society," *Arab Studies Quarterly* 9, no. 1 (Winter 1987), p. 2.

93. Ibid., p. 3.

94. Ibid., p. 4.

95. Ibid., p. 5.

96. Ibid.

97. Ibid., p. 15.

98. Ibid., pp. 15–16.

PART THREE:
SPECIAL TOPICS IN ARAB STUDIES

5 The State of the Art in Studies of Middle Eastern Urbanization

JANET ABU-LUGHOD

THERE HAVE BEEN three different genres of scholarly works on cities of the Middle East, in particular the Arab World. The purpose of this chapter is to identify these approaches referring, albeit not exhaustively, to works that exemplify each approach, and to raise some fundamental criticisms concerning their limitations.

The three basic approaches that dominate the literature on urbanization in the Arab World may be identified as: 1) generalizations about the characteristics of the "Islamic City" and, to a lesser extent, the mechanisms that created this form of city-building, focusing almost exclusively on preindustrial/medieval cities; 2) biographies of individual cities in the Arab world designed to show—for varying time periods and durations— the ways they grew and changed and the types of problems they faced; and 3) statistical and often comparative work on the levels of urbanization (that is, the percentage of population living in cities) in various countries of the Arab region, often with the intent of demonstrating certain "abnormalities" in the Arab urban hierarchy.

The work that falls in the first genre has been done largely by western Orientalists who began in the early twentieth century to lay out what they assumed to be the quintessential characteristics of "The Islamic City." Recently, there has been an efflorescence of revisionist work done by Muslim urbanists (largely from the Gulf area/Saudi Arabia) who are seeking, in the cities of the past, models for creating "true" Islamic cities today.

The work in the second genre has been more varied in provenance and scope. Some has been done by Western historians interested in reconstructing the nature of given cities (either their physical form or their social and political organization) at some time in the past. Some has been done by Western anthropologists examining the present and trying to connect contemporary patterns to their historical roots. Some has been done by practicing planners in the Arab world who pay greater attention to contemporary problems of housing, utilities, and, less commonly, of employment, levels of living, and political power. Very little work has been done by social scientists broadly grounded in urban studies.

Finally, the work in the last category has, for the most part, been produced by demographers whose chief focus has been on certain "abnormalities" in the demographic structure of Arab urbanization—such as "overurbanization," "primacy," and the like. While some of this work has been done by sociologists and urbanists who have empirical grounding in the region and a familiarity with what such levels of urbanization actually mean in terms of way of life, much has been produced in a rather mechanical fashion, using data from the Middle East to test generalizations derived either from theory or from empirical findings elsewhere. (I shall not cite the poor studies in this survey.)

THE LITERATURE ON THE ISLAMIC CITY

The etiology of the concept of the Islamic City shows an increasingly solidified "gloss" about topographic and political structures of medieval cities in the Middle East and North Africa based largely on a few cases (mostly North African) studied "on the eve" of European domination. The writings of Georges Marcais (1940; 1945), William Marcais (1928), Roger Le Tourneau (1949; 1957 and 1965), and Gustave von Grunebaum (1955) figure large in the construction of this urban myth about a common form for the medieval city in Islamic realms, while the legal and political bases for such an urban form were sought by Spies (1927) and Brunschvig (1947) in legal texts and fiche. More recently, both western historians (Hourani and Stern, 1970; L. Carl Brown, 1973) and Muslim urbanists (al-Hathloul, 1981; Hakim, 1986) have been expanding this investigation into the relationship between legal precedents and the form of cities.

While puzzling over the distortions that the Orientalist myth of "the" Islamic City introduced into the study of Middle Eastern cities, it is apparent that most producers of this genre have not been urbanists. Therefore, they lacked both an understanding of the universal processes whereby cities are created and recreated and a comparative perspective against which to judge what was general and what was unique about medieval cities of the Middle East. It is as if the only cities they had known were those of medieval Islam. Thus, they attributed to the "religion" many urban characteristics which were actually due to the preindustrial level of technology, the hot dry climatic zone, the pre-Islamic tradition of city building, and even the material used for construction.

It is just this knowledge which seems so lacking in the Orientalists who set out to "define" the Islamic city. They failed to recognize how many of the things they were finding were typical of cities during the preindustrial era, regardless of cultural region or religion. An item such as the division of the commercial district into subzones of economic specialization was as typical of European cities in the Middle Ages as it was of cities in the Middle East. Similarly, the famous "courtyard house" design was (and is) typical in many urban centers built in very hot dry climates, regardless of religion; indeed it was found throughout the pre-Islamic Middle East as far back as Sumarian times. Furthermore, walking cities all tend to have somewhat meandering streets, particularly when wheeled carts are not in use. The most likely explanation for the extreme narrowness and irregularity of the street pattern in medieval cities in the Middle East and North Africa was not Islam so much as it was the absence of wheeled carts—a function more of costs and new methods of harnessing camels than of religion. Building materials, in themselves, often dictate the form of buildings, especially in the absence of any cultural imperative. Thus, cities and buildings in tropical Indonesia look more like those in other Asian places and structures than they resemble "Islamic" ones.

I do not mean to suggest that there were no special characteristics of Middle Eastern cities which were due to Islam. There clearly were. Gender segregation was one. The legal pattern—the divisibility of property rights, the greater responsibility to close neighbors, and the importance of waqf as a factor leading to poor maintenance—was another. It is possible that religious segregation was a third, but only under certain conditions.

Students of the Islamic city (for example, Lapidus, 1967, as well as von Grunebaum and W. Marcais) also posited that it had a special political form of organization, or rather, lack thereof. They failed to note that many of the characteristics they singled out as specific to Islamic cities were not atypical of non-Islamic cities in other times and places. Ever since the position was set forth by Max Weber, it has been an accepted truism that oriental and occidental medieval cities were fundamentally different. Lapidus, for example, starts from this premise. Max Weber, in his famous section on the stadt (English trans., 1958), contended that only western cities, with their presumed municipal autonomy and their laissez-faire form of civil/political administration, were "true cities," and then, only during medieval times. In contrast, oriental cities were "merely" cities within empires, as if this was some sort of deficiency. The position, when one thinks about it, is strange, since clearly a metropolis is more developed than a city-state. Certainly, the capital of a world empire is no less a city than a city-state such as present-day Kuwait or medieval Lubeck or Genoa; it is simply a different kind. It is definitely not Islamic.

Nor were the European medieval communities, so admired by Weber, as self-ruled nor their economies as "laissez-faire" as Weber claimed. The state interfered and regulated business perhaps even more than was the case in medieval Islamic cities, and many of the institutions considered part of the self-government of European cities (such as the prevot of the market, etc.) were also present in Arab cities of the Middle Ages.

The division of the polity into groups having somewhat different rights and responsibilities, and the tendency to segregate residentially these groups from one another, was also not a unique characteristic of Arab cities in the preindustrial period. I have been doing research on medieval cities of Europe and find similar political institutions. At least in the great trading centers, foreign merchants often occupied their own buildings and even quarters; they were given special dispensations and privileges with respect to the legal court system, often adjudicating their own disputes. Interestingly enough, in Chinese port cities during the same period, a similar system prevailed. In China, Muslim merchants lived in their own quarters under their own laws, just as Jews were segregated in many European cities, both occupationally and residentially. In a manner similar to the millet system, Arab merchants in Chinese ports were often held collectively responsible for their own communally-administered neighborhood (see Abu-Lughod, 1989).

In short, had the Orientalists describing the Islamic city known more about premodern cities elsewhere in the world, they might have found fewer unique elements. But they would have been able to appreciate the few there were, and they would have been forced to explain through Islam those elements which truly distinguished Arab cities from others.

BIOGRAPHIES OF ARAB CITIES

This genre of work is perhaps the most commonly found. Think over the cities that have received such treatment: Cairo (Clerget, 1934; Raymond, *inter alia* 1973–74; Abu-Lughod, 1971; Staffa, 1977; Wiet, 1964, to mention only a few); Damascus (Sauvaget, 1934; Ziadeh, 1964; Lapidus, 1967; Rafeq, 1966); Aleppo (Sauvaget, 1940; Lapidus, 1967); Algiers (Lespes, 1930); Casablanca (Adam, 1968); Beirut (Khalaf and Kongstad, 1973; Khuri, 1975; Fawaz, 1983); Rabat (Abu-Lughod, 1980); Sale (Brown, 1976); Boujad (Eickelman, 1976); Tlemcen (Lawless, 1976); Tunis (Daoulatli, 1976); Fez (le Tourneau, 1949, 1965); Baghdad (Wiet, 1971); Sanaa (Sergeant, 1980, 1985); Mecca and Medina (Esin, 1963), to mention only ones that come readily to mind. Most of these works have not been done by urbanists.

Many have been written by journalists or historians specializing in the Middle East. Only rarely is there a scholar like Sauvaget who understands intuitively what a city is. A few studies have been done by architectural historians who tend to grasp the physical forms best while being only dimly aware of the social forces that gave rise to them. The best, I think, are the studies done by social scientists, for they recognize that cities are living entities—shaped by the social life within them and in turn modifying and influencing that life. None, to my knowledge, has been done by an economist, which seems a grave deficiency.

A second set of entries in this category would contain the special-purpose studies of aspects (usually problematic) of a given city, usually written by engineers or city planners in the Arab world itself—practical people with very practical agendas. More restricted in scope and almost exclusively confined to the contemporary period, they are largely descriptive, quantitative, and only weakly policy-oriented.

Both of these types of works tend to suffer from myopia, a disease which comes from examining a single case too closely. Whether descriptively historical or focused more narrowly on a given "problem," they cannot help but be weak in explanation, for their authors' eyes often have blinders which exclude crucial events and forces that lie *beyond* the given urban environment being studied.

This is a particularly serious fault when one wishes to explain cities in the Arab World, and the error becomes progressively greater as one approaches the present time. To explain the rise and fall of cities in the period of Islamic greatness one needs to know not only what was happening in the cities themselves but what was happening to world trade routes and to the rise and fall of other cities and empires. Similarly, to understand the sources of today's problems in Arab cities, one needs to comprehend the after-effects of imperialism and colonialism, both internally within a country and externally with reference to the metropole. Students of contemporary Arab cities who do not take into account the articulation of the Arab World with the rest of the world system *can never* explain adequately the causes of urban problems nor can they prescribe effective solutions.

It amazes me that so little of the literature on Arab cities is guided by any theoretical understanding of outside systems and how they impact upon urban growth and problems. This is not true of the urban literature on other parts of the Third World. Dependency theory, generated in Latin America and applied powerfully to urban studies there, has been virtually unapplied to the Middle Eastern context. Imperialism—and the Middle East suffered as much as any region from it—is seldom invoked to explain the type of parasitic urbanization that evolved in the Arab World, although no student of African (or, today, even Indian) urbanization is ever allowed to ignore it. Colonialism is usually ignored, except to note that it created "dual cities" throughout the region. Nor do the urban studies on the Middle East pay much attention to the way such cities articulate either with the Arab region around them or with the world economic system which defines their role in the international division of labor.

I would make a few exceptions to this blanket criticism. Kenneth Brown's study of Sale (1976) and my own of Rabat (1980) benefited from the researches of Miege (4 volumes, 1961–63) which demonstrated how western capitalist penetration of Morocco took place. Given that fundamental source, it was impossible to ignore the urban consequences. It was the cities that felt the ultimate impact of the process of industrial involution and of the massive dislodgement of transhumants and peasants that came in the wake of a restructured and subordinated economy. Leila Fawaz's (1983) study of Beirut in the nineteenth century is also sensitively aware of how outside forces influenced the physical and social structure of a dependent Arab city.

But where is that awareness of the world among Arab urbanists struggling to solve contemporary problems? What housers and planners in Egypt appear aware of the external causes of their difficulties? When I was in Egypt in March, 1985 I gave a lecture entitled "The Coming Crisis in

Arab Cities" which tried to relate changes in the international market for oil to the types of urbanization which have occurred in the past decade and to the economic and urban difficulties now beginning to be felt in various Arab countries and their cities. This is what seems to be missing from the descriptions of catastrophe that pepper the work of Arab engineers and city planners. This understanding does not usually inform their analyses nor guide their policy recommendations. (See, for example, the old book edited by Berger, 1963, but not fully corrected in the much later collection edited by Blake and Lawless, 1980.)

STATISTICAL STUDIES OF COMPARATIVE LEVELS OF URBANIZATION

The final genre to be covered is produced by demographers who focus their attention on the percent of population in Arab countries who live in cities. Through their statistical comparisons they identify two major types of problems: first, the one called over-urbanization, which comes from comparing the levels of urbanization in the Arab region with those in other regions of comparable "development"; the second, called hyper-cephaly or "primacy," which comes from comparing the relative sizes of cities within a given country. Much of this work has been valuable, for example the general findings of Kingsley Davis and Hilda Golden (1954, 1969, 1972), and the more regionally-specific studies of Parke (1954), Thomlinson (1975), Bonine (1980), El-Shakhs and Amirahmadi (1985), Ibrahim (1975), and Abu-Lughod (1960, 1973).

There can be little doubt that the deviations these scholars have found are significant. In comparison to other Third World regions, Middle Eastern countries do have a higher percentage of their populations living in cities than seems "warranted" by their levels of industrial development, the proportion of their populations in agriculture, and their literacy levels. Similarly, many Arab countries suffer from what has been called the problem of primacy, with the largest city containing a "disproportionate" percentage of the urban population.

The major critique I would level against this work is that all too often it has been purely quantitative and descriptive. It has tended to accept what the particular government defines as "urban" without making cross-national adjustments for comparability. It has assumed an unchanging relationship between size and the quality of "urbanity," without noting that in sparsely settled regions even a small town can serve "urban functions," while in densely settled agrarian countries like Egypt a village can attain great size without being recognizable as an "urban" place. Secondly, this type of work has been statistically flawed because it has taken the nation state as the unit of analysis. It has therefore compared units of widely different sizes, from city-states of a few hundred thousand to giants of many millions, without recognizing that there are certain scale and regional prerequisites to the achievement of balanced hierarchies of cities or of "proper" levels of urbanization. As I said in a very early article on primacy in Egypt (1965), demographers would find primacy even in the United States if they considered only the relationship between the size of the New York metropolitan area and the state of New York.

Such mindless statistical manipulations are indicative of the real defect in this approach, namely, that it makes no attempt to classify and to explain. Again, in much of my recent work on Arab cities (1984 and 1985) I have tried to develop a typology of Arab countries, based upon their size, economic base, and relationship to the international division of labor, and to use this classification system to predict the types of cities that develop, the levels of urbanization that are likely to be found, and to explain the causes of the urban problems that follow from these.

CONCLUSION

As suggested earlier, it is better to end on a more positive note. I think things are beginning to get better in the study of urbanization in the Arab World. The changes in the nature of the work now being done are, I think, in the right direction (for example, some of the work being done in the Durham school). In order to do the kind of work we need on Arab cities, we need to move toward studies that:

a) explain as well as describe;
b) relate the work to theoretical perspectives in the social sciences, especially those that have been generating in other Third World regions;
c) place city developments in a larger economic and political context;
d) not "gloss" from Orientalists' stereotypes but examine a wide range of cases to explore variations as well as similarities;
e) become more comparative, not in a mechanical way but for the pur-

pose of understanding how variations in underlying forces give rise to different empirical consequences;

f) explore the meaning to and functions of Arab cities for their inhabitants.

If we can begin to do these things better, I am very hopeful that the field of Middle Eastern urban studies will catch up with urban studies being done on other regions and will start making its proper contributions to a larger field which, thus far, has not integrated material on the Middle East into its framework.

SOME BIBLIOGRAPHIC REFERENCES FOR FURTHER STUDY

The Islamic City

Abu-Lughod, Janet. 1987. "The Islamic City: Historic Myth, Empirical Reality, Conceptual Essence," *International Journal of Middle East Studies* 17, pp. 155–76

———. 1989. *Before European Hegemony: The World System A.D. 1250–1350.* New York and London: Oxford University Press.

———. 1975. "Comments on the Form of Cities: Lessons from the Islamic City." *Janus: Essays in Ancient and Medieval Studies,* edited by L. Orlin (Ann Arbor), pp. 119–30.

———. 1983. "Contemporary Relevance of Islamic Urban Planning Principles." In Aydin Germen, ed., *Islamic Architecture and Urbanism* (Dammam: King Faisal University), pp. 64–70.

Brunschvig, R. 1947. "Urbanisme medieval et droit musulmane." *Revue des Etudes Islamiques* 15, pp. 127–55.

Eickleman, Dale. 1974. "Is There an Islamic City?" *International Journal of Middle East Studies* 5, pp. 274–94.

Germen, Ayden, ed. 1983. *Islamic Architecture and Urbanism.* Dammam: King Faisal University.

Grunebaum, Gustave von. 1955. "The Structure of the Musim Town." Memoir 81 of The American Anthropological Association, Ann Arbor. Reprinted in *Islam: Essays in the Nature and Growth of a Cultural Tradition* (1961).

Hakim, Basim. 1986. *Arabo-Islamic Cities: Building and Planning Principles.* London: Routledge and Kegan Paul, distributors.

al-Hathloul, Saleh. 1981. "Tradition, Continuity and Change in the Physical Environment: The Arab Muslim City." Ph.D. dissertation, M.I.T.

Hourani, Albert and S.M. Stern, eds. 1970. *The Islamic City.* Philadelphia: University of Pennsylvania Press.

Lapidus, Ira. 1967. *Muslim Cities in the Later Middle Ages.* Cambridge: Harvard University Press.

Le Tourneau, Roger. 1957. *Les villes musulmanes de l'Afrique du nord.* Algiers.

Marcais, Georges. 1945. "La conception des villes dans l'Islam," *Revue d'Alger* II, pp. 517–33.

———. 1940, reprinted 1957. "L'Urbanisme musulmane." Reprinted in *Melanges d'histoire et d'archeologie de l'occident musulman,* Algiers I, pp. 219–31.

Marcais, William. 1928. "L'Islamisme et la vie urbaine." *L'Academie des Inscriptions et Belles-Lettres, Comtes Rendus,* Paris (Jan.–March), pp. 86–100.

Massignon, Louis. 1920. "Les corps de metiers et la cite Islamique." *Revue Internationale de Sociologie* 28, pp. 473–87.

Serjeant, R.B., ed. 1980. *The Islamic City.* Paris: UNESCO.

Spies, Otto. 1927. "Islamisches Nachbarrecht nach schafaitischer Lehre." *Zeitschift fur vergleichende Rechiswissenschaft* 42, pp. 393–421.

Weber, Max. 1958. *The City.* English trans. edited by Don Martindale. Originally part of *Economy and Society.* Glencoe: Free Press.

Urban Biographies and Collections

Abu-Lughod, Janet. 1971. *Cairo: 1001 Years of the City Victorious.* Princeton: Princeton University Press.

———. 1980. *Rabat: Urban Apartheid in Morocco.* Princeton: Princeton University Press.

Berger, Morroe, ed. 1963. *The New Metropolis in the Arab World.* Delhi: Allied Publishers.

Blake, Gerald and Richard Lawless, eds. 1980. *The Changing Middle Eastern City.* London: Croom Helm.

Brown, L. Carl, ed. 1973. *From Medina to Metropolis.* Princeton: Darwin Press.

Brown, Kenneth. 1976. *People of Sale: Tradition and Change in a Moroccan City, 1830–1930.* Cambridge: Harvard University Press.

Chevallier, Dominique, ed. 1979. *Espace social de la ville arabe.* Paris: G.-P. Maisonneuve et Larose.

Daoulatli, Abdelaziz. 1976. *Tunis sous les Hafsides; Evolution urbaine et activite architecturale.* Tunis.

Eickelman, Dale. 1976. *Moroccan Islam: Tradition and Society in a Pilgrimage Center.* Austin: University of Texas Press.

Esin, Emel. 1963. *Mecca the Blessed, Madina the Radiant.* New York: Crown.

Fawaz, Leila. 1983. *Merchants and Migrants in Nineteenth Century Beirut.* Cambridge: Harvard University Press.

Khalaf, Samir and Per Kongstad. 1973. *Hamra of Beirut.* Leiden.

Khuri, Fuad. 1975. *From Village to Suburb: Order and Change in Greater Beirut.* Chicago: University of Chicago Press.

Lawless, Richard and Gerald Blake. 1976. *Tlemcen: Continuity and Change in an Algerian Islamic Town*. London and New York: Bowker for the Centre for Middle Eastern and Islamic Studies of the University of Durham.

Lespes, Rene. 1930. *Alger: etude de geographie et d'histoire urbaine*. Paris: Alcan.

Rafeq, Abdul-Karim. 1966. *The Province of Damascus, 1723–1783*. Beirut: Khayat's.

Raymond, Andre. 1973–74. *Artisans et commrrcants au Caire au XVIIIe siecle*. Two vols. Damascus: Institut Francais de Damas.

Sauvaget, Jean. 1940–41. *Alep: Essai sur le developpement d'une grande ville Syrienne, des origines au milieu du XIXe siecle*. Paris, in two volumes.

———. 1934. "Esquisses d'une histoire de la ville de Damas," *Revue des Etudes Islamiques* 8, pp. 421–80.

Le Tourneau, Roger. 1949. *Fes avant le protectorat: etude economique et sociale d'une ville de l'occident musulman*. Casablanca.

———. 1965. *La vie quotidienne a Fes en 1900*. Paris.

Wiet, Gaston. 1971. *Baghdad: Metropolis of the Abbasid Caliphate*. Norman: University of Oklahoma Press.

Wiet, Gaston. 1964. *Cairo: City of Art and Commerce*. Norman: University of Oklahoma Press.

Ziadeh, Nicola. 1964. *Damascus under the Mamluks*. Norman: University of Oklahoma Press.

Statistical Studies of Urbanization

Abu-Lughod, Janet. 1965. "Urbanization in Egypt: Present State and Future Prospects." *Economic Development and Cultural Change* (April), pp. 245–53.

———. 1972. "Problems and Policy Implications of Middle Eastern Urbanization." *Studies on Development Problems in Selected Countries of the Middle East*. New York: United Nations.

———. 1984. "Culture, 'Modes of Production,' and the Changing Nature of Cities in the Arab World." In Agnew, Mercer and Sopher, eds. *The City in Cultural Context*, pp. 94–119. Boston: Allen & Unwin.

———. 1985. "Urbanization and Social Change in the Arab World." In John Walton, ed., *Capital and Labour in the Urbanized World*, pp. 126–45. London: Sage Publications.

Bonine, Michael. 1980. "The Urbanization of the Persian Gulf Nations." In A.J. Cottrell, ed., *The Persian Gulf States: A General Survey*, pp. 225–78, Baltimore: The John Hopkins Press.

Davis, Kingsley and Hilda Hertz [Golden]. 1954. "Urbanization and the Development of Pre-Industrial Areas." *Economic Development and Cultural Change* 3, pp. 6–26.

Davis, Kingsley, 1969; 1972. *World Urbanization 1950–1970*. University of California Population Monograph Series no. 4; no. 9.

El-Shakhs, Salah and Hooshang Amirahmadi. 1985. "The Integrative Role of the Urban System in the Spatial Transformation of the Middle East and North Africa." Presented to M.E.S.A. meetings, New Orleans, November.

Ibrahim, Saad Eddin. 1975. "Overurbanization and Underurbanism: The Case of the Arab World." *International Journal of Middle East Studies* 6, pp. 29–45.

Parke, Robert. 1954. "Overurbanization in Egypt." Unpublished paper.

Thomlinson, Ralph. 1975. "The Primate City in Morocco: Casablanca or Rabat or None?" *Population Review* 19, nos. 1–2, pp. 24–33.

6 Old Wine, New Bottles

Reflections and Projections Concerning Research on Women in Middle Eastern Studies

Cynthia Nelson

INTRODUCTION

THE METAPHORS "old wine and new bottles" suggest that despite a great deal of contemporary feminist discourse, the epistemological problem of woman as Other, continues to pose a challenge—ideologically, theoretically and methodologically—for those of us engaged in the construction of knowledge about Middle Eastern societies and cultures. When asked: "Why study women," we are forced to admit that the dominant social science paradigms not only have excluded women from theoretical analyses but also have rendered our various social realities non-problematic. Hence, the continual seeking for "new paradigms" through which to apprehend and account" for the ever ephemeral social realities of "women" in the Middle East.

When we choose to focus on *women* in our research we tend to shift the level of discourse away from complex society (or those so-called theoretical realities embedded in institutional arrangements) to social actors within specific historical and existential situations. It is not that we are analytically fragmenting an integrated social reality—all theory does this by definition. It is that women never have been, until recently, "theoretically interesting."[1]

The major focus of this chapter is to examine contemporary scholarship on "women in Middle Eastern studies" and explore how women scholars attempt to analytically integrate women into an understanding of our fragmented social reality. Specifically: What are the ideological, theoretical and methodological issues revealed when women become the focus of our intellectual concerns? I make no pretense to be all inclusive or exhaustive of the vast amount of published material on "women in Middle Eastern studies."[2] A detailed analysis of that genre of Middle East scholarship from a feminist perspective is beyond the scope of this paper.

My objectives are somewhat more limited: 1) to select examples from a broad spectrum of social science discourse by women on or about Middle Eastern women in order to highlight the dominant themes reflected in the literature; 2) to examine the "paradigmatic shifts" taking place from the late sixties in Western social science (particularly in anthropology) in order to illustrate the intimate connection between our paradigms and the knowledge we construct about Middle Eastern women; to look at these new paradigms in the context of the contemporary social realities of Middle Eastern women and to suggest possible future research directions.

Assumptions

The assumptions underlying my selection of scholarship on "women in the Middle East" raise certain epistemological issues that have influenced the analysis. First I have opted to look at the work (primarily anthropological) of women (Western as well as Middle Eastern) about women in the Middle East. It is my assumption (and the published record seems to support it) that in their research, women more than men consider women "theoretically interesting." This raises the question of whether being woman studying women overcomes the androcentrism of conventional social science.[3]

Second, I have chosen to comment more directly on the published material of the 1970s and 1980s on the assumption that a period of major intellectual crisis among Western as well as Middle Eastern scholars emerged in the late sixties that had a profound impact on the subsequent scholarship on women in the Middle East. This crisis involved unprecedented self criticism and radical rethinking in the social/human sciences in response to the political turmoil abroad as well as in America including the feminist challenge. Conventional scholarship on the Middle East prior to the sixties tended to exclude women and feminist issues from theory and method. Even Edward Said's masterful critique of "Orientalism" was silent on the problem of woman as Other except for a few lines about Kuchuk Hanem.[4] This time frame also covers the period of my own involvement in the "construction of knowledge" about women in Middle Eastern societies, particularly Egypt from 1963 to the present and raises a third epistemological issue—being part of the problem being studied.

As a Western (i.e., an American) woman I am Other to the society within which I live and work, not only because I am a woman, but also an alien woman. However as an Other who questions and criticizes the Western discipline which accepts and legitimates man's experience and views of social reality as the bedrock of ethnographic data, I share an Otherness with those Middle Eastern scholars who question these Western theoretical stereotypes about women in Middle Eastern society. As self-conscious intellectuals we are all confronted with the challenge of relevance and authenticity, although we may experience this differently. As Geiger[5] has cogently stated:

> If feminism is understood as theory of women's point of view and if feminist method is understood to be the collective critical reconstitution of the meaning of women's social experience as women live through it, it is readily apparent that this theory must account for and encompass the diversity of that experience. Further, women's conscious perceptions of that experience must constitute our most critical and complex data.

It is in the context and spirit of this mandate that the following reflections on scholarship related to women of the Middle East is undertaken.

Reflections on Scholarship

In presenting this material, given my initial assumptions, I chose a chronological schema believing it provides a more heuristic strategy within which to discuss the various themes. I have grouped these themes into different periods which overlap with certain historical changes which have had and continue to have an impact, however indirectly, on the study of women in the Middle East since World War II until the present. From the post World War I era through the 1950s is the period of *the awakening* of interest in the Middle Eastern woman. It is also the time of the rise of independence struggles, the processes of decolonization and the beginning of the Palestinian tragedy and its consequent impact on the "politicization of women." Throughout the sixties is the period of *the empirical gaze* primarily by western male scholars. The Middle Eastern woman is rendered public but primarily through western images and stereotypes. The political struggles of the oppressed peoples of the Third World, the crisis of conscience among the western "dissenting academy," and the *nakba* of 1967 with its impact on Arab intellectuals ushered in the 1970s and the era of *the critical response*. Finally the decade of the eighties—the assassination of Sadat, the emergence of Islamic fundamentalism, the Gulf War, unprecedented labor migration, heavy US/AID involvement in development programs—has engendered *the indigenous quest*.

These ideological trends do not come into being and alter as neatly and as regularly as the decades suggest. However, it offers a way to illustrate the dialectic relationship between the production of scholarship and its historical context.

The Awakening

Prior to the Second World War one discovers very little systematic scholarship on women in the Middle East and those few are restricted to studies on pre-Islamic women.[6] Except for Blackman's study of upper Egyptian fellahin and Granqvist's studies of the Palestinian village of Artas, there is virtually no empirical research being conducted by women on women in the Middle East until well after World War II.[7] But the whole post World War II "decolonization" process, reflected in national independence movements such as the insurrection against French colonial rule in Algeria, witnessed the increased participation of Arab women struggling for social and political freedom—including their own. Many "feminist struggles" erupted in the post war era such as that reflected in the life and work of Doria Shafik.[8]

After World War II and throughout the fifties we observe an awakening interest in women of the Middle East, particularly how the broader processes of socio-political change and transformation were influencing the status of women and her role in the family and wider society.[9] Characteristic of this scholarship was the uncritical assumption of the intimate linkage between changing women's status and modernizing Middle Eastern society. Typical of the ideological stance of the period is this statement:

Middle Eastern society has come a long way on the road to modernization. The notion of male superiority has been balanced with the emancipation of women and it is the women's movement which is the most significant single factor in the changing Middle East, even, as the status of women is everywhere the most significant measure of civilization and human progress.[10]

Men were viewed as the shapers and repositories of tradition—women as the vanguard of change. And the ideological emphasis was on creating *The New Woman* rather than recognizing the many new types that would emerge. Middle Eastern women's reality, therefore, was perceived through the lens of western stereotypes of what was assumed to be "modern," "civilized" and "progressive" as contrasted to what was considered "traditional," "Islamic" and "conservative."

THE EMPIRICAL GAZE

The period of the 1960s continues this trend and is characterized as rendering Middle Eastern women more visible but primarily through the "gaze" of western theoretical (and thus androcentric) paradigms. As Louise Sweet[11] pointed out:

> It is interesting that while much of the research has been done by men, perhaps more women have involved themselves in this area than in others of the world scene. It is an area in which corporate patrilineality predominates together with the stereotypes of masculine dominance, patriarchism, "subordination" of women, and a sharp division of labor between the sexes, classes and ethnic groups. Most women engaged in research in the area have *selected the same problems men have* and on only a few occasions have the stereotypes been challenged.

From an examination of a number of bibliographies summarizing the existing research on women in the Middle East[12] one is immediately struck by the number of articles focusing on themes of the changing status, position and role of women. There is a suggestion that the "improvement of the position of women" necessitates the "breaking of tradition" in order that women can become "more free." Islam, specifically the Personal Status Law, is perceived as some ahistorical factor determining women's Being and where women's rights are concerned perceived by its critics as retrograde and repressive.[13] Supporters of Islam, on the other hand, point to extra Islamic culture or *tradition* as the determinant of women's status.[14]

Whatever the stance toward Islam, there is a very strong tendency, among both western and Middle Eastern scholars to use ideology as the determinant factor of women's situation.

The 1960s is also the era of the first ethnographies on the Middle East by women.[15] It also sees full length studies on women by men.[16] This is the period in which the first international social science conference is held on the "Role of Women in Mediterranean Society" (Mediterranean Social Science Council, Athens, Greece, 1966). Titles of the papers reflect the dominant themes of the time: "Changing Male and Female Relations in a Changing Society" (Nelson); "Position of Women in Tunisian Society" (Abu Zahra); "Consequences of Segregation Among Women in Cyrenaica" (Peters); "Bedouin Women in Towns" (Bujra). Reiterating these themes but reflecting different scholars was the first collected volume of essays by women on women challenging the stereotypes about Middle Eastern women, edited by Louise Sweet. Under the title "Appearance and Reality: Status and Role of Women in Mediterranean Society" (*Anthropological Quarterly* 40, no. 3: 1967) the papers focused on "Key and Peripheral Roles of Noble Women in a Middle East Plains Village" (Aswad); "Legal Status of Women Among the 'Awlad Ali" (Mohsen) and "The Women of 'Ain al-Dayr" (Sweet). In a previous issue (40, no. 2: 1967) Dobkin published "Social Ranking in the Women's World of Purdah: A Turkish Example."

The fifties and sixties were a prelude to the seventies and eighties in terms of the increased production of knowledge about Middle Eastern women. The themes of change looms large in the literature of the 1960s but the categories of thought are the conventional concepts of androcentric and positivistic social science. For the most part scholars are not "aware" of their own ideological perspectives—an awareness that the historically constructed image of the Middle East in the West often subtly and, perhaps, more often blatantly, distorted the western vision of Muslim women and of her whole society. The only essay I found in the 1960s that engaged in a reflective stance toward being a western field researcher in a Muslim society and analyzed its implication for the kind of knowledge that can be constructed was Papanek's "The Woman Fieldworker in Purdah Society."[17] She uses the concept "role flexibility" to suggest that women "in a purdah society can do a better job of scientific transvestism than can a man"—an assumption that becomes part of the feminist critique of scholarship during the seventies and eighties.

THE CRITICAL RESPONSE

From the early seventies onward the scholarship on women in the Middle East begins to reflect the "crisis" that was setting in around Western social science particularly in anthropology during the late sixties.[18]

> As responsive and responsible anthropologists how could we not question normal science when the so-called Third World began to define its own historical destiny and then its people commenced to talk back at the social scientist.[19]

This questioning produced an increasing number of Middle Eastern women's voices critiquing western androcentric social science paradigms as well as the patriarchy of the Islamic Middle East.[20] This was echoed by several review articles examining gender as well as discipline bias in contemporary scholarship on women in the Middle East.[21] The old paradigms did not provide any resonance for the new structure of sentiments that was emerging—neither in the west where, among other challenges, the feminist reawakening was forcing a reexamination of ideas about gender, female sexuality and women's appropriate social roles; nor in the Middle East where the 1967 defeat was forcing Arab intellectuals to rethink the foundations of their own knowledge about themselves and their society and its relation to the western world.

Many indigenous scholars were pursuing their graduate training in the west and returning to their own societies to conduct field research during this period. A new book examining Arab women's reflections on doing research in their own society is *Studying Your Own Society: Arab Women in the Field,* edited by S. al-Torki and C. Solh. The converging interests of these critical responses to the western empirical gaze were the critical questions: who participates in the construction of knowledge about women in the Middle East and who controls the process. As June Nash[22] has cogently remarked:

> We are now in a liminal state of the social sciences. The values on which our selective criteria are premised are being questioned by people who never before were a significant enough part of the profession to challenge them. These include women and natives of the cultures scrutinized.

This liminal state resembles most closely to what Kuhn would call a scientific revolution which is not based on gradual increments of knowledge but on rejecting old paradigms for new ones. Paradigmatic change entails reevaluating existing data and reformulating theory that cannot adequately explain recurrent anomalies. Kuhn used paradigm in at least two senses: as models, or "concrete puzzle-solutions"; and as "the entire constellation of beliefs, values, techniques, and so on shared by the members of a given scientific community."[23] Crises in science, according to Kuhn, may be handled in one of three ways: by resolving the problem with traditional paradigms; by concluding that no solution is possible at the present time; or by developing new paradigms with the ensuing battle over its acceptance.

By examining the scholarship on women in the Middle East during the seventies we discover the paradigms of role, status and position are beginning to be replaced with the paradigms of power, patriarchy and production. Basically what is being called into question are prior theory and data that presented an ahistorical model of male dominance and female subordination in so-called "traditional" Arab culture. Typical of this type of model-building is Jamil Hilal's.[24]

Male domination in the Arab culture is maintained through the creation of two worlds. Thus men and women can be said to "inhabit" two different and, in some sense, dualistic social worlds. The sexual division cuts across all other divisions. Men dwell basically in the "public" world of work, property, politics and religious practice. Women on the other hand dwell in the "private" world of domesticity, child-rearing and the household. The dualistic nature of the two worlds is evinced by the association of the first with "culture" and the second with "nature." The divergent orientations of the two worlds are expressed and mediated tangibly and symbolically, and their segregation is maintained and regulated in a number of ways.

Within this paradigm, women were invisible in studies of politics, which is assumed to be a male domain. Failure to recognize the diversity of women's political roles is built into the background assumptions of male dominance and man's monopoloy of power. These assumptions are further reinforced by the notion that politics occur beyond the domestic sphere associated with women. According to this view, women are parochial or disinterested in the public world of male politics; in other words women are nonpolitical. Models of political organization are influenced by dualisms of public/private spheres and political/nonpolitical action. These dichotomized relations assume a theoretical and ideological opposition between nonpolitical, domestic woman and the political, public man.

WOMEN AND POWER

These assumptions of public and private equated with male dominance and female subordination were uncritically taken for granted in the ethnographic descriptions of women in the Middle East until the early seventies when several women social scientists in the Middle East began to rethink our notions of power and recognize its special features as a particular kind of social relation—reciprocity of influence—rather than as an embodied quality institutionalized in kinds of social structures. The previous tendency of ethnographers to use jural models emphasizing formal role relations and institutions, overlooked informal political roles of women. Illustrative of the search for new paradigms was the exploration with the phenomenological idea of "negotiated social order."[25] Looking at power from this perspective, we are forced to raise different sets of questions— questions that recognize the ongoing dialectical process of social life. What are the constructs that facilitate, limit and govern negotiation? What are the sanctions open to women? In what ways can and do women influence men? How is control exercised by women? How conscious are women of their capacity to influence? In other words what are women doing in this reciprocity?

For the most part the research on women in the Middle East during the seventies represents different answers to such questions and as researchers begin to construct empirical knowledge about the variety and diversity of women's lives in the Middle East a new understanding of women's power emerges. For example, within the Syrian village of Tell Toqaan "women bring with them a long tradition of reponsibility for the performance and management of social and economic activities and of manipulation of political relations between segments of the society."[26] Or within the Moroccan hamlet of Aghzim "women increase the significance of the systems of social stratification which continue to have economic and political importance, partly because it is only through women that the majority of people can derive benefits from the market and from government, via patron-client relationships."[27] Or within the organization of domestic groups in the Saudi-Arabian city of Jiddah "women have always exercised significant control over decisions of their male agnates relating to the arrangement of marriages. Given the particular, social, political and economic role of marriage in Arabian society, this control, in turn, has had consequences beyond the realm of domestic relations.[28] Or within the neighborhood street of Borj Hammoud "networks of neighboring women constitute critical units of the social order, shaping street life and assuming significant social functions in the context of Lebanese society."[29] Or within the Egyptian village of Fateha "power relations are intimately related to the onset of folk illness and to explanations of illness causation; and that explanations for the differential incidence of spirit possession should be sought in *social relations of power differential affecting both males and females.*"[30] Or within the medinas of Fez and Meknes "a closer examination of the structure and operation of the household reveals the presence of a considerable measure of 'unassigned power,' which women compete for and utilize to further their own needs and wishes."[31]

This is not to conclude that the research conducted by women on women in the Middle East during the seventies eliminated the notion of different social worlds with its inherent male domination and female subordination, but rather drew our attention to the variety of strategies available to women to manipulate position and status to achieve their own ends. The research also emphasized the significance of cultural and historical specificity in research. The abstract concept "the Muslim Middle Eastern woman" is being replaced by empirical specificity of historical time and cultural place as well as social class. But most importantly it suggests alternative paradigms by which to understand women's experiences within the context of concrete social realities.

WOMEN AND PATRIARCHY

A related but different line of inquiry illustrating the paradigmatic shifts of the seventies, is the reexamination of the concept "patriarchy"— understood in the broadest sense to mean the institutionalized forms of male dominance and female subordination whether in terms of political power, family and personal status or the control of economic resources. The principle challenge to older conceptualizations is the recognition that patriarchy is not simply a system of male domination in which women are perceived as helpless pawns at the mercy of coercive males, but rather as a complex phenomenon constraining men as well as women in a mutually dehumanizing ideology. As Abu-Azhra[32] has pointed out:

> The whole institution of the modesty of women (viz patriarchy) can be fully understood only in relation to the values of both male and female. Whether they like it or not women have to pretend that they are modest and men to pretend that they are virile. It thus creates more fears and more challenge for men, since according to social values men have to prove their masculinity, and so women have to defend their modesty.

Throughout the 1970s the ideology of patriarchy became a focus of research.[33] Themes appearing in this literature range from the modesty code as a means whereby men can maintain their image of virility; to a criticism that feminists have tended to neglect the roots of the problem of patriarchy "which lie not in the formal rules of Islamic law but rather in a number of cultural practices and conservative attitudes shared by both men and women;"[34] to provocative analyses of the Muslim concept of female sexuality in which "sexual segregation is a device to protect men, not women;"[35] to thick descriptions of the self image of bint-il-balad "as a man among men;"[36] to comparative analyses of sexual ideologies in the forging of female consciousness, promoting of female solidarity and the generating of change in male-female relations.[37] Throughout this research westerners are reminded of the need to reexamine their stereotypes about Middle Eastern patriarchy as well as their models for change.[38]

WOMEN AND PRODUCTION

The journal literature on women and production published in the seventies reveals the broad range of women's productive roles, from their contributions in economies of subsistence or of simple commodity production to economies characterized by advanced stages of capitalism. It also reveals the impact of patriarchy upon productive roles, and changes in these roles as a society moves from one economic stage to another.

Some of the common issues emerging from the published work on women and production focus on: the invisibility of the nature and scope of women's productive roles in official sources; the problem of conceptualizing "work" to fit societies where the division between work and leisure is

not rigid; the difficulty in obtaining data on property rights and owner-
ship among women; women's manipulation of patrimony for long term
security and protection; assessing the impact of income-generating work
on the status of village women; the patriarchal constraints of sex segregation and female seclusion on women's participation in the work force; international aid in the service of the patriarchy; women's work in family
production; how women use courts to activate family responsibility especially support for female family members; women and labor migration.[39]

Such issues became the focal point for theory construction about the
problem of the interactions between class and sex within different Middle
Eastern economies. Debates center around the most appropriate "paradigm" (theoretical perspective)—class analysis or patriarchal analysis. On
the one hand are those studies reflecting a historical materialist bias and
the latter a cultural idealist bias. Illustrative of the former line of inquiry is
Gran's[40] analysis:

> the curious and somewhat contradictory fact that despite the entry of
> large numbers of Egyptian women into the labor force since World
> War II, the lower middle class women have become professionally liber-
> ated surpassing their upper middle class counterparts, while remaining
> socially conservative.

She explains this by showing how this phenomenon is linked to the development of Egypt's relationship to the world market and queries
whether the gulf between the two strata, one socially liberated but professionally "unliberated," the other professionally liberated but socially and
sexually conservative, continue to exist? Her answer:

> If economic pressure on the petite bourgeoisie induces misogynist ideo-
> logical reactions in the short run, in the long run is makes women's
> work outside the home more indispensable than ever. The rampant in-
> flation encouraged by Sadat's policies has eaten deeply into the incomes
> of the lower middle classes and threatens the upper middle class as well.
> In response, many Egyptian professionals—men as well as women—are
> migrating to other Arab countries to find work.[41]

Tucker's research on "Egyptian Women in the Work Force" supports
this kind of analysis when she argues that women's work in Egypt appears

to vary in form and scope in relation to the economic phases in Egyptian history. The pattern of female labor—including labor which is inconsistent with female seclusion—differs from one historical period to another, even when social structures and values remain more or less constant.[42] In her larger study of *Women in Nineteenth Century Egypt* (Cambridge: Cambridge University Press, 1985), Tucker further develops this position. Focusing on lower class women, she traces changes in the work role and family life of peasant women in the countryside and craftswomen and traders in Cairo and explores the varied effects of capitalist transformation on women, their family life using material from Islamic court records. For Tucker, to explain female participation solely as a product of a certain set of cultural biases "does not really clarify the problem." A theme that Mona Hammam also has addressed in her research on women and industrial work in Egypt.[43] Through the case of Chubra el Kheima, Hammam examines what happened to women in Egypt, the first Arab country to undergo protracted capitalist transformation. Despite structural and institutional constraints, women are drawn into the wage labor market at different stages in the process of economic transformation. She demonstrates that even the most ideologically entrenched and culturally prescribed tradition of sex division in society gives way to the force of economic determinants. Also Hammam's study of "Labor Migration and the Sexual Division of Labor" presents an historical materialist framework for developing a more coherent understanding of women's economic activities in the Arab social formations. She conceptualizes these activities are:

> a continuum that spans market (including petty commodity/informal sector production and trade) and nonmarket production, as well as wage, casual, migrant and unvalorized labor. This continuum is conditioned by the cycle of capital accumulation which separates the sphere of reproducing labor (physically, materially, socially and ideologically) from the general circuit of social reproduction.[44]

Mernissi, arguing from a cultural idealist patriarchal perspective, emphasizes in her analyses the impact of capitalist development on women.[45] As Mernissi states:

> It is only through the analysis of the historical conditions which have determined how the sexual division of labor is perceived that solutions

can be suggested because the great blockage in the Arab Muslim's countries' approach to the situation of women (perceived as a very serious
problem since the second half of the nineteenth century) is *an ideological
blockage before it is an economic one.*[46]

For Mernissi the object of her study is to force a fundamental reversal of
the models, practices and values of development which she argues is carried out as a male phenomenon. She was forced to explain one of the most
significant results of her inquiry—"the fundamental *contradiction* between
the statements of the peasant women on development, and those of the
planners, directors and agents of this development, the vast majority of
whom are men."[47] Through a series of case studies of women and daily life
in a Moroccan village, Mernissi attempts a theorization which would explain why development is experienced in such radically different ways by
the male decision-makers and by the peasant women. Her paradigm: The
low status of women as a manifestation of sex and class in Arab Muslim society. In her conclusion she states:

> It is obvious that the solutions are first of all an ideological sort. No iso-
> lated and limited attempt to create profitable jobs for women will
> change the situation in a radical way. The problem lies above all in the
> way in which society perceives and evaluates manual labor in general,
> and manual labor carried out within networks called traditional—
> networks in which exploitation in the relations of work reveals a more
> ferocious character when women are involved.[48]

Mernissi is aware that her analysis "reopens the familiar debate on
which factors are the determining ones—the ideological or the economic
ones?" She believes this debate is largely out of date not only because of
the appearance of more and more subtle analyses, which have revealed the
complexity of the ramifications and links between ideological and economic factors, but also because the studies on sexuality and its connection
with economics in the developed economies have demonstrated the great
weight of ideology.

Ideology, far from being negligible, is revealed to be, in certain historical circumstances, of very great importance as we note the appearance
in the Arab world of a whole analytical tendency that stresses ideology

as the basis for study and action to clear up the stagnation from dependence.[49]

With that observation Mernissi reopens the debate on one of the central issues underlying the scholarship of the 1980s.

THE INDIGENOUS QUEST

> Political freedom was won more than a generation ago; the fight for economic independence is being fought; the battle for the mind has scarcely begun. Only when the intellectual doors of perception are cleansed will the Third World be able to gamble with the fundamental realities.[50]

Nowhere is this battle being more ferociously waged than in the Middle East. And no issue in this cleansing process is more heatedly debated than that of women's status. And no religious symbol personifies this debate more than "the veil." This linkage of women's status and religion in a culture where the spheres of religion and politics are not fully separate make the "women's question" a political one in the real sense of the term. No wonder then that everywhere today the problem of women's status is one of the politically most sensitive issues from Morocco to Saudi Arabia. Perhaps it has always been the case, but the recent scholarship on "women in the Middle East" seems to reflect a much greater awareness that to understand the status of Middle Eastern women today in all its variations and permutations, one has to analyze the specific modalities of religious ideology, social and economic organization and political rule.[51] This is by no means an easy task but the challenge seems to demand a very different kind of scholarship than that which typified the research of the earlier decades. If "a new wind of cultural decolonization is blowing through the Middle East," which is having a profound impact on the lives of women, then we should expect a new scholarship to emerge in order to grasp and understand it. Those scholars who are attempting to understand and explain this very phenomenon (some are committed to changing it as well) are also confronting their own cultural identities and modes of knowing in ways that never previously were considered to be part of the research "problematique." It is in this context of the challenge of authenticity and relevance of one's own research to the broader political struggle of decolonizing the mind that the scholarship of the 1980s must be examined.

The research on women in the Middle East published in the last few years reveals an increasing number of Middle Eastern women scholars engaged in the critical assessment of social science research on women in the Middle East. Also appearing are more ethnographic fieldwork studies by Middle Eastern women analyzing women's situation in their own societies.[52]

This is not to say that western women scholars are less in evidence in their publications on women in the Middle East. The 1980s has witnessed a number of full length monographs by western women scholars.

The strategic question that emerges as one reviews some of this literature of the 1980s is whether there are any significant differences in terms of the questions posed or paradigms offered as more Middle Eastern scholars turn their gaze inward upon their own societies and ultimately upon themselves. In other words, how do scholars—Middle Eastern and non-Middle Eastern—confront the challenge of "cleansing the intellectual doors of perception," when it comes to the construction of knowledge about women? To suggest possible directions in answering that question are two recent studies on women in the Middle East, one by a Saudi Arabian anthropologist (al-Torki) studying elite women of Jiddah; and the other by an Arab-American anthropologist (Abu-Lughod) studying Bedouin women of the Western desert of Egypt.[53]

I have selected these two studies for several reasons: 1) Each author explicitly states that she is concerned with the issue of sexual segregation and its consequences on the lives of women in the community she is studying; 2) Each community reflects a different ecological, historical and cultural niche within the broader Arab-Islamic tapestry of the Middle East and therefore allows us to examine the specific modalities of a common phenomenon throughout the Middle East—female seclusion; and 3) Each analysis provides conceptual and methodological insights to the issue of "indigenizing research."

How does each describe the phenomenon of seclusion and how do they approach its study?

In these families separation of the sexes leads to radical seclusion of women from public life. This segregation finds its cultural compensation in the elaboration of formal and informal networks of friendship and kin. Social visits are the major means for women to reduce their isolation. It is thus not surprising that they are more elaborate among women and are taken more seriously by them than by men.[54]

Bedouin women live in a separate community that could be considered a sub-society: separate from and parallel to men's yet cross cut by ties to men and encompassed in the larger world defined by kinship in tribal structure: characterized by complex and intense personal relation; and maintained by shared secrets, conveyed most poignantly through poetry.[55]

Whereas al-Torki's study is:

of continuity and change among elite domestic groups in Jiddah through a comparison of behavior and ideology of three generations of that city's prominent families.[56]

Abu-Lughod

wished to study interpersonal relations (those between women and men in particular) and the ideology of social life, topics that could not be studied without people's willingness to talk openly about their personal lives and feelings.[57]

Whereas al-Torki worked within the cosmopolitan city of Jiddah, Abu-Lughod worked in the sedentarized Bedouin camp of the Awlad Ali, yet each was constrained by their gender in very similar ways.

Since domestic groups were the only field of social relations accessible to me as an unmarried woman, most of the data was gathered from women. I could not gather data about men in these families as they related to other men in friendship networks, in business activities, and in daily interaction in the public world.[58]

Although in the first phase of my fieldwork I moved back and forth from the men's world to the women's, I soon realized that my contact with men—boring and frustrating because of barriers to conversation about personal matters created by rules of propriety and the formality of men's gatherings—also foreclosed the possibility that the women would trust me. I chose to declare my loyalty to the women.[59]

The conclusions that the two scholars reach about the meaning of seclusion in the modalities of everyday life are strikingly similar. Al-Torki states:

Even where norms of seclusion for women were more restrictive of women's mobility and the resultant dependency on men greater, women invested time, energy, and money in sustaining networks of friendship with other women in other households. They thereby widened their social horizons and reduced the precariousness of their status in society. The strategies here involved cooperation with other women and provided women with information vital to both men and women but actually controlled exclusively by women.[60]

Abu-Lughod maintains:

Sexual segregation is not inherently bad for women. In this case it seems clear that the separation of the worlds mitigates the negative effects of sexual inequality and women's dependence... women escape the direct experience of their subordination and gain the respect accorded to those who uphold the social order. Women enthusiastically support the segregation that allows them to carve out significant fields for autonomous action in their relatively unsupervised and egalitarian world.[61]

The main insight coming from both al-Torki's and Abu-Lughod's research is:

by shifting our gaze and assuming the perspective of those for whom this community of women is the primary arena of social life, we get a more accurate and nuanced view not only of its connections to the men's world, but of *the nature of women's experience and relationships within the community.*[62]

I was a conscious witness to my own resocialization as an Arab woman, and thus learned many aspects of this role in the best manner possible. I became what can be best described as an observant participant.[63]

Each in her own way has contributed to "cleansing the intellectual doors of perception"—first by self consciously being interested in women's subjective experience of themselves; and secondly allowing their models to come from the mouths of their informants. The message I hear from these two voices is that greater empirical validity is being accorded to indigenous cultural perspectives than to the conventional western social science models, and one's gender has more significance than one's nationality in gaining access to women's subjective experience. Hence the question is posed as to whether indigenizing research has not more to do with our paradigms than our passports.

CONCLUSION: BRINGING OURSELVES INTO THE DISCOURSE

Many women scholars doing research on women in the Middle East have thought they were rectifying the androcentric bias of conventional research by focusing their attention on the "women's situation." Despite this focus, the conceptual and methodological approaches they have used have been grounded primarily in a positivist epistemology. As Robert Murphy[64] so cogently stated:

> Thus we speak of the need for "objectivity," which means, in part, that we should not be led astray by our subjective states regarding people under study. At the same time, however, we strive for "empathy" with our subjects, which can be downright perilous for the maintenance of our objectivity. We want to be inside our informant's head and emotions, but we wish to stand aside and be aloof from them. This is what Levi-Strauss has called being *engagé* and *degagé* at the same time. It is the dialectics of reducing people to objects while trying to achieve understanding of them and of converting ourselves into instruments while struggling to maintain our identities.

In the 1950s and 1960s not only were women's voices and experiences muted in social science discourse on the Middle East but also the ethnographic "self" was concealed. The authoritative voice of the 1950s and 1960s—predominantly the male western voice—never questioned the ontological status of the anthropological fact. Questions of gender, of self and the construction of knowledge were never raised. With the feminist challenge to conventional social science discourse has emerged the "paradigmatic shifts" of the 1970s and 1980s.

Feminist inquiry questions the established premises of male dominated science.[65] The feminist inquiry necessarily involves a reflexive stance. The complex dialectic of self-evaluation, cross-cultural experiences, researcher/informant relations, and the role of ethnographers as interpreters of others' behavior, links the anthropological enterprise to feminist inquiry.[66]

The emergence of women's lives and experiences in recent writings on the Middle East[67] is a result of paradigm induced changes in values, perceptions, methods, and conceptual frameworks. The formerly muted voices of women are being heard as feminist anthropology *sensitizes fieldworkers to the reflexive awareness* of the research process, researcher/informant relationships, and to the dynamics of intracultural variation and gender differences within specific social systems. "The constitutive role of the social scientist is, from a paradigmatic point of view, crucial to the actual determination of his or her scientific 'object' and to the critical understanding of any knowledge whatsoever."[68]

The Kuhnian crisis in social science, particularly anthropology, can be resolved with the emergence of new paradigms at many levels of discourse and analysis. These shifts have also resulted in a greater critical awareness of ethnocentric bias in western social science perceptions of Middle Eastern social reality.[69] They have also prompted some Arab scholars to "Search for a New Identity of the Social Sciences in the Arab World."

No single framework is capable of explaining the entire spectrum of female realities across cultures, let alone the human condition. Formulations of new paradigms and redefinitions of the goals and methods of social science are a positive affirmation—and a challenge to—the many disciplines. Feminist scholarship is more than just adding new information to old *paradigms*. It forces us to ask different questions and to construct new frameworks that contribute to an integrated understanding of fragmented human experiences. This requires sensitivity to gender differences in perception and values and to the complexity of women's lives across diverse histories, cultures and classes.

NOTES

1. F. Edholm, O. Harris, and K. Young, "Conceputalizing Women," *Critique of Anthropology* 9/10, no. 10 (1977), pp. 100–30; I. Illich, *Gender* (New York: Pantheon, 1982).

2. I will not enter here into the discussion as to whether there exists a coherent body of knowledge and methodological approach that is specific to something called "Women in Middle Eastern Studies." For the purposes of this paper I shall be dealing primarily with women's scholarship on Arab women as reflected in the discipline of anthropology. For it is within that discipline that the feminist challenge is having its critical impact. See S. Tiffany, "Paradigms of Power: Feminist Reflections on the Anthropology of Women in Pacific Island Societies," *Working Paper 79 of Women in International Development Series* (East Lansing: Michigan State University, 1985).
3. N. Scheper-Hughes, "The Problem of Bias in Andocentric and Feminist Anthropology," *Women's Studies* 10 (1983), pp. 109–16.
4. E. Said, *Orientalism* (London: Routledge and Kegan Paul, 1978), pp. 6, 186–88, 207.
5. S.N. Geiger, "Women's Life Histories," *Signs: Journal of Women, Culture and Society* 11, no. 2 (Winter, 1986), pp. 334–51.
6. N. Abbott, *Aisha, The Beloved of the Prophet* (Chicago, 1942); N. Abbott, "Women and the State in Early Islam," *Journal of Near Eastern Studies* 1 (1942), pp. 341–68; B. Amiruddin, "Women's Status in Islam: A Moslem View," *Muslim World* 28 (1938), pp. 153–63; I. Lichtenstaeder, *Women of the Aiyam al-Arab: A Study of Female Life During Warfare in Pre-Islamic Arabia* (London: Royal Asiatic Society, 1935); D.G. Phillips, "The Growth of the Feminist Movement in Egypt," *Muslim World* 18, no. 3 (1926), pp. 277–85; D.G. Phillips, "The Awakening of Egypt's Womanhood," *Muslim World* 18, no. 1 (1928), pp. 402–8; R. Pierre, "L'evolution de la Femme Musulmane en Egypte," *En Terre d'Islam* (1933), pp. 277–87, 297–310; G.H. Stern, *Marriage in Early Islam* (London: J.G. Forlung Fund, Royal Asiatic Society, 1939); R. Woodmall, *Moslem Women Enter a New World* (London: Allen, 1936); S. Zwemer, *Moslem Women* (West Medfort: Central Committee for the United Study of Foreign Missions, 1926).
7. W. Blackman, *The Fellahin of Upper Egypt* (London: George C. Harrap, 1927); H. Granqvist, *Marriage Conditions Among the Arabs* (Helsingfors: Akademische Buchhandlung, 1931–1935); W. Blackman, *Birth and Childhood Among the Arabs; Studies in a Humammaden Village in Palestine* (Helsingfors: Soderstrom, 1947); W. Blackman, *Child Problems Among the Arabs: Studies in a Muhammadan Village* (Helsingfors: Soderstrom, 1950); M. Ayoub, *Endogamous Marriage in a Middle Eastern Village* (Cambridge: Unpublished Doctoral Dissertation, Radcliffe College, 1957); M. Ayoub, "Parallel Cousin Marriage and Endogamy: A Study in Sociometry," *Southwestern Journal of Anthropology* 15, (1959), pp. 266–75; J. and K. Douglas, "Aspects of Marriage and Family Living Among Egyptian Peasants," *Marriage and Family Living* 16, (1954), pp. 45–48; R. Woodsmall, *Study of the Role of Women, Their Activities and Organizations in Egypt, Lebanon, Jordan, Syria and Iraq* (Woodstock: Elmtree, 1956); F. Ziadeh, "Equality (Kafa'ah) in the Muslim Law of Marriage," *The American Journal of Comparative Law* 6, no. 4 (1957), pp. 503–17.

8. C. Nelson, "The Voices of Doria Shafik: Feminist Consciousness in Egypt 1940–1960," *Feminist Issues* 6, no. 2 (Fall, 1986), pp. 15–31.
9. N. Abbott, "Women," in R. Anshem, ed., *Mid-East: World Centers, Yesterday, Today and Tomorrow* (New York: Harper Brothers, 1956); L. el-Hamamsy, "The Changing Role of Egyptian Women," *Middle East Forum* 33, no. 6 (1958), pp. 24–29; G. Joly, "The Women of Lebanon," *Journal of the Royal Asia Society* 38 (1951), pp. 17–23; I. Lichtenstaeder, "The New Woman in Modern Egypt," *Muslim World* 38 (1948), pp. 163–71; and "An Arab Egyptian Family," *Middle East Journal* 4 (1952), pp. 379–99, and "The Muslim Woman in Transition: Based on Observations in Egypt and Pakistan," *Sociologus* 7, no. 1 (1957), pp. 23–28.
10. Abbott, "Women," p. 200.
11. L. Sweet and T.J. O'Leary, *Circum-Mediterranean Peasantry: Introductory Bibliographies* (New Haven: HRAF Press), p. xviii.
12. S. Abdel Kader, "A Survey of Trends in Social Science Research on Women in the Arab Region," *Social Science Research and Women in the Arab World* (Unesco Paris/London: Frances Pinter, 1984), pp. 175–97; A. al-Qazzaz, *Women in the Middle East and North Africa: An Annotated Bibliography* (Austin: Center for Middle East Studies at the University of Texas, 1977), and "Current Status of Research on Women in the Arab World," *Middle East Studies* XIV, no. 3 (October, 1978); S.R. Meghdessian, *The Status of the Arab Woman: A Selected Bibliography* (London: Mansell, 1980); M. Raccagni, *The Modern Arab Woman: A Bibliography* (New Jersey: Scarecrow Press, 1978); M. Rihani, *A Bibliography of Recent Research on Family and Women in the Arab States* (Beirut: Institute for Women of Beirut University College, 1976); I.M. Ruud, *Women's Status in the Muslim World: A Bibliographic Survey* (Koln: E.J. Brill, 1981).
13. F. M'Rabet, *Les Algeriennes* (Paris: Maspero, 1967).
14. Ziadah, "Equality."
15. E.W. Fernea, *Guest of the Sheikh* (New York: Doubleday, 1965); A. Fuller, *Buari: Portrait of a Lebanese Muslim Village* (Cambridge: Harvard University Press, 1961); F. M'Rabet, *La Femme Algerienne Suivi par Les Algeriennes* (Paris: Maspero, 1969); L. Sweet, *Tell Toquaan: A Syrian Village* (Ann Arbor: University of Michigan, 1960); G. Tillion, *Le Harem et Les Cousins* (Paris: Seuil, 1966); J. Williams, *The Youth of Haouch el Harimi: A Lebanese Village* (Cambridge: Harvard University Press, 1968).
16. H.H. Hansen, *The Kurdish Women's Life* (Copenhagen: Nationalmuseetsskrifter, 1961); D. Gordon, *Women of Algeria: An Essay on Change* (Cambridge: Harvard University Press, 1968).
17. H. Papanek, "The Women Fieldworkers in Purdah Society," *Human Organization* 23, no. 2 (1964), pp. 160–63.
18. T. Asad, *Anthropology and the Colonial Encounter* (London: Ithaca Press, 1973); G. Berreman, "Is Anthropology Alive? Social Responsibility in Social Anthropology," *Current Anthropology* 9 (1968), pp. 391–96; F. Fanon, *Wretched of the Earth* (New York: Grove Press, 1965); K. Gough, "World

Revolution and the Science of Man," in T. Roszak, ed., *The Dissenting Academy* (London: Chatto and Windus Ltd., 1967), pp. 135–159; A Gouldner, *The Coming Crisis in Western Sociology* (New York: Basic Books, 1970); T. Kuhn, *The Structure of Scientific Revolutions* (Chicago: 1970); A. Mafeje, "The Problem of Anthropology in Historical Perspective: An Inquiry into the Growth of the Social Sciences," *Canadian Journal of African Studies* X, no. 2 (1976), pp. 307–33; C.W. Mills, *The Sociological Imagination* (London: Oxford University Press, 1959); B. Scholte, "Epistemic Paradigms: Some Problems of Cross Cultural Research on Social Anthropological Theory and History," *American Anthropologist* 68, no.5 (1966); 1192–1201; B. Scholte, "Toward a Reflexive and Critical Anthropology," in D. Hymes, eds., *Reinventing Anthropology* (New York: Random House, 1974), pp. 430–57.

19. Scholte, "Paradigm Concept," p. 235.

20. N. Abu-Zahra, "On Modesty of Women in Arab Muslim Villages: A Reply," *American Anthropologist* 72 (1970), pp. 1079–88; S. al-Torki, "Family Organization and Women's Power in Urban Saudi Arabian Society," *Journal of Anthropological Research* 33 (1977), pp. 277–87; A. Baffoun, "Femmes et Developpement dans le Maghreb Arabe: Socioanalyses des Origines de l'Inegalite," Unpublished paper presented at the seminar on Decolonizing Research (Dakar: Centre de Recherche pour le Developpement International, 1977); S. el-Missiri, "Self Images of Traditional Urban Women in Cairo," in L. Beck and N. Keddie, eds., *Women in the Muslim World* (Cambridge: Harvard University Press, 1978), pp. 522–40; A. Farrag, "Social Control Among Mzabite Women of Beni Isguen," *Middle Eastern Studies* 3 (1971), pp. 317–27; S. Morsy, "Sex Roles, Power and Illness in an Egyptian Village," *American Anthropologist* 5, no. 1 (1978), pp. 137–50; F. Mernissi, *Beyond the Veil: Male-Female Dynamics in a Modern Muslim Society* (New York: Schenkman, 1975); F. Mernissi, "Virginity and Patriarchy," in A. al-Hibri, ed., *Women and Islam* (Oxford: Pergamon Press, 1982), pp.183–92; F. Sabah, *Woman in the Muslim Unconscious* (New York: Pergamon Press, 1984); N. Saadawi, *The Hidden Face of Eve: Women in the Arab World* (London: Zed Press, 1980); N. Saadawi, *Women at the Point of Zero* (London: Zed Press, 1980).

21. A. al-Hibri, "A Study of Islamic Herstory: Or How Did We Ever Get Into This Mess?" in A. Al-Hibri, ed., *Women and Islam* (Oxford: Pergamon Press, 1982), pp. 207–20; D. Kandiyoti, "Emancipated but Unliberated?" Unpublished Paper (San Francisco: Middle East Studies Association Meetings, 1984); N. Keddie, "Problems in the Study of Middle Eastern Women," *International Journal of Middle East Studies* 10, (1979), pp. 225–40; S. Morsy, "Zionist Ideology as Anthropology: An Analysis of Joseph Ginat's Women in Muslim Rural Society," *Arab Studies Quarterly* 5, no. 4 (Fall, 1983), pp. 362–79; C. Nelson, "Public and Private Politics: Women in the Middle Eastern World," *American Ethnologist* 1, no. 3 (August, 1974): 551–63; F. Sayigh, "Roles and Functions of Arab Women: A Reappraisal," *Arab Studies Quarterly* 3, no. 3 (Spring, 1981), pp. 258–74; J. Tucker, "Problems in the Historiography of Women in the Middle East," *International Journal of Middle*

East Studies 15 (1983), pp. 321–36; D. Waines, "Through a Veil Darkly: The Study of Women in Muslim Societies," *Comparative Studies of Society and History* 24, no. 3 (1982), pp. 642–59.

22. J. Nash, "Introduction," in J. Nash and H. Safa, eds., *Sex and Class in Latin America: Women's Perspectives on Politics, Economics, and the Family in the Third World* (New York: Bergin), p. 15.

23. Kuhn, *Structure of Revolutions*, p. 175.

24. J. Hilal, "The Management of Male Dominance in Traditional Arab Culture: A Tentative Model," *Civilizations* XXI, no. 1 (1971), pp. 85–95.

25. Nelson, "Public and Private Politics," and L. Rosen, "The Negotiation of Reality: Male-Female Relations in Sefrou, Morocco," in Beck and Keddie, pp. 637–58.

26. L. Sweet, "In Reality: Some Middle Eastern Women," in C. Mathiasson, ed., *Many Sisters: Women in Cross Cultural Perspective* (New York: Free Press, 1974), p. 381.

27. V. Maher, *Women and Property in Morocco: Their Changing Relation to the Process of Social Stratification in the Middle Atlas* (Cambridge: Cambridge University Press), p. 2.

28. al-Torki, *"Family Organization,"* p. 277.

29. S. Joseph, "Women and the Neighborhood Street in Borj Hamoud, Lebanon," in Beck and Keddie, pp. 541–57.

30. S. Morsy, "Sex Differences and Folk Illness in an Egyptian Village," in Beck and Keddie, pp. 611–14.

31. A. Rassam, "Women and Domestic Power in Morocco," *International Journal of Middle East Studies* 12 (1980), pp. 171–79.

32. Abu-Zahra, "On the Modest," p. 1087.

33. S. Mohsen, "The Egyptian Woman: Between Modernity and Tradition," in C. Mathiasson ed., *Many Sisters*, pp. 52–67; Mernissi, *Beyond the Veil;* D. Dwyer, *Images and Self Images: Male and Female in Morocco* (New York: Columbia University Press, 1978); D. Dwyer, "Ideologies of Sexual Inequality and Strategies for Change in Male-Female Relations," *American Ethnologist* 5, no. 2 (1978), pp. 227–40.

34. Mohsen, "The Egyptian Women," p. 58.

35. Mernissi, *Behind the Veil*, p. 4.

36. el-Missiri, "Bint-al-Balad," p. 534.

37. Dwyer, "Ideologies."

38. C. Nelson and V. Olesen, "Veil of Illusion: A Critique of the Concept 'Equality' in Western Feminist Thought," in C. Nelson and V. Olesen, eds., *Catalyst* 10/11 (Summer, 1977), pp. 8–36.

39. S. Davis, *Patience and Power: Women's Lives in Moroccan Village* (Cambridge: Schenkman, 1982); S. Ferichou, "L'aide internationale au service du patriarchat: L'example tunisien," *Unesco Report* (1978); M. Hammam, "Egypt's Working Women: Texile Workers of Chubra el Kheima," *Merip Reports* (1970), pp. 3–7; M. Hammam, "Women and Industrial Work: The Case of Chubra el Kheima," *Arab Studies Quarterly* 11 (1980), pp. 50–59; C.

Makhlouf, *Changing Veils: Women and Modernization in North Yemen* (Austin: University of Texas Press, 1979); M. Mundy, "Women's Inheritance of Land in Highland Yemen," *Arabian Studies* 5 (1979), pp. 161–87; C. Myntti, "Yemeni Workers Abroad: The Impact on Women," *Merip Reports* 15, no. 4 (1984), pp. 11–16; E. Taylor-Awny, "Egyptian Migration and Peasant Wives," *Merip Reports* 14, no. 5 (1985), pp. 3–16; J. Tucker, "The Decline of the Family Economy in Mid-19th Century Egypt," *Arab Studies Quarterly* 1, no. 3 (1979), pp. 245–71; H. Zurayk, "Measuring Women's Economic Production," *The Measurement of Women's Economic Production* (Beirut, 1979), pp. 5–38.

40. J. Gran, "The Impact of the World Market on Egyptian Women," *Merip Reports* 58 (1977), pp. 3–7.

41. Ibid.

42. J. Tucker, "Egyptian Women in the Work Force," *Merip Reports* 50 (1977), pp. 3–9.

43. Hamman, "Egypt's Working Women," and "Women and Industrial Work."

44. M. Hamman, "Labor Migration and the Sexual Division of Labor," *Merip Reports* 95 (1981), p. 3.

45. F. Mernissi, "Women and the Impact of Capitalist Development in Morocco, Part I," *Feminist Issues* (Fall, 1982), pp. 69–104 and Part II, *Feminist Issues* (Spring, 1983), pp. 61–112; F. Mernissi, "Zhor's World: A Moroccan Domestic Worker Speaks Out," *Feminist Issues* (Spring, 1983), pp. 3–31.

46. Ibid., p. 77.

47. Ibid., p. 69.

48. Mernissi, "Zhor's World," p. 13.

49. Ibid., p. 22

50. G. Bell-Villada, "Decolonizing the Mind," *South: The Third World Magazine* (January, 1983), p. 19.

51. Beck and Keddie, "Women," and Tucker, "Problems in Historiography."

52. See the essays in al-Hibri, *Women and Islam* and the papers by A. Baffoun and A. Rassam in Unesco, ed., *Social Science Research* (London: Frances Pinter, 1984); S. al-Torki, "The Anthropologist in the Field: A Case of 'Indigenous Anthropology' from Saudi Arabia," in H. Fah, ed., *Indigenous Anthropology in Non-Western Countries* (Durham: Carolina Academic Press, 1982), pp. 167–75; Unesco, *Social Science Research;* F. el-Guindi, "Veiled Activism: Egyptian Women in the Contemporary Islamic Movement," *L'femme de la mediterranee, peuples mediterraneens* 22–23 (June, 1983), pp. 79–89; S. al-Torki, *Women in Saudi Arabia: Ideology and Behavior Among the Elite* (New York: Columbia University Press, 1986); M. Hatem, "Underdevelopment, Mothering and Gender Within the Egyptian Family," *Arab Studies Quarterly* 8, no. 1 (Winter, 1986), pp. 45–61; M. Hatem, "The Enduring Alliance of Nationalism and Patriarchy in the Musim Personal Status Law: The Case of Modern Egypt," *Feminist Issues* 6, no. 1 (Spring, 1986), pp. 19–44; L. Ahmed, "Feminism and Feminist Movements in the Middle East; A Preliminary Exploration," in al-Hibri, *Women and Islam*, pp. 153–68. In this context

it is relevant to point out that the Department of Sociology-Anthropology at The American University of Cairo has accumulated a good deal of "indigenous research" over the past twenty-five years in the form of unpublished MA theses—most of which contain ethnographic description about some aspect of women and changing Egyptian and Middle Eastern society.

53. al-Torki, *Women in Saudi Arabia* and L. Abu-Lughod, "A Community of Secrets: The Separate World of Bedouin Women," *Signs: Journal of Women, Culture and Society* 10, no. 4 (1985), pp. 637–59.
54. al-Torki, 1986, p. 99.
55. L. Abu-Lughod, *Veiled Sentiments: Honor, Modesty and Poetry in a Bedouin Society* (Berkeley: University of California Press, 1986), p. 639.
56. al-Torki, 1986, pp. 637–59.
57. Abu-Lughod, *Veiled Sentiments,* pp. 638–39.
58. al-Torki, 1986, pp. 6.
59. Abu-Lughod,*Veiled Sentiments,* pp. 638–39.
60. al-Torki, 1986, pp. 162.
61. Abu-Lughod,*Veiled Sentiments,* pp. 657.
62. Abu-Lughod,*Veiled Sentiments,* pp. 637–38.
63. al-Torki, 1986, p. 2.
64. R. Murphy, *The Dialectics of Social Life: Alarms and Excursions in Anthropological Theory* (London: George Allen and Unwin Ltd., 1972).
65. E.F. Keller, "Feminism and the Analytic Tools for the Study of Science," *Academe* (September/October, 1983), pp. 14–21.
66. Tiffany,"Paradigms of Power."
67. N. Atiya, *Khul-Khal: Five Egyptian Women Tell Their Stories* (Syracuse: Syracuse University Press, 1981); E.W. Fernea and B.Q. Berzigan, eds., *Middle Eastern Women Speak* (Austin: University of Texas Press, 1977); Mernissi, "Zhor's World."
68. B. Scholte, "Cultural Anthropology and the Paradigm Concept: A Brief History of Their Recent Convergence," in L. Graham et al., eds., *Functions and Uses of Disciplinary Histories*, Vol. VII (Hague: D. Reidel, 1983), pp. 229–78.
69. L. Ahmed, "Western Ethnocentrism and Perceptions of the Harem," *Feminist Studies* 8 (1984), pp. 521–34.

7 Science, Ideology and Authoritarianism In Middle East Economics

NADIA RAMSIS FARAH

THE STUDY OF Middle East economics is based on science but is permeated by ideology. Economists seem to rarely agree. The reason is simple. While economics is a science, it is heavily influenced by political, social and ideological perceptions. Two main competing paradigms influence economic analysis: liberal economics and Marxist economic thought. Within each of the main theoretical paradigms, different schools of thought add to the methodological confusion and complexity. The student of economics has to determine which approach to use: classical, neo-classical, Keynesian, post-Keynesian, institutionalist, traditional Marxist, neo-Marxist, dependencia, or World-systems. The diversity of approaches forces economists to make clear choices in terms of paradigms and schools. The choice is rarely based on the scientific qualities of a particular paradigm or approach. The choice is ideological. Such a choice identifies the economist's social and political priorities and therefore it determines his/her political identification with a certain class and/or social group. Economists are ideological interpreters of different classes, social groups and/or international forces. The polarization between classes, social groups and rich and poor nations is paralleled by the polarization between economists.

Middle East economics is no exception to this state of affairs. The literature is replete with the different paradigms, schools and approaches. Nevertheless, Middle East economics is marked by a distinctive difference in analysis between internationalist and nationalist economists. The internationalists, who are more often than not economists working for international organizations such as the International Monetary Fund, the World

Bank or such similar organizations, apply to the study of Middle East economics a traditional, neo-classical approach. Behind the battery of statistics, econometric models and complex graphs, the internationalists' approach implies the following propositions:
1) Middle East economic systems are identical or should be identical to the free-market Western systems;
2) There is only one scientific approach to economics: the neo-classical approach;
3) Problems encountered in Middle East economies are explained away by unfortunate state interference in the workings of the self-adjusting free-market mechanisms;
4) Therefore, if only the states of the Middle East adopt the premises of the free-market system—competition and comparative advantages—and follow the advice of the international economic organizations, economic development will follow.

Nationalist economists, while using all the tricks of the trade, applying different and sometimes widely divergent approaches and paradigms, are weary of the internationalists' position. The nationalists' knowledge of Middle East economic systems, and their own experience in the field, make them either question economic theory, or at least, use this theory in a novel way in an attempt to accommodate Middle East economic realities.

This basic difference between internationalists and nationalists sets the tone for the study of Middle East economics. Internationalists and nationalists clash on almost all basic topics and major issues of economic policy. Basic debates of contention involve the nature of the Middle East economies, development strategies, and the role of the state in economic development. This list does not exhaust all topics discussed in Middle East economics. However, most controversies center around these issues.

Nevertheless, there is a lack of an attempt to properly identify the nature of Middle East economics. Attempting to apply the known models fails to grasp the intricacies, complexities and specificity of the Middle East. In fact, we rather think that Middle East economics are unique in that economic policy is not influenced by straight-forward economic rationality pertaining to the free-market system or otherwise. Economic policy is geared towards the maintenance and security of existing regimes. What seems to be an irrational economic policy, if we apply purely economic criteria, makes sense only if we take into account the noneconomic factors that influence economic policy-making. Authoritarian economics is a brand of economic policy and economic decision-making that defies the precepts of recognized economic theories. Once we acknowledge this, we may be able to put to rest some of the controversies that have raged for years.

If Middle East economics are authoritarian economics, as we contend, should economists relinquish economics as a science? The identification of Middle East economics as authoritarian economics is the first step to reestablish the scientific nature of economics. The recognition of the overtly political and state-security oriented character of Middle East economics will coalesce the economist's efforts at rationalizing the process in a strive for real sustained development where economic decision-making is liberated from the requirements of maintaining regime stability and security.

ECONOMICS AS A SCIENCE AND ECONOMISTS AS IDEOLOGICAL INTERPRETERS

Economics as a science started with the publication of Adam Smith's *The Wealth of Nations* in 1776. What differentiated Adam Smith's treatise from previous writings dealing with the economy was his attempt to deduce general laws from his observations of the British economy. He investigated such questions as value, price and rent. His contemporaries and followers enriched economic theory with their assiduous investigations. From Ricardo to Malthus to John Stuart Mill, economic theory grew as a consistent body of thought dealing with the intricacies of the economy. Under the persistent efforts of the classical economists, economics emerged as a distinct science separate from the fields of religion and ethics. Classical economics were in essence a formulation of the laws of the vigorous capitalist system which dawned on Europe in the eighteenth century. However, the classical economists were not shy in declaring their political and ideological positions. When Smith and especially Ricardo mercilessly attacked the feudal landowners, they attempted to prove that rent is unearned income. Therefore, rent could be fully taxed for the benefit of industrial capital accumulation. The rent controversy was not simply economic. Clearly, the classical economists, by identifying rent as unearned income, were involved in the struggle between the feudal landlords and the nascent industrial bourgeoisie over state and therefore economic hegemony.

Smith and Ricardo were on the side of the industrialists. The battle waged against the feudal landlords was couched in seemingly iron-clad economic laws pertaining to nature. The labor theory of value elaborated by Ricardo was meant to discover the causes of value and the creation of profits. Coupled with Ricardo's law of wages, this theory was forged to keep wages at a minimum, to maximize the profits of the new bourgeoisie and accelerate capital accumulation. In this case, Ricardo was a true ideological interpreter of the capitalist class, while Malthus defended vehemently both capitalists and landlords against workers and tenants. If workers and tenants were poor, it was their own fault. They tended to propagate rapidly and overpopulation was seen to lead to poverty and moral laxity.

Karl Marx used classical political economy to build a devastating critique of the capitalist system. Using Ricardo's labor theory of value, he arrived at drastically different conclusions. Labor exploitation in addition to class struggle were the Marxist ideological weapons to wage the war on the capitalists for the benefit of the working class.

As a reaction to the harsh Marxist critique, economic theory developed into a more elaborate and mathematical paradigm with the rise of marginalism and the neo-classic school. Economics were divorced from politics and became reified as elaborate laws attempting to discover the determinants of both producer and consumer behavior.

Neo-classical theory experienced a crisis due to the Great Depression of the 1930s. Keynesianism was the miraculous solution that discovered that the state has an important role to play in the maintenance of the free-market system. The result was the welfare state which reigned supreme until the deep international crisis of the 1970s. With the new crisis, Keynesianism lost its appeal and the proponents of the new capitalist order were set to destroy the welfare state that gave so many rights to the workers and the poor. Monetarism is the attempt of the capitalists to get rid of high taxation, to cut wages and social benefits and to use the crisis in altering the power relations between rich and poor in favor of capital-owners.

This quick survey indicates that economic theory moved progressively from one school to another in response to the objective requirements of capitalist development. Economists, by defending certain class positions, had to prove these positions by formulating laws and theories. Paradoxically, it is this kind of ideological conflict that led to the sharpening of economic tools, striving to move economics from advice shrouded in religious and ethical arguments into a social science.

Socialist economics faced a challenge with the victory of the Bolshevik revolution in the Soviet Union. The Bolshevik state adopted socialism as its ideological and political paradigm. While Marxism laid scientific rules in its critique of capitalism, it did not set the criteria for building a socialist state. Apart from the general guidelines of the abolishment of private property and state control of economic resources, Marx did not advance any detailed economic policy. The Soviet state had to experiment and develop appropriate economic tools to carry out its socialist program. Slowly, methods of planning were developed to deal with the problems of a state-controlled economy.

While both liberal and Marxist economics are based on clear ideological premises, the development of economics as a science proceeded in both paradigms. In both the liberal and the Marxist traditions, the ideological premises are taken for granted. Accordingly, the development of rational economic tools consistent with the political and ideological requirements of liberalism and socialism was possible. Liberal and Marxist economics managed to create a rational economic policy largely separate if not divorced from the ideological and political spheres in which context they evolved.

In the case of Middle East economics, we are still at the stage of political and ideological formulations. The main arguments in Middle East economics reflect the ideological polarization between the proponents of the liberal tradition or the socialist perspective. The debates fail to recognize the nature of Middle East economics. Consequently, no scientific or rational policy development is possible. Middle East economics has not yet matured into a science.

BASIC DEBATES

A clear indication that Middle East economics is still at the stage of ideological formulation, are the continuously debated issues of the nature of the economy, the appropriate development strategy and the role of the state in the economy. Debates are shrouded in thick ideological formulations in which the proponents of each point of view usually attempt to discredit opponents by using noneconomic criteria. For example, they often accuse each other of a lack of patriotism, of being alienated, westernized, corrupt or, more simply, of nonconformity with the religious edicts of the Islamic Shar'ia. However, a close scrutiny of these debates reveal that we are still at the stage of ideological polarization. Economists are content to confront each other with the ready-made theories existing in the literature. No real efforts are focused on the study of the economies in question. Usually economists, to reinforce their point of view, would refer to the experiments of England, the United States, the Soviet Union or to the Japanese, South Korean and Chinese models of development. Granted that we can learn from other countries' economic histories, the greatest lack in Middle East economics is an in-depth study of Middle East economic structures in themselves and for themselves.

The Nature of the Middle East Economics

Internationalists consider the Middle East economic structure as an extension of the capitalist economy. For example, one stated:

> Middle Easterners have long since proved themselves as acquisitive as we Westerners, as skillful at calculation of comparative costs and advantages in various fields of investment, and as possessed as we of capitalist inclinations. In its simpler applications Western doctrine seems distinctly relevant to the Middle East."[1]

Another argued:

> . . . The Egyptian government has been discussing with the IMF and the World Bank a program of economic reform that includes 1) decreased expenditures and increased revenues; 2) an exchange rate unification; 3) a reform of interest rate structure; 4) energy price increases; 5) reduction of government-control in the agricultural sector including increasing farmgate prices; and 6) an adjustment of industrial policy during the next five year plan.[2]

These two quotations reflect the internationalist attitude. If the people of the Middle East prove that they can respond to changes in prices or respond to profitable opportunities of investment, then they are fit and capable to deal with the laws of the capitalist economy. It is almost as if prior to capitalism, people in the Middle East did not know about supply and demand and were not possessed by the acquisitive spirit! In fact, the opposite is true; the whole economic history of the Middle East prior to the emergence of the capitalist system depended on long distance trade. If anything, the Arabs perfected and refined the rules governing trade, and centuries ago their thinkers were discussing the problems of inflation, scarcity, demand and supply, profits, etc. In the voluminous historical works of Al-Maqrizi and Al-Jabarti, constant references are made to situations of inflation, scarcity and monopoly practices.

Being possessed of the acquisitive spirit is not a unique feature to capitalism nor is it the property of Western civilization. However, while Meyer accepts in principle the applicability of Western capitalist theory to the Middle East economy, he is fully aware that the theory, as it is, is rarely applicable in the Middle Eastern context. Instead of searching for the answer in the specificity of the Middle East economic structure, Meyer thinks that a mere accommodation of the existing economic tools is sufficient to make Western theory fully equipped to deal effectively with the problems of these economies.

If we think that Meyer is overstretching the applicability of the capitalist model to the Middle East, international organizations' economists usually do not even bother to discuss the nature of the Middle East economies. It is taken for granted that the Middle East economy is purely and simply a capitalist economy, and if it is not, it should be.

The IMF and World Bank program of economic reform of Egypt reads as a first-hand application of neo-classical economics. The Egyptian economic crisis is seen as a classic case of a crisis created by past economic policies which defied the sacred laws of the free market.

> The Egyptian economy suffers from the legacy of economic policies dating from the 1950s. These policies were characterized by ration cards, subsidies, price regulation, a dominant public sector and state control. Having established control over prices, the government has tried to maintain many at fixed, nominal levels, protecting the average Egyptian from the shocks in the international economy. Egyptian consumers have not faced world prices for energy or many basic commodities for years. As the gap between market and administered prices has grown, it has become more costly and difficult to maintain the system.[3]

This analysis is made with no reference, knowledge or even desire to know if the free-market rules can be operative in the Middle East economy in the same way they are in advanced Western societies. There is a complete neglect of noneconomic constraints on economic policy. Little attention is paid to the social burdens such a program entails for the majority of the population. The neglect of these factors react back negatively on economic policy-making. And more often than not, the application of the classic IMF and World Bank methods have resulted in worse economic crises than the one they thought to remedy.

Nationalist liberal economists, while being basically convinced of the capitalist character of the Middle East economy, tend to be more sensitive to the different characteristics of the indigenous economic structures and the social and political constraints enveloping economic policy-making.

The prominent Arab economist, Yusif Sayigh, best expresses this kind of nationalist sensitivity to the general applicability of the capitalist model.

> ... emphasis should be placed on self-reliance in the drive for development—instead of the uncritical adoption of alien development models or the undiscriminating belief in the universality of some stage sequence simply because it suits the history of the West or satisfactorily describes its experience.[4]

In his analysis of Arab financial surplus, Hazem Al-Biblawi tries to use Keynesian economics in analyzing the financial behavior of the Arab Gulf Oil states. However, Keynesianism was not conducive to Al-Biblawi's clear preference for placing Arab funds in Third-World markets, nor in explaining the pattern of Arab financial investments. Instead of abandoning the Keynesian paradigm, Al-Biblawi attempts to adapt the theory in such a way as to explain this pattern through what he calls "The placement case." Thus he demonstrates the nonprofitability of this pattern of investment to the Gulf states and thereby he could argue for investing the financial surplus in Third-World development as a more profitable economic activity.[5]

If liberal economists are not grappling with the nature of the economic structure of the Middle East, the problem is more acute with radical economists.

During the 1950s and 1960s, radical economists were mainly interested in the problems of transformation of a traditional to a modern economic structure. The noncapitalist road to development was theoretically formulated to take account of the rapid transformations in Middle-East economic structures under state control. Clinging to the orthodox Marxist notion of stages, radical economists were confronted by attempts of the new independent states in the Middle East and in the Third World at independent development via state control (Nasser's Egypt, Boumedienne's Algeria, Iraq and Syria). In response, they formulated the concept of "skipping" or substantially curtailing the capitalist stage in the development of a largely "so-called" feudal structure to a socialist economic system.[6]

This belief in the capability of the state to transform the economic structure was shattered by the sharp turn in the economic policies of most countries of the Middle East in the 1970s. The policies of economic re-internationalization, of "Open Door Policies" pursued by the most radical of Arab states, notably Egypt and to a lesser extent Syria, Iraq, and Algeria, demonstrated the naivety of the notions of historical determinism and the inevitability of progress held by most radical economists. A search into the reasons for the breakdown of the radical Arab regimes and the failure of their economic programs led to a wholesale adoption of the neo-Marxist school of dependency. It is noteworthy that dependency theory during its heyday in the 1960s was practically ignored by Middle East economists. While the thesis of dependency was on the decline in Latin America (where it originated) in the 1970s, it gained wide popularity in the Middle East. This can be explained by two main factors. First, dependency was used as a means to reject complete responsibility for the failure of the populist system based on an attempt at economic independence through state-controlled development. Second, the dependency thesis stressed the external factors for underdevelopment. The use of the dependency thesis underlies the dangers of the "open-door policies" or reinternationalization programs known under the euphemism of export-oriented industrialization.

> The insistence on explaining all important Arab developments, from the defeat of 1967, to the increase in oil prices, to the radical change in Arab economic policy—to the change in the nature of economic and political inter-Arab relations, to the outbreak of the civil war in Lebanon, to the Camp-David treaty between Egypt and Israel, as mere reflections of bad, internal conditions, or an expression of an independent Arab will, cannot lead except to more mystification and perplexity.[7]

Professor Galal Amin, while not neglecting the internal factors responsible for change, claims that the explanation of the current economic situation in terms of internal factors only, reveals a masochistic attitude.[8]

By determining the economic structure of the Middle East as a dependent economic structure, radical economists are clearly attributing the underdevelopment of the Middle East and the perpetuation of its underdevelopment to the external economic relations tying the Middle East to the old imperialist centers (Europe) and the center of new imperialism (USA).

However, criticisms of this approach are increasing. The most important of these criticisms stressed the fact that the Middle Eastern economy was not penetrated by European capitalism until the *nineteenth* century. Meanwhile dependency theorists claim that underdevelopment started from the *sixteenth* century with the era of European mercantilism. While this is true of Latin-America where the dependency school originated, it is not true of the Middle East.[9] Second, while external factors of dependency have a role in shaping the economy of the Middle East, internal factors such as existing class alliances have a crucial role in the formation of that structure. Third, overstressing the role of the external factors in the shaping of the Middle East economic structure reflects a Euro-Centric view of economic processes. It simply means that the Third-World, including the Middle East, is unable to develop unless the centers of growth (i.e., Europe and the US) change in character and structure to allow a similar change in the periphery.[10]

The dissatisfaction with the dependency paradigm resulted in recent attempts at applying the concepts of modes of production and social formations.

The proponents of the modes of production approach have either used the Marxist concept of the Asiatic mode of production or, more generally, the concept of articulation of modes of production, in order to determine the specific nature of Middle East economies.[11] The social formations theorists look for an explanation for the failure of capitalist transformation in the Middle East. Part of the explanation lies in the historical fact of capitalist incorporation of the Middle East in the *nineteenth* and *twentieth* centuries. While European penetration transformed some sectors, it failed in carrying a full capitalist restructuring of the Middle East economy. This failure can be explained in part by the interests of metropolitan capitalism. Existing precapitalist modes of production subsidize capitalist growth in the center by providing cheap raw materials, cheap labor supply or migrant workers. At the same time, internal forces profiting through the precapitalist modes are also perpetuating these modes, resisting thereby the process of capitalist transformation.[12]

While the social formations thesis offers an explanation of the nature of the economic structures of the Middle East, it is still at an early stage of formulation. However, more in-depth empirical research is needed if this school is expected to yield any meaningful explanation of the nature of the Middle East economic structure. It is in the framework of this last school, that we place our thesis of the nature of Middle East economics as authoritarian economics.

Development Strategies and the Role of the State

The ideological polarization regarding the nature of the Middle East economy is reflected in the debate about development strategies. In the 1950s and 1960s, nationalist economists advocated the strategy of import substitution industrialization as the means for an independent and self-sustained development. The state had the main functions of capital accumulation, protection of national industries and the satisfaction of the population's basic needs. Through measures such as land reform, nationalization of foreign and national capital, a tight policy of controls and subsidies, the radical states of the Middle East pursued development and social equity. Influenced by the popularity and weight of the radical states (i.e., Egypt, Syria, Iraq and Algeria), many other Arab states followed suit in emphasizing redistribution with growth.

In the heyday of import-substitution industrialization, the dominant ideology of development in the Third World, even the liberal economists did not dispute the relevance of the policy. Bent Hansen and Girgis Marzouk,[13] after a critical appraisal of the nationalization measures taken by the Egyptian government in the 1950s and early 1960s, suggest only in a very indirect way that maybe more traditional methods of directing investment and redistributing income could have been more beneficial. However the authors did not disagree in principle with the good motives of the policy. In their discussion of industrialization in Egypt, Hansen and Marzouk are directly defending the policies of protectionism as the means for industrialization.[14]

However, by the early 1970s, we see marked disenchantment with the strategy of import-substitution and the large role of the state in economic development. Galal Amin in his very important book, *The Modernization of Poverty*, expresses this kind of disillusion.

It is indeed remarkable how Arab countries starting from such different points and following such different routes have achieved such similar results. With or without land reform, the land-lords and tribal chiefs have been largely deprived of political power but the agricultural population continues to be discriminated against. With or without socialist slogans, the public sector is growing but the rate of saving is not. The domination of the traditional form of foreign economic interests has either vanished or is on the decline, even in oil, but is rapidly being replaced by that of a new native class. Rich or poor in agricultural resources, all of them, except Syria, have a growing food deficit, and Syria's surplus is declining. They have all plans and have been investing much higher rates than Europe ever did during the last century and have been urbanizing much faster, without making, except for Egypt, any significant change in economic structure. They have received vast funds from foreign governments or companies of which they, without exception, have managed to waste considerable portions and in almost all, the government has been more wasteful than the public.[15]

The import-substitution strategy in the Middle East was questioned sharply by both proponents and antagonists after the 1967 Arab defeat. The populist regimes, especially in Egypt, established their legitimacy on the basis of building a strong state. The economic strategy of import-substitution was a component in the creation of an independent Arab world able to confront foreign and especially Israeli threats. The failure of populism (i.e. Nasserism) led to the reemergence of strong currents in the economic literature advocating a more liberalized economy. The economic problems facing the Middle East are explained as a result of the intervention of a corrupt and inefficient state. Armed with the examples of South Korea, Singapore, Hong Kong and Taiwan, internationalist and liberal economists questioned and challenged the import-substitution strategy for development.

In addition, internal and international developments in the Middle East in the 1970s led to spectacular increases in oil prices, a development which made possible the inflow of huge financial resources to the Arab region. Both oil-rich and poor Arab states tried to benefit from the boom by liberalizing the economy. In the case of the radical states of Egypt, Syria, Iraq and Algeria, this attempt led to the renouncement of any strategy for a self-reliant economy. The "Open-Door" policies adopted by these states were an attempt at sharing in the oil wealth.

In this context, the believers in import-substitution and self-reliance became a minority. The debates in the economic literature of the 1970s are in fact debates between the proponents of liberalization and the proponents of nationalist, auto-centric development.

The liberalization of the Arab economy is advocated as an essential step to move from import-substitution to an export-led strategy. In order to have access to foreign markets, there is a need for foreign capital, advanced technology and know-how. Barriers against foreign trade have to be abolished. Incentives have to be given to foreign and Arab capital. State intervention has to be curtailed and private entrepreneurship encouraged.

Radical economists on the defensive counter by stressing the dangers of this policy. The literature of the last two decades is dominated by harsh critiques of the effects of the liberal economic policies adopted by the majority of Arab states.[16] The relative decline in industrial and agricultural productivity in favor of oil and services gave birth to the thesis of the rentier economy. The Arab states are living off oil rent. The high salaries of migrant workers compared to the scale of salaries in their home countries are described as rentier incomes.[17] Egyptian economists maintain that, regardless of oil and rapid growth as measured by the rate of increase in the gross national product, income inequalities are increasing. The liberalization of the economy resulted also in the emergence of a new class which is making its fortunes through shady or illegal activities: a parasitic class.[18] High inflationary pressures and increased liquidity resulted in the mushrooming of the informal sector and nonproductive activities at the expense of the commodities sectors. Finally, the policy led to a staggering international debt for the poor Arab states and a decline in the financial surplus of the rich states.

For the radical economists, there is a need for a reexamination of the "open-door" policies. The solution would be a return to the strategy of import-substitution. For liberal and internationalist economists, the actual crisis of the Arab World results from the still large role of the state in the Arab economy. More liberalization is needed and state intervention has to be curtailed. Hence the calls for the sale of public sector enterprises, the reinstitution of free-market mechanisms, the cancellation of state subsidies and a sharp decrease in state public expenditures.

The real debate is in essence a debate on the role of the state in the economy; hence the ideological polarization most clearly demonstrated in the economic literature of the last decade. This polarization is symptomatic of an economy in transition. Both, either the one wholly condemning the role of the state in the economy or the one supporting it, have yet to come to grips with the nature of Middle East economics. A consensus on that may lead to a consensus on what economic strategy to adopt. However, the current economic debates, while highly motivated by ideological and class positions, have prompted Arab economists to probe into recent economic phenomena. This analysis is yielding valuable insights into the economic dynamics of the Middle East. Our knowledge of the Arab economy has undoubtedly gained from such debates. The theses of the rentier economy, the parasitic new capitalist class and the dynamics of the informal sectors are net additions to development theory. They bring us closer to a better understanding of the role of the state in the Middle East.

However, the basic role of the state in the Middle East is not that of the protection of private economic activity as envisioned by liberal economists. It is also not that of leading the development process as extolled by radical economists. The role of the state in the Middle East has been and is still that of redistribution in order to maintain state security. The two interrelated functions of redistribution and security are at the basis of what we call "Authoritarian Economics."

AUTHORITARIAN ECONOMICS IN THE MIDDLE EAST

Authoritarian economics has certain properties that may seem irrational if we apply strict economic criteria. The main defining characteristic of authoritarian economics is that the state uses its economic power to maintain regime stability. The role of the state in the economy is substantial. Yet authoritarian economics is not simply an outcome of the role of the state. The state in both advanced free-market and socialist economies is undertaking a dominant and determining role. However, economic policy in advanced countries follows a definite economic rationality. Whatever the ideological underpinnings, economic policy has evolved into a clear set of economic priorities, based on a long-term view of societal development. This is not the case in most Third-World and especially Arab states. The majority of Arab states passed through successive stages of economic transition and pursued development strategies, often contradictory, without laying strong foundations for either a stable economic structure or economic policy. The basis for the fragility of the economics in the Arab World corresponds to a unique form of economic practices, where regardless of the professed ideology of the state (i.e., capitalist or socialist), the state is the chief economic actor in society. The main economic function of the state is not that of production either directly or indirectly. Its main economic function is that of redistribution. The redistribution policies of

Arab states have the main goal of regime security by holding the balance between different classes and social groups. To maintain security, the role of redistribution is backed by the use of force.

In order to achieve the goal of security, the state follows certain practices that may seem incoherent from an economic point of view. While Arab states have professed the rational economic goals of independent development and increased welfare for its citizens, its economic practices usually act against these goals. Accordingly, a chief characteristic of authoritarian economics is the adoption by the state of multiple and often opposing rules in regard to the same issue area. Examples of these contradictory policies abound in the Arab World. The Algerian regime adopted a policy of heavy industrialization to lessen its dependence on the oil and natural gas sector; however, a hefty share of the major state investment went to the hydrocarbon sector. The percentage of investment in that sector was no less than 28% from 1967 to 1978. At the same time, investment in agriculture declined from 16% in 1969 to 4.5% in 1978. This policy, instead of decreasing dependency, led to more dependence on the hydrocarbon sector in the generation of gross domestic product. Algeria is forced to import more than 50% of its food needs. Food imports are costing Algeria for the moment more than its total revenues from the exports of hydrocarbons. To maintain internal political stability, the state is forced to subsidize food prices and other basic needs. The subsidies reached 3.8 billion dinars in 1982, which accentuated the crisis of the government budget deficit.[19] The deficit is usually financed by inflationary methods which lead to more deterioration in living standards which in turn inflate the volume of subsidies. Instead of achieving an independent development and an amelioration in the standards of living, Algeria is more deeply entrenched into the international capitalist economic system and its dependence on primary-product exports (oil and natural gas) is increasing rather than decreasing. On the other end of the spectrum, oil-rich countries nationalized the international oil companies in an attempt at economic independence. Saudi Arabia received tremendous returns for its oil exports after 1973. Independent development attempts in Saudi Arabia resulted in self-sufficiency in wheat production (at five times its international price) and the building of an ultra-modern capital-intensive petrochemical industry. Petrochemical products face high protectionist measures from advanced countries in terms of quotas and high tariffs. Meanwhile Saudi Arabia still depends on the revenues of oil exports which form 96% of its gross national product.[20] The huge financial surplus, and its recycling in American and European markets, led to more dependency of the Saudi economy on international market forces.

Contradictory policies regarding the same issue area are also clear in sectoral economic policies. Egypt, after changing abruptly its economic policy from the strategy of import substitution to that of economic liberalization, "Infitah," is conducting contradictory policies regarding every sector of the economy. In agriculture, the old lands are still under the Nasserist laws of controlled rent and mandatory marketing boards for strategic crops (i.e., cotton, wheat, rice, etc...) while the new lands are completely uncontrolled. Prices in the "infitah" sector of agriculture are set according to supply and demand. Vegetables, fruits and flowers are exempted from taxation. The result is the deterioration of agricultural production, the import of over 65% of Egypt's food needs and the devotion of agricultural land to untraditional crops (i.e., clover, vegetables and fruits). The same is true for all other sectors, where Nasserist rules control part of the sector's economy, while the other is left to the new free market open door rules.

We cannot credit such policies to any kind of economic rationality, either capitalist or socialist. The raison d'être of such policies is not economic but political, which brings us to the second main characteristic of authoritarian economics, that of the primacy of distribution over production.

The state's uses of economic power are not only incoherent from an economic point of view, but they are also reactive and eclectic. If the characteristic feature of authoritarian politics is exclusion and depoliticization of society, authoritarian economics can be qualified as arbitrary redistributional policies. The arbitrary nature of the authoritarian economics of redistribution stems from several factors. Like some other economic philosophies, distribution for authoritarian economics takes an over-all precedence and supremacy over production. But unlike most of these philosophies, the distributional criteria and the shares allocated to various groups are not usually based on, neither are they justified by, systematic criteria pertaining to roles or contributions in the generation of wealth or production. These distributional policies do not conform either to any humanist or progressive sense of fairness or social justice. In addition, the policies of distribution or the criteria to allocate shares in the social wealth are usually contradictory and inconsistent. Individuals performing the same role in the economy or the bureaucracy are rewarded differently according to the significance of the target group to which they belong in the "security map" of the authoritarian regime. Hence, authoritarian economics are by and large economics of bribery and corruption. Accordingly, authoritarian economics are by definition economics of waste.

The nationalization of key enterprises in Egypt in 1961, Iraq in 1964 and Syria in 1965 led to the emergence of a huge public sector. The new directors of the public sector were not chosen for their managerial efficiency. They were appointed either for security reasons, or as a reward for services rendered to the state, or as a means of gaining the loyalties of some prominent families and/or social group. Some of the key positions in the public sector were granted to prominent military officers either to secure their loyalties or to exclude them from the armed forces if they posited some kind of threat to the regime. Previous private owners were appointed as directors and managers especially in Nasserist Egypt. Finally, technocratic elements were included to maintain middle class loyalty to the regime in power.[21] While the major enterprises were nationalized, a substantial private sector was maintained, including medium to small-size enterprises. Most construction was left in private hands. The interpenetration between public and private sector created a conduit of illegal wealth to some of the directors of the public sector. The granting of licences, the provision of subsidized inputs to the private sector became the means for quick fortunes to the decision-makers and directors of key public sector enterprises. The economics of corruption and bribery created a special dynamic of distribution of wealth. The state used this system to reward certain social groups and/or individuals for their loyalty to the regime or as means to exclude or punish others.[22]

After the adoption of the Open-door policy in the 1970s and under the impact of oil wealth, the radical Arab regimes returned to a policy of reintegration in the international economic system. An Open-door sector was superimposed on the highly state-controlled sector. The new sector, especially in Egypt, is free of state controls especially in terms of wages. Employment opportunities in the free sector of the economy are sought after. The wage rate in the "infitah" sector exceeds the wage rate in the public sector sometimes by ten to fifteen fold for the same job. Access to employment in the open door sector depends in a majority of cases on the power of the applicant. That power is usually derived from important positions in the government or state sector. Nepotism and patron-client relationships are the dynamics of employment in the new free sector. Again here, the "infitah" sector is providing high incomes to the family members of the

powerful state personalities. The Open-door sector is a means of redistribution for the elites including the bureaucratic elites of the 1960s.[23] The
state controls the open-door sector, not directly but by the power it has
over its very existence. The laws which allowed this sector to come to existence can be reversed if it does not satisfy the interests of the state elites. In
this way, the "infitah" sector is a state creation that prospers as long as it
serves state interests.

Finally, authoritarian economics can also be described as the form of
economic practices that coincide with the preeminence of the "security
perspective" to state functions. This is partly reflected in the inflated budget of security institutions (e.g., the army, regular police forces, secret police, para-military forces, etc.). Economic policy is more or less subject to
the commanding power of security policies. This explains the special care
given to the economic requirements of security exigencies, and it is reflected in the great share of the armed forces in government budgets.
Egypt, which concluded the peace treaty with Israel in order to divert resources to economic development as officially proclaimed by the regime,
allocates over 28% of its government expenditures to the army alone. This
preoccupation with security leads to sudden changes in economic policy.
Allocations for investment projects could be suddenly cancelled to finance
external and internal security needs. During the Yemen war, the Egyptian
regime pressed by the high financial burden of the protracted war decided
to finance the war from the investment funds rather than restrict public
and private consumption. The populist regime of the 1960s maintained
the political support of the masses through a battery of welfare policies. In
order not to antagonize the masses, the regime chose to maintain existing
consumption levels at the cost of a halt in economic growth during the
second half of the 1960s.[24]

To maintain social peace, Arab governments in Tunisia, Morocco,
Egypt, Syria and the Sudan may cancel new projects to finance a temporary rise in consumption levels through subsidies or wage increases which
in turn are vacated of real content through the feeding of inflationary pressures and manipulation of monetary policies. The determining factor in
disposing of resources is essentially the need for rearranging social configurations according to security needs.

In brief, the authoritarian economics of the Middle East are simply an
irresponsible practice by states whose definition of the role of the state is
not the construction of a "social and economic" system with stable repro-
ductive mechanisms and institutions. It is a form of economics which aims

at running the daily affairs of a society within the framework of a short-run philosophy of stability and security, whatever the long-run consequences. Authoritarian economics is not geared towards development. It is in essence the economics of regime survival.

If we recognize the particular characteristics of authoritarian economics, then a first step to move from ideology to science in Middle East economics hinges on the economists' ability to discover the mechanisms of this peculiar structure of economic policies. The job of the Arab economist is to offer to the public and active political forces in the Arab World, a clear diagnosis of state economic policies. The second task is to differentiate the special form of authoritarian economics, which is politically over-determined, from the need for a rational state role in the economy. A critique of authoritarian economics should not be used as a ploy to curtail the state role. The state has a definite role in leading the development process. What is needed is to divorce the economic policy of the state from its security needs. The most pressing task for Arab economists is the depoliticization and the rationalization of Arab economic policy.

NOTES

1. A.J. Meyer, *Middle Eastern Capitalism: Nine Essays* (Cambridge, Massachusetts: Harvard University Press, 1959), p. 112.
2. American Embassy, *Economic Trends Report: Egypt* (Cairo, Egypt: December 1986): pp. 2–3.
3. American Embassy, p. 7.
4. Yusif A. Sayigh, *The Determinants of Arab Economic Development* (London: Croom Helm, 1978), pp. 12–13.
5. Hazem Al-Biblawi, "The Predicament of the Arab Gulf Oil States: Individual Gains and Collective Losses," in M. Kerr and S. Yassi (eds.), *Rich and Poor States in the Middle East* (Boulder, Colorado: Westview Press and Cairo, Egypt: AUC Press, 1982), pp. 165–224.
6. V. Khoros, *Populism: Its Past, Present and Future* (Moscow: Progress Publishers, English text, 1984).
7. Galal Amin, *The Arab East and the West,* Third Edition (Beirut, Lebanon: Center of Arab Unity Studies), p. 13 (in Arabic).
8. Amin, p. 14.
9. Mohamed E. Said, "Dependency As an Explanation for Arab Underdevelopment," *Al-Mustaqbal Al-Arabi* 62 (1984) (in Arabic).
10. Said; and Nadia Farah, "Social Formations and Arab Social Systems," *Al-Mustaqbal Al-Arabi* 91 (1986) (in Arabic).
11. See, for example, Ahmed Sadek Saad, *The Asian Mode of Production: Egypt's Social and Economic History* (Beirut: Ibn Khaldoun Press, 1979) (in Arabic).

12. Farah.

13. Bent Hansen and Girgis Marzouk, *Development and Economic Policy in the UAR (Egypt)* (Amsterdam: North-Holl and Publishing Company, 1965).

14. Hansen and Marzouk, pp. 151–55.

15. Galal Amin, *The Modernization of Poverty* (Leiden: J. Brill, 1974), p. 108.

16. See, for example, Kerr & Yassin (eds.).

17. Mahmoud Abdel-Fadil et al., *The Transition of the Egyptian Economy Under the New Open-Door Policy (1973–1983)* (London: Oxford University Press, 1985).

18. Fadil et al.

19. Abdel-Latif Ben-Shinho, "The Algerian Experiment: Economic Dynamics and Social Development," in Fergany et al., *Independent Development in the Arab World* (Beirut: Center for Arab Unity Studies, 1987), pp. 189–515 (in Arabic).

20. Mohamed Hisham Khawagia, "The Experiment of Economic Development from the point of view of Independence and Dependency in the Kingdom of Saudi-Arabia," in Fergany et al., *Independent Development in the Arab World* (Beirut: Center for Arab Unity Studies, 1987), pp. 547–91.

21. See Essam Khafagy, *The State and Capitalist Development in Iraq: 1968–1978* (Cairo: Dar Al-Mustaqbal Al-Arabi, 1983); Adel Ghoneim, *The Egyptian Case of a Dependent State Capitalism* (Cairo: Darl Al-Mustaqbal Al-Arabi, 1986) (in Arabic).

22. Nadia Farah, "Development and the Crisis of Political Transformation," *Al-Manar* (June 1985) (in Arabic).

23. Samia Said Imam, "The Social Roots of the 'Open-Door' Elites in Egyptian Society," Unpublished M.A. thesis, Faculty of Economics and Political Science, Cairo University, 1985.

24. Nadia R. Farah, "Western Theory and Arab Development," *Al-Mustaqbal Al-Arabi* 64 (June 1984) (in Arabic).

8 The Dilemma of Modern Arab Economic Thought

Basil al-Bustany

Since the end of World War Two, the cause of Arab Unity has been the central objective pursued by Arab "Nationalists." On the economic front, this has been directly reflected in the continued call by Arab economists for the attainment of economic integration, as it was deemed the critical means by which such unity can be achieved.

At the same time, however, both interrelated goals proved to be quite elusive. This fact is clearly demonstrated by the record of economic cooperation and coordination among the Arab states since the mid-1940s. For, despite the continued hammering by the Arab economists on the merits and needs for economic intergration, as well as the enactment of a number of important measures in the sphere of mutual economic cooperation, the goal of economic unity remains unattainable.

Why has economic integration proven to be a difficult objective to reach? What are the factors causing the ever-present gap between expectations and achievements? Within the context of future Arab economic development, these are critical issues which need to be examined.

FANCY

Generally, the "theme" of economic integration as presented by Arab economists contains two main aspects. It seeks to outline the attributes of economic integration including the examination of the meaning, forms and elements of the integration process mostly presented in a comparative dress. The major constraints to the realization of the goal of integration among the Arab countries also are identified and analyzed.

A number of factors are advanced in support of the merits and benefits of Arab economic integration. As exemplified by the literature on the subject, the main benefits include the following:

a) That the Arabs represent one nation that is unified by a complex of historical and cultural forces, the interaction of which gives the nation its "identity."

b) In an international economic environment where interdependence as well as competition prevail, survival can only be secured through large economic units.

c) Since no single Arab country can sustain the course of independent development (mainly due to the limitations of the resource base), economic integration would then present itself as the only viable alternative constituting the "necessary condition" for securing such development.

d) Above all, economic integration enjoys wide popular support as it represents the backbone of the long sought objective of Arab unity.

The scope of actual economic (and noneconomic) cooperation among Arab countries is extensive indeed. This takes many forms including mainly a number of official agreements, regional and specialized institutions, as well as other measures. Within this context, the agreement establishing the Arab League in 1945 represents no doubt the all-embracing framework for mutual economic cooperation. This overall set up was reinforced on the economic field by two other major agreements, that of Arab Economic Unity in 1957 (but actually becoming effective only in 1964), and the agreement creating the Economic Unity Council in 1964.

The substantial increase in Arab financial resources in the early 1970s, thanks to the "Oil Revolution" and its aftermath, was quite instrumental in enhancing the resources and the multiplication of pan-Arab institutions and organizations. At present, there are at least twenty such specialized set ups operating in the economic sphere.

A number of constraints to effective economic cooperation among Arab countries are identified in the vast literature on economic integration. They include structural, institutional, legal, planning, and others relating to the implementation mechanisms.

It is argued that, despite the relative availability of human, financial and natural resources in the Arab World, the economic pattern had failed to redress the structural imbalance which clearly identifies the Arab economy. Features such as the still relatively important agricultural sector, where traditional methods and low productivity prevail; the limited nonoil industrial base; and the overwhelming importance of the oil sector in many such countries, represent the dominant characteristics of their economies. The failure of achieving the necessary structural transformation has resulted in deepening the degree of openness, hence dependency upon the external sector, both economically and financially. Further, it is contended that the main effect that the "Oil Revolution" had on the Arab economy was essentially quantitative rather than qualitative, and thus was unable to support the transformation process.

Despite the presence of a vast network of pan-Arab institutions operating on the economic plateau, they suffer from a number of severe limitations. Most evident of these include lack of adequate flexibility in responding to a continuously changing environment; duplication of functions, which is a source of frequent conflict; and, recently, rising shortages of the necessary operating funds.

Legally, it is argued that the nature of the decision-making and implementation process in most of these institutions seriously hamper effective economic cooperation. The requirement of the "unanimity rule" of voting has been blamed for the prevailing chronic indecision as well as postponement of a number of issues deemed vital to the performance of economic cooperation. This was further aggravated by the absence of a reinforcement mechanism of whatever decisions were agreed upon. And although a number of serious suggestions and efforts were made in order to replace the present voting mechanism by a majority system, none has so far succeeded. Consequently, the records of performance of most of these institutions show clearly that while "agreed" decisions abound, actual commitments are quite limited.

On the planning level, a country-by-country basis has been the distinctive feature of economic planning in the Arab economy. Although many efforts and attempts were spent at translating the "general consensus" for some form of planning into a formal apparatus embracing all Arab countries, little has so far been secured. As a result, contradictions, indeed conflicts, have arisen out of such country-based planning, ones which are often regarded by Arab economists as fatal to the setting up of an overall planning apparatus.

It is generally contended by Arab economists that the absence of a "true" mechanism within the economic integration process has been the underlying factor impeding the effectiveness of the decision-implementation process. Because effective popular participation is not forthcoming or is prohibited, the whole mechanism fails to reveal the hopes and desires of the population. In other words, the mechanism is nondemocratic. Further, such lack of positive participation has severely restrained the possibility of mounting pressure on those officials involved in the integration and cooperation process.

Besides these constraints, there is general agreement among Arab economists that the political factor, i.e., the "lack of political will" represents the most critical element preventing the realization of the economic integration objective. For aside from being an area of "hyper-sensitivity" among the Arab states, the continued political conflicts reveal a unique feature of spreading over other forms of relationships, particularly in the economic field. And in an effort to contain the influence of this dynamic but disturbing factor, the call is unanimous among Arab economists for the "neutralization" of the political element in mutual economic dealings among Arab countries.

FACTS

A substantial increase in economic relations among the different Arab countries took place in the 1970s. This took mainly the form of sustained financial flows from oil to nonoil countries, a reverse flow for labor, as well as a variety of other actions relating specially to economic policy coordination.

The same period, however, was also witness to increased economic (and noneconomic) problems. The continuation of the Iraq-Iran war, the Lebanese civil war, the Arab-Israeli conflict, the rebellion in Southern Sudan, and other inter-Arab conflicts, all had serious economic repercussions. Aside from deepening political divisions, hence economic disunity within the Arab ranks, they had substantially drained their respective economies of much needed human, material and financial resources.

Further, and as the thrust of the oil boom continues to fade, inter-Arab economic problems started to mount. The large decline in oil revenues, due to curtailed output and exports, caused matching declines in the levels of economic expansions enjoyed by all Arab countries, oil and nonoil alike.

Besides, the fall in the financial flows from the donor countries produced a massive exodus of labor, particularly from the Arab Gulf countries, both Arab and non-Arab.

The final outcome of the interaction of the economic, social and political forces was clearly reflected by the pattern and course of economic development. Aside from failing to achieve self-sustained development (if not deepening dependence), it created a wide wealth and income gap between the different Arab economies. The divergence between rich and needy economies is vividly demonstrated by the prevailing imbalance in the size of gross domestic income, per capita incomes, and, for the nonoil economies, increased budgetary, trade and balance of payments deficits, as well as mounting external debts.

FRUSTRATION

The widening gap on the integration front between aspirations and realizations produced by the development course had exerted a massive, if not devastating, impact on Arab economic thinking. Now that Arab economists are more seriously appreciative of the mounting challenges that their demands for economic integration pose, they also are almost unanimous in their consensus that the best that could be done at present is to hold the state of deterioration from further worsening. They do this rather than expounding new ideas on integration.

This "frustrated reaction" by Arab economists has generally assumed three trends, which may be identified as follows:

FIRST, the "Pragmatists" who have resigned themselves to accepting whatever circumstances may yield. This is clearly a case of negative retreat.

SECOND, the "Utopians," are those who, seeing their economic integration dreams turning sour, drifted ever deeper in their abstraction. Here again a case of retreat but towards idealism.

THIRD, the "Realist-Unionists," who, although fully appreciating the impact of the forces working against their objectives, nevertheless, still regard economic integration both on the subjective (i.e., ideological) level as well as the objective (i.e., economic rationale) level as constituting the only viable course for the future.

Does this state of frustrated reaction amount to a dilemma? We would argue that it does. The essence of it all stems from the fact that most Arab economists do not fully appreciate or even comprehend the "uniqueness" of the process of Arab economic integration itself. The properties of this uniqueness may best be demonstrated with reference to three inter-related issues: the "special case" of Arab unity; relevance to other integration cases; and the role of the political factor.

It may well be argued that the Arab as an individual experiences a state of "internal conflict." This state of disequilibrium is produced by the gulf between his national aspirations for Arab Unity as an objective and his daily living and practice as a member of a "state." In aggregative terms, it is the coexistence of the Arabs as belonging to one nation that is in reality divided into many sovereign states; a contradiction in identity. Further, this state of contradiction would remain as long as unity aspirations are not fulfilled.

The uniqueness of the special case of Arab economic integration also reveals itself in comparison with other cases of integration, both in developing and developed countries. For these countries, surely there is no crisis of national identity. Thus when economic integration is sought, it constitutes only a "means" by which certain economic objectives may be attained. In other words, economic integration remains a relationship between identifiable national entities, and thus whether it becomes permanent or transitory would not pose a threat to this settled national identity.

The case for Arab economic integration is quite different in the sense that it constitutes not only a means but also an "objective or end" in itself. As a means, it is no different from other integration cases. But as an end, it does differ and here lies the essence of the Arab integration process: it represents the backbone for the achievement of Arab unity, thus overcoming the very cause of the national identity crises prevalent in the Arab World; it is the vehicle of harmony.

Most Arab economists in the search for an escape from this dilemma have blamed the political factor for their troubles, arguing that if the "political will" was present, things would turn far better for their objectives. Hence comes their call for the neutralization of the political elements.

But can this be done? We would again argue that it is neither plausible nor rational. For as long as economic integration as an end constitutes a course of action towards reaching unity, it must by-pass existing sovereign entities—i.e., existing Arab states. In other words, its coming into being is not a transitory but a permanent act where all of these states would merge into one economic as well as one national unit. And this is a course which has been, and still is, resisted by most of these states.

FUTURE

On a purely economic basis, the rationale for economic integration in the Arab economies seems quite convincing. At the same time, however, given the prevailing circumstances, the possibility of realizing it is difficult indeed. This is obvious enough; it is a central issue that involves not only economic but political as well as ideological considerations.

Can Arab economists escape their present dilemma? Once again it seems that, apart from the possibility of unforeseen major events, they will have to live with it for some time to come. And yet the area is pregnant with such events. And if the opportunity occurs, particularly if it would involve popular participation, the prospects for economic unity may get a strong boost. Only then the main source of the dilemma, i.e., the "national identity crisis" would have disappeared. For there is no escaping from the conviction that a self-sustained course of economic development can only be secured through an integrated economy for the whole area.

SELECTED REFERENCES

Abdullah, I., et al. 1979. "Studies in Arab Development," *Arab Issues* 8: 167–332.

Al-Baily, O. 1985. "Research and Development," *Arab Affairs* 5: 148–63.

Al-Bitar, N. 1982. "Role of Scientific Unity Theory and Mutual Arab Affairs," *Arab Issues* 10: 7–16.

Al-Bitar, N. 1975. "The Economic Path Towards Unity: A Critique," *Arab Studies* 5: 3–21.

Al-Bustany, B. 1985. "The Philosophy of Arab Unity," *Arab Issues* 5: 7–16.

Al-Dajani, et al. 1984. "The Arab Mind: A Critical Review," *Arab Future* 12: 128–49.

Al-Sayegh, Y. 1980. "Development Strategy in the Arab World," *Arab Studies* 5: 3–27.

Al-Sayegh, Y. 1982. "Arab Development and the Critical Triangle," *Arab Future* 7: 6–19.

Arab Fund for Economic and Social Development, "Arab Development: Achievements and Prospects," *Arab Affairs* 11: 45–81.

Idrees, M. 1983. "The Arab World in the Eighties: Between Modernization and Development," *Arab Issues* 6: 105–36.

Issa, M. 1986. "Consumption and Arab Nationalistic Behaviour," *Arab Studies* 3: 3–17.

Khalil, K. 1983. "Arab Development: A Review," *Arab Issues* 6: 45–64.

Kolan, J., et al. 1979. "The Arab Economy: Development Issues," *Arab Issues* 12: 107–208.

Muhafaza, A., et al. 1982. "The Arab League," *Arab Future* 7: 65–142.

Muhammed, Y. 1983. "The Issue of Development in the Arab World," *Arab Issues* 6: 65–76.

Mursey, F. 1983. "The Impact of Inflation on Arab Economic Development," Arab Affairs 2: 6–14.

Mursey, F. 1985. "Re-evaluation of Arab Economic Integration," *Journal of Arab Economic Unity Council* 6: 7–26.

Mutar, J. 1986. "The Tragedy of Arab Mutual Economic Decision," *Arab Future* 4: 16–24.

Rabee, H. 1983. "Development Problems in the Arab World," *Arab Affairs* 6: 77–90.

Zalzala, A. 1980. "Arab Economic Development and Its Challenges," *Arab Future* 11: 6–21.

9 Biased Science or Dismal Art?

A Critical Evaluation of the State of the Art of Arab Foreign Policies' Analysis

BAHGAT KORANY

THE PROVERB "All that glitters is not gold" is doubly relevant for foreign policy theory-building and for the analysis of Third World foreign policies as an area of specialization.

This chapter begins by surveying studies published between 1965 and 1985 on the foreign policies of the eight African countries which are members of the Arab League (countries which in fact constitute the majority of the Arab population). The result is 143 items in all, not even an average of one study per country per year. Why such a dearth, similar to the barrenness of the Sahara? The chapter discusses problems of data accessibility and obstacles (technical and social) to field research. These should be the main ones since—according to Rosenau—by 1976:

> all the evidence points to the conclusion that the comparative study of foreign policy has emerged as a *normal* science. For nearly a decade many investigators have been busily building and improving data banks, testing and revising propositions, using and departing from each other's work... Our differences now are about small points."[1]

Kegley and Skinner agree that "a field of scientific foreign policy analysis has not only emerged but is also proceeding in the 'mopping up' activities of 'normal' science."[2] Not so is the view exposed in this chapter. The second part of this paper chronicles foreign policy analysis from the 1962-Decision-Making framework of Snyder et al. to Rosenau's 1984-ISA (International Studies Association), Presidential Address where his Pre-

Theory is revisited. The field is found to be conceptually ethnocentric, methodologically flawed and certainly noncumulative.

One seeming exception is that island of research around politicial psychology. Industrious teams of researchers have applied concepts and accumulated data to explain foreign policy behavior by the leader's perceptual traits, belief system or personality dispositions. If some of its findings were questioned occasionally, this was not the case in the Third World where its "theorems" were deemed to be always applicable. Brecher and Rosenau differed on almost all basics, but agreed on the primacy of this variable in Third World policy analysis. Wilkenfeld and associates—as the authors of the latest published sophisticated project IBA (Inter-State Behavior Analysis)—analyse the relative potency of four sets of variables determining foreign policy behavior (societal, interstate, global, and psychological). Their findings emphasized that whereas the global set of indicators were the most potent in explaining the foreign policies of the 53 nations sampled, the psychological variables were particularly potent in the explanation of the foreign policy behavior of Third World countries.[3] For these societies then, political psychology reinforced the conventional wisdom coming from such traditional endeavors as the art of biography or even crude psycho-history. It was thus accepted as "The Theory" in Third World foreign policy analysis. This approach is partial and simplistic, confusing intervening variables with sources of foreign policy, and equating visibility with potency. Moreover, the approach tends to aggravate—rather than attentuate—our data problems. A complement—if not an alternative—is needed to offset the unhealthy monopoly and limitations of this approach.

Yet we have to remember that during the last two decades we have been guilty of starting from scratch so many times—a manifestation of the complex of always wanting to be first. The question in the last part of the chapter then was how not to simply exclude this approach and other acquisitions of the Comparative Foreign Policy movement which would have been the easy way out. The challenge rather is how to integrate these recent advances into a general guiding perspective—both relevant and applicable to Third World foreign policy analysis.

To attain this objective, two strategies are suggested: a) clarification of fundamentals of foreign policy analysis to facilitate stock-taking and make the different islands of research cumulative, thereby achieving a consensus of sorts; and b) international political economy as an umbrella integrative perspective to guide research priorities and prescribe a mode of data interpretation. The emphasis is put on its interdisciplinary character, the po-

TABLE 9.1   Publications on the Foreign Policies of Eight African
Countries 1965–1985

Algeria	35 items
Egypt	60 items
Libya	27 items
Mauritania	1 item
Morocco	6 items
Somalia	1 item
The Sudan	7 items
Tunisia	6 items

tency of the world hierarchy, and the influence of transnational networks on the decision-making process. "Great men" and elites and their data are thus analysed, not as psychological atoms but as social phenomena.

LITERATURE SURVEY: THE DEARTH OF MATERIAL

The underdevelopment of this field is immediately evident in the dearth of published material on the eight African countries which are members of the Arab League. My former survey concerned studies published between 1965 and 1981[4] for comments on sources covered and procedure followed. The survey results confirmed the initial impression of a dearth of material on the subject. For the purposes of this essay, I extended the period covered by the survey to 1985.

Table 9.1 tabulates the number of items on the foreign policies proper of eight African countries from 1965 to 1985. The total number of items inventoried was higher, but some were excluded from this analysis because they dealt with what we can term system dynamics: process and structure of the African or Arab regional systems, or the interaction between the two. Some other items were also excluded because—though touching on foreign policy—they did not offer a reasonably systematic analysis. Thus there is a total of 143 items accepted and recorded in the above table for the eight countries in the twenty-year period, i.e. not even an average of one study per country per year.

An obvious characteristic of the data is its uneven distribution. Egypt seems to be relatively over-published, possessing 60 times as many items as

Mauritania or Somalia (the Ogadan War notwithstanding); and 10 times as many as Morocco (an influential African power with a strategic location on both the Mediterranean and the Atlantic) or Tunisia, the headquarters of the Arab League since 1979. On the other hand, Libya—whose population is about one-eighth that of Morocco—has three times as many studies on its foreign policy.

The data trend—much more an order of magnitude than a precise measurement—is clear at this level. But can we discern any common reason for this uneven distribution. Egypt's "overpublished" case is probably the easiest to account for: it was the first independent African country (Ethiopia's particular case apart), and an influential bridge between the center of the Arab World and sub-Saharan Africa. But Libya did not enjoy these elements of power.

Thus, rather than a function of traditional elements of power, the number of published studies on a country's foreign policy seems to be correlated with an active pattern of behavior in the world system or in the region. Qadhaffi's radicalism and revolutionary ethos arouse curiosity in many and attract attention to his country, petrol or no petrol. This is also the case with Egypt, where studies on its foreign policy generally multiplied with the increasing activism of its charismatic leadership under Nasser (with Ismael's 1971 study as a revealing indicator in this respect). This correlation between number of publications and a country's activism rather than with its elements of power is confirmed by the relatively high number of studies on the foreign policy of Algeria, four and one-half as many as those on neighboring Morocco which—moreover—gained its independence six years before. Contrary to Morocco, Algeria's posturing as an ideological model and its championing of Third Worldism and global restructuring gave it an international status disproportionate to its material elements of power. (Incidentally, cases in sub-Saharan Africa like Nkrumah's Ghana or Nyrere's Tanzania seem to confirm that the trend applies in other regions too.) This great influence of "current affairs" and "market demand" could account for the journalistic tone and lack of rigor in many of the studies on Arab foreign policies.

However relatively overpublished some of these countries are, the general dearth of material should not be overlooked. For we had to wait until 1976 to see the first theoretically-inspired book on Egypt's foreign policy,[5] and until 1984 to have a full study on Algeria's.[6] Interestingly enough, both books were originally Ph.D. dissertations at the universities of London and Paris respectively. Moreover, a standard and relatively systematic textbook on Middle East foreign policy[7] did not deem it relevant to include any Arab-African cases except Egypt, even when it went into its second edition seven years later.

ACCOUNTING FOR THE DEARTH OF MATERIAL

The reasons for this dismal state of affairs may be easily guessed at. They can be classified into two main categories: 1) empirical: problems related to data-accessibility and the occasional lack of an environment conducive to field research; and 2) conceptual: the ability—or lack thereof—of present concepts in the subfield of comparative foreign policy to act as intellectual lenses to raise the relevant questions and guide us to investigate phenomena to answer these questions. Each of these groups of difficulties merits comment.

Data and Field Research Problems

The question of data can be dispensed with relatively easily, for many of us are familiar with, and frustrated by it. We are familiar with the blanks in various tables on income distribution, life expectancy or even literacy rates in the publications of such rich and imposing organisations as, for instance, the World Bank. And demographers could maintain heated debates about such relatively "easy" data as the total population of Nigeria, or even China, and certainly Saudi Arabia—where the margin of error until the early 1980s was 100%—(i.e., the difference between the estimates of four or eight million people).

The problem with foreign policy data is of course worse, since this aspect of behavior is supposed to deal with "vital national interest" and is thus shrouded in secrecy. To get around such a narrow concept of security[8] and obtain information necessitates high level connections. Even when obtained, some of this information can be of modest quality and even contradictory, either because it is doctored or politically-oriented. Moreover, given the discreet character of the information sources, some of the evidence cannot be checked and evaluated in rigorous scientific fashion.

The data problem is not solved if we limit ourselves to past events in order to avoid contemporary and burning issues. Archival facilities are still very modest in most of these countries. A short story could drive the point home. When Egypt's foreign minister (1968–1971) and later Secretary-

General of the Arab League (1972–1979), Mahmoud Riad, was writing his memoirs, he needed to consult some of his own documents for which he had no copy. He recounts that after much wheeling and dealing, his erstwhile collaborators who were only too eager to serve him, brought him into a huge room where key official documents were piled up and gave him the liberty to consult as much as he wanted. Discouraged by the magnitude of the effort of sorting-out and the uncertain payoffs of such an endeavor, he did not even enter the room so preciously guarded.[9]

The story of Mr. Riad hints at an important data source: the profitability of interviews as an information-gathering technique. Interviews are of course time-consuming and usually require "pulling strings" to get to the "right people." But even when successful in getting to the crucial sources, the researcher could come up against data problems of a different order, e.g., social taboos as to what questions he/she can ask and of course how to ask them. This problem could also exist in some "developed" countries, but in many Third World countries what constitutes the private domain is far more encompassing and thus limits the areas where the researcher can probe. If the researcher is too curious or inquisitive, doors can easily be closed again since there is not the equivalent of a "Freedom of Information Act." Thus the researcher can sometimes end by being at the mercy of his information sources, which must be preciously nurtured.

Another socio-political risk in conducting interviews and field work generally is that the researcher has to navigate cleverly among the different factions and groups, in order to avoid being mistrusted by either or all of them. The researcher may sometimes end up in a no-win catch 22 position, because he has to be personable and agreeable to get the information while at the same time avoiding over-familiarity for fear of being engulfed by the wheeling and dealing among the different influential groups.

And, of course, when the researcher has acquired the necessary credentials, and is about to complete his data tables, there is nothing that prevents a surprise military coup, the declaration of a state of emergency, the confiscation of all tapes and data sheets. At best the researcher must leave the country in a hurry, and be satisfied with whatever data he has, no matter how incomplete or modest in quality.

These data-accessibility problems (both technical and social) are well-known to researchers bent on systematic field inquiry rather than academic tourism. But bonuses do exist; flexible application of legal barriers may unexpectedly turn up mines of information. Even if a researcher is unlucky enough not to receive such bonuses and the above-mentioned pessimistic portrait literally takes place, there is still an anomaly to be solved. For instance, why have researchers of other so-called closed systems still fared well in meeting these data problems? Why have minutely-documented studies on the foreign or defence policies of the USSR by Americans and other Westerners been possible? Of course, archival facilities are much better developed in this case, and there exists a whole army of Kremlinologists in addition to impressive translation services of even the Pravda *in toto*.

It is also true that the Cold War dictat and the superpower status of the USSR make this "Soviet watching" almost a necessity. But then why have our colleagues in Comparative Politics, for instance, managed to produce thoroughly-documented studies on party transformation,[10] elites' structure and circulation[11] or even the mechanism and personnel of a military coup.[12] This question directs attention to the state of foreign policy theory itself.

Conceptual Problems

The study of Third World foreign policies generally cannot be separated from what is happening in the general field of analysis dubbed Comparative Foreign Policy. The 1960s seem to have been the watershed in the "scientific" analysis of this subdiscipline. In 1962 Snyder et al. published in book form their 1954-privately circulated ideas on how decisions are made, and they suggested a framework for their analysis. The study had an enormous impact and was soon cited in different works ranging from the treatment of disturbed communication to the analysis of judicial behavior.

Almost at the same time, a publication from the other side of the Atlantic but going in the same direction, tried to order the different factors shaping foreign policy-making.[13] Though not having the same impact, Frankel's study was shorter and more accessible in language. It also made the approach less limited to the US and thus foreign policy decision-making looked like a universal school in its own right. In the words of J. Rosenau:[14]

> ... the habits it challenged have been largely abandoned and the new ones it proposed have become so fully incorporated into the working assumptions of practitioners that they no longer need to be explicated or the original formulation from which they came cited.

Yet, it was precisely Rosenau who, in 1966, believed that the field of foreign policy analysis was so much behind that it was too early and/or overambitious to aim at a theory: "There can be no real flourishing of theory," Rosenau affirmed, "until the materials of the field are processed, i.e., rendered comparable, through the use of *pre*-theories of foreign policy."[15] He thus assumed the task of elaborating such a pre-theory that would provide a basis for comparison in the examination of external behavior of various countries in various situations.[16]

At the same time, other North American researchers were engaged in the same endeavor.[17] But contrary to many theory-builders, Brecher went ahead to apply it in a huge three-volume 1800-page study on Israel's foreign policy and he is now—with the collaboration of researchers in Europe, Israel, and North America—developing his International Crisis (Decision-Making) Behavior model world-wide.

All such academic activities could indicate that foreign policy theory-building was comfortably cruising toward its destination, as the jubilant quotations by Rosenau and some of his disciples mentioned in the chapter's introduction seemed to presage. But I have contended elsewhere[18] that this optimism was premature. In fact, some elementary but basic issues of foreign policy analysis remained unresolved and even passed unnoticed, e.g., the definition of what we are trying to explain.[19]

Not surprisingly then, Rosenau had to attenuate his optimism and to observe that the seeming convergence of different conceptual efforts was slowing down and that researchers even of his own school "are going our own separate ways."[20] In other words by the late 1970s the field was still in a "muddle."[21] Rosenau, however, had then in mind only methodological and conceptual issues, and epistemological problems of the universal applicability of the present models were not yet on the agenda.

Though it is laudatory on the part of an established authority to reconsider his views and to be frankly innovative, there is a price to be paid for the disciples and for the evolution of the field in general. For if ideas are considered too casually and thus reconsidered frequently, the field can fall prey to noncumulation and conceptual anarchy. But in 1984 it was, anyhow, timely for Rosenau to "revisit" his pre-theory 20 years after its presentation at a Northwestern University Conference. In his reconsideration of the pre-theory, he synthesized at least ten organizing themes that "warrant[ed] revisitation."[22] But this important recent effort goes further to attract attention to two crucial points:

a) That our theories could be deficient not only because of our conceptual and/or methodological limitations, but also because of the epistemological ones and the intrusion of values in scientific endeavor.

> We can no longer assume—as the original Pre-Theory did—that we are static observers, that our values and concepts remain constant throughout our careers, that our personal lives evolve independently of our professional successes and difficulties, and that explication consists merely of being clear about these constancies. Instead, we need to treat ourselves as open systems, as actors undergoing continuous development and change in response to the very changes in the world we are seeking to grasp and influence.[23]

In other words, we need to go beyond our ethnocentric limits to make our "general" theory and conceptual constructs much more universal in application. Since—as Rosenau himself acknowledges—I have dealt with this problem in detail before; I need not belabor the point here.[24]

b) That a general overarching theory might still be an over-ambitious objective.

> And now it is also clear that a broadly shared paradigm is presently beyond our grasp and that the dialectic dialogues that have emerged instead of consensus may actually stimulate progress toward greater comprehension.[25]

Thus partial theories, or islands of theory, are not only beneficial, but might well be at this juncture the only road left to us. This is indeed making a virtue of necessity.

POLITICAL PSYCHOLOGY AS A PARTIAL THEORY: THE UNHEALTHY MONOPOLY OF A CONVENTIONAL WISDOM

Precisely one of these islands of theory, especially in the type of societies that interest us here, is the psychological or idiosyncratic, or what I called elsewhere "the great man theory of history." Practitioners and academicians, classicists and behavioralists, journalists, travellers and number-crunchers have concentrated on the man at the top to explain a country's behavior. The approach is thus shared by such divergent schools of thought as authors of best-seller biographies, psycho-history, and specialists of cognition and perception.

It is also to be remembered that established foreign policy theory builders, despite their major differences, have been almost unanimous in their agreement on the primacy of the psychological-idiosyncratic factor in dealing with the foreign policies of Arab and other Third World countries (e.g., Brecher and Rosenau, differing on many basics, agreed on the primacy of this factor). So consensual and hence so important is this island of theory that its detailed evaluation is necessary.

A caveat, however, needs to be mentioned. The diversity and richness of this approach should not be underestimated. The fact that in the limited space available here we emphasize the general "forest" rather than the particularistic "tree" aspects should not make us unaware of intra-school varieties and debates. Such variety can be ascertained, limited only to a sub-school of political psychology: cognitive approaches to decision-making.

Still, for the sake of evaluation these sub-schools could be regrouped since they share basic premises concerning the primacy of the role of the individual in explaining foreign policy. In his well-quoted study on *International Relations in the New Africa,* William Zartman[26] put this premise explicitly:

> ... The declarations of the president become the national ideology, consecrated into—"isms" formed on the leader's name—such as Bourguibism, Nkrumahism, and ben Bellaism. Specific, even minute decisions are made by the President... His anger and his ardor, his whims and his convictions become the mood of his country's policy, and his friendships and acquaintances mark its limits.

More recently, two prominent pillars of this school reiterated it nicely:

> ... nations have more than national attributes; nations have particular kinds of leaders with preferences for specific types of decision groups and regime organisations. It is individuals who make foreign policy decisions; knowing something about such individuals singly and in groups may give us a better understanding of the foreign policy behavior of nations.[27]

It is true that this approach has much to commend it as a means of opening the "black box" which is indeed a prerequisite to any serious explanatory endeavor. But precisely my question is, how can concentration on the individual—even if he is the great man at the top—produce the needed explanation? The problems are many, and they remain unresolved after so many decades of energy and investment. They can be synthesized around six main points:[28]

1) Its overemphasis on the psychological environment has led—at least at the empirical level if not explicitly at the conceptual level—to the exclusion of the operational environment (i.e., "the real world" as distinct from the image or perception of this world). This research strategy imbalance, in turn, has resulted in a psychological reductionism verging on monovariable analysis—a major handicap in any serious endeavor at theory building.

2) By basing its advance on detailed answers to complex psychological questions related to the decision-maker's perceptions, stress, and coping, pscyhological reductionism has complicated rather than eased the problem of data accessibility in Third World foreign policy analysis. For instance, one of the main researchers involved in the applications of Brecher's worldwide international crisis behavior model to Zambia warns us that "much of the primary evidence needed for any exhaustive analysis is unattainable, unrecorded or beyond the recall of the principal participants."[29] Another researcher, working on the same project but concerned with an Arab country, invested several months in research only to find himself unable to collect the needed data. He confided to me that he needed to live several days and nights with the head of state, his family, his secretary, and perhaps other members of the immediate entourage. (Indeed, my own research confirms such difficulties.) But does this mean that the required data can be obtained only through individual feats of resourcefulness, perseverance, long-term investment, and lucky high-geared connections such as those exhibited by Snyder and Paige (1958) in their analysis of the Korean decision or by Brecher in his work on Israel? These feats have not yet been matched by other researchers; hence the model's reapplicability remains inert. This is the crucial issue of the approach's cost-effectiveness, i.e., the resultant gain in understanding given the time spent on gathering data.

3) Content analysis (the other technique, in addition to interviews, favored by this school) is even less helpful. Egypt and Syria, for instance, at the time of the 1973-October War, were engaged in a carefully planned deception campaign. What was said and published during this campaign was geared not only to camouflage the preparation of the

imminent attack until the last minute but also, in fact, to indicate exactly the opposite—namely, the absence of such preparations. Moreover, and as the Hermans cogently said, it is not sure whether content analysis of interviews even with heads of government reveal personality data or only a preferred public image.[30] This question could leave us if not without an explanation, at least with a spurious one.

4) Even if these data problems are tackled, and even if we manage to accumulate enough information to analyze the attitudes of decisionmakers, the crucial problems involved in the attitude-behavior correlation must still be faced. That is, we know that a change in leadership is not always followed by a change in behavior. We also know that in many cases of politics, as well as in daily life situations, there is a difference between "said" and "done," between expressed attitude and actual behavior—an inconsistency that psychological research has been struggling with for some time. But rather than facing this problem, which is at the basis of the conceptualization and findings of the psychological model, the psychological model has chosen to ignore it. Indeed, it has *assumed* an attitude-behavior correlation rather than demonstrated it.

5) Related to this last problem is the absence of any answer—although the question has not really been asked—as to why individual decisionmakers sometimes act out of character. To continue the Egyptian example, if any behavioral change took place in President Sadat's style of dealing with the Arab-Israeli conflict up until the October War, it occured in the direction of narrowing, rather than widening, the differences between his behavior and his predecessor's (militant) behavior. It was, after all, the "moderate" Sadat who had to launch the 1973 War—hence the implication that psychological variables are only a residual determinant, superseded by "operational environment" factors that, in the final analysis, condition the decision.

6) Equally perplexing is the explanatory potential claimed by the psychological model. If psychological factors explain the need for action (in this case, the need to launch the October War), why did not the war take place earlier? For instance, in 1971 Egypt's crisis was so acute that Sadat had to declare 1971 "the year of decision," only to be ridiculed later on and to lose yet more credibility for not carrying out his threat. And why did the country feel compelled to go to war at the time it did? More important, what were the factors that made Egypt switch from the long-respected Arab strategy of total war to plan and launch a limited offensive? What were the real goals as distinct from the declared

ones? Last but not least, why did the war take the form it did? Which groups or individuals participated in its elaboration, and how did they succeed or fail in advancing different points of view? These are some of the basic questions to be asked in any analysis of the decision-making process. But the psychological model not only leaves them unanswered, it fails even to raise them. Perhaps the psychological model is guilty of functionalist logic, which engages in a form of tautology instead of full-fledged explanation. Functionalist logic answers a question such as "Why did X die?" by stating that "X died because his heart stopped beating." Technically, the answer is correct, but it fails to indicate, for instance, either the properties of the disease or the mechanisms that led finally to death.

Does this mean that this psychological level should be brushed aside as irrelevant? On the contrary, what needs to be done is to integrate the serious findings of this school of research in a general perspective applicable to the Third World.

There are at least two prerequisites for such an integration:
1) Clarification and consensus of sorts on basics;
2) Agreement on a general perspective within which the different islands of theory can be integrated. Such a perspective will help make them cumulative rather than criss-crossing.

REFORMULATION OF OUR RESEARCH STRATEGY AND INTERNATIONAL POLITICAL ECONOMY AS AN INTEGRATIVE PERSPECTIVE

To recapitulate, not only Arab foreign policy analysis, but also the general field of Comparative Foreign Policy seems to be still groping. There are some advances and islands of research are becoming increasingly specialized and even sophisticated. But it seems as if the price of some advance was to gloss over some basic issues. Hence, it is mandatory to reiterate and clarify basics. Even Rosenau—"with the advantage of hindsight"—agrees on such a strategy at present. "Now it seems obvious to me," he says in his 1984 Presidential Address commemorating the 25th Anniversary of the International Studies Association, "that to aspire to theoretical breakthroughs we need to return to fundamentals, to take nothing for granted. . . . "[31] In this respect, we need to agree on the main building blocks of a general foreign policy theory, especially what they mean, and which conceptual resources are most beneficial for what specific aspects. Three organizing blocks can be suggested here.

Three organizing blocks are prerequisites for consensus on fundamentals

THE WHAT QUESTION: At a certain time not only was foreign policy output undefined, but the question was not really raised. The foreign policy to be explained was sometimes general objectives and strategies; at other times it was routine actions or behavior (especially with the rise of events data), and in yet other cases it was decision, as with Snyder et al., Frankel, Brecher and the psychological school generally. A foreign policy can be all of these together, on condition that we are explicit about the distinctions. Indeed, being explicit about such distinctions can open a whole range of interesting questions about the different relations between the different components of the foreign policy output. For instance, from its official declarations Algeria's revolutionary elan and its insistence on world restructuring are too well-known to emphasize. Yet, it is the US, the "height of world imperialism" and the guardian of the "anarchronistic status quo" that was Algeria's chief commercial partner during the 1970s. Algeria's graduate students, its future managers and governing elite, flock in increasing numbers to North American universities. In 1970, there were 46 Algerians in North American graduate programs; in 1978, there were 1,720. Does this reveal a contradiction or inconsistency in Algeria's foreign policy between "say" and "do"? If so, is this inconsistency merely tactical or strategic, and how can it be measured?

A plausible island of research capable of helping us to answer these questions is role theory, and K. Holsti's pioneering application proved beneficial for foreign policy students.[32] Present applications, combined with the use of more than one technique of analysis, show the theory's adaptability and its applicability to Third World foreign policy problems.[33] Based on this research experience, four assets can be briefly mentioned in this respect: a) by applying the distinction between role-conception (corresponding to foreign policy orientation) and role-performance (corresponding to foreign policy behavior and decisions), we address ourselves to the relationship between "say" and "do" in the country's foreign policy output; b) the use of this island of research links our work with the different social sciences (e.g., anthropology, sociology, social psychology) and allows us to capitalize on the advances of social theory; c) it allows researchers to exploit the assets of some modern techniques developed in foreign policy analysis and combine them with other social science techniques (events data, "crucial indicators," content analysis); d) no serious problems of usage were revealed in its application to Third World cases.

THE HOW QUESTION: This is the crucial opening of the blackbox to anatomize the mechanism of policy-making: who does what, when, with, or against whom. The importance of raising and hopefully solving the "How" question should not be slighted, for—only by knowing the answers to the "How?" questions, questions that will often involve mastering rather tedious and recondite technicalities particular to the subject matter, can one even begin to formulate the more puzzling "Why?" question.

The political psychology island of theory (e.g., Brecher, Di Rivera; M. Hermann, O. Holsti, Janis; Pruit) has concentrated on this aspect as its prime objective, and provided us with specific concepts and even rich data. We should continue to capitalize on its resources, provided we are conscious of its limitations and attempt to go beyond them. Even some industrious and insightful leaders of this school are helping in this direction by throwing their nets wider to catch the complexity of the decision-making process. As the Hermanns put it:

> Group factors can affect what the predominant leader will urge on the government, regime factors can influence what the single group will do, and leader characterstics may become important when multiple groups are making a decision.[34]

We are thus getting increasingly conscious of the danger of psychological reductionism. But—as the Hermanns wisely warn their school members—there is still "much left to do." For it should be reiterated that the man at the top, though the most visible, is not necessarily the most important in making policies, not always the decision-maker, but probably only the decision-taker.[35] These constraints can also apply to the decision group itself, the bureaucratic politics model notwithstanding.[36] Consequently, while focusing on the decision-making group, we should widen considerably the mesh of our net so that we do not divorce this group from a) the regime, with its structural bases and characteristic processes[37]; b) the dialectics between state and society which will allow us precisely to profit from the increasingly sophisticated insights of works on the state and historical state-formation; and c) global dependency networks characteristic of penetrated societies. In this respect the emphasis on informal group interactions is very relevant because foreign members can be indirect—but influential—participants in the decision-making group.

Formal national sovereignty and state boundaries notwithstanding, the emphasis on such internal/external linkages will bring us nearer to tackling the most important question of all: the determinants or sources of foreign policy.

THE WHY QUESTION: The search for causality is the primordial and final objective both for understanding "current affairs" or Arab foreign policies, as well as for foreign policy theory-building. In all sciences (social as well as "natural") explanation is a complicated process. But strangely enough many foreign policy theorists have delved into this question from the start without specifying beforehand what type or component of the foreign policy output they were focusing upon. This might well be one of the reasons for the obstacles to present theory-building. Should we not be like doctors who observe the patient carefully before proceeding with the diagnosis and prescribing the relevant treatment?

Thus, rather than listing foreign policy sources across the board and leaving the reader to guess the independent/dependent variable or cause/effect linkage, we should tailor the most potent determinant to the specific foreign policy output. For instance, deciding that the leader's personality dispositions are the most potent in crisis decisions, might not exclude the potency of other factors for other types of foreign policy output (i.e., orientation or routine behavior) or indeed for other types of decisions (e.g., noncrisis). We might then relatively soon accumulate enough data to show us that when dealing with orientation, historical factors and geographical location should be privileged and initially focused upon; and in dealing with routine behavior, regime characteristics might be the most potent; whereas group dynamics and informal networks might be the most immediate influences in shaping the final decisions.

The frequent delving into foreign policy sources—though intuitive and often crude—has, however, important beneficial side-effects for present theory-building. Practioners and journalists, traditionally-oriented power theorists and behaviorally-inclined political scientists offered us lots of recipes and frameworks to ponder over and possibly choose from—provided we leave aside for the moment the controversial question of potency. Rosenau's pre-theory—especially in its revisited version (1984)—might be a functional starting point, for its attempts to be comprehensive and parsimonious, without falling into simplism. Such evaluation applies also to the CREON project, since it has been influenced by the pre-theory in its formulation, but tries certainly to be more rigorous and operational.[38] More recently,[39] Wilkenfeld et al. (1980) has produced the framework at the basis of their Inter-State Behavior Analysis (IBA). Though sophisticated and empirically-oriented, with its data-bank, regression and factor analysis, it does not show any epistemological progress for the countries of interest here and therefore its applicability is in doubt. A good start for the enterprizing graduate student might well be McGowan's and Shapiro's survey of comparative foreign policy studies until the early 1970s.[40] The importance of this introductory inventory for our purposes here is that to classify their 118 propositions, the authors had to make explicit 13 categories of foreign policy sources. Despite its obvious need for updating, this study offers the student both a stocktaking of the main literature and also a suggested framework for classifying possible foreign policy determinants.

With such specifications of our dependent and independent variables and the mapping out of their linkages we will be in a better position to build upon the advances of the different islands of theory. But to make these really cumulative rather than criss-crossing, we need a general perspective within which the different research findings may be brought together, otherwise we will end up with a pile of stones but not a house.

International Political Economy as an Integrative Perspective

This integrative perspective, to use the fishing metaphor, fixes the meshes of the nets in ways that allow us to select different ponds, fish at different depths and catch different sizes of fish. Even before the catch itself, the integrative perspective could guide us on what phenomena to observe and interrelationships to investigate, and thus provide a rough scale of research priority and even variables' potency. A comparison with the competing perspective of political psychology is in order here and would drive this point home. In the following quotation, notice what assumptions—in this latter perspective—guide our understanding and analysis of foreign policy phenomena to observe, the independent/dependent variable relationship hypothesized and the methodology used to reach an explanation.

It is possible to learn about a leader from *how* he/she says something. From an analysis of how the material is said, we can gain information about the leader's emotional state (in particular how stressful the situation seems to be)... [M. Hermann 1979] has reviewed the various signs which indicate stress in verbal material, including the use of "ah" repetitions, and changes in thought in mid-sentence. Weigle [1982] has employed a voice analysis methodology to examine the expressions of stress of US presidents during international crises, utilizing their public speeches during the crisis as the sources of data. Voice analysis, which focuses on physiological voice characteristic variations, assumes that a recording of the speech or interview is available.

With access to a videotape of a political leader's behavior, we can use the vast number of nonverbal indicators which psychologists have identified to infer the emotional experience of the leader in a particular situation... For example, a comparison of President Nixon's spontaneous (nonpurposive) movements and self-adaptive gestures (nose rubbing, head scratching) during his televised 1974-State of Union address and his extemporaneous several minute discussion of Watergate following showed a seven-fold increase in these nonverbal indicators of stress during the presentation of the Watergate material.[41]

An advocate of political economy might quite conceivably contest the relationship between voice variations, nose rubbing, head scratching (as indicators of the leader's stress) and foreign policy. He/she will certainly raise the issue of cost-effectiveness and rational resource-allocation in deciding on research priorities. To understand a Third World country's foreign policy sources and processes, should he/she start with leader's stress or rather with the regime's legitimacy crisis, the pressure of the military to conclude an arms agreement, the demands of influential religious or ethnic groups for an "authentic" foreign policy, the famine or the debt problem and how IMF/World Bank "advice" determine the type of participants and bargaining within the decision-making group; the structure of negotiations with the multinational companies in one of the banana republics?

Rather than being obsessed with formalistic and psychologistic-reductionist analysis, we should combine relevant data collection with the analysis of informal groups and relations, social dynamics based on kinship, marriage, friendship or other social bonds. The perspective's interdisciplinarity and generality will allow us precisely to observe and analyse these group dynamics from "inside" the culture so to speak. In this case the ethnocentric danger[42] of our analysis will be much less. But there is another advantage of the perspective not less important than emphasis on informal group dynamics. The perspective's emphasis on international hierarchy[43] and transnational networks as a source of policy and an influence on decision making push us to analyse group membership across national frontiers. For if economic anthropology conceptualizes patron-client relations within the small community, there is nothing to prevent us from considering patron-client relations as part of national/international linkages. In other words, the "real patron" might be the external super-patron, whether he is the main decision-maker on arms in Washington, Moscow, Paris or London, an executive of the IMF or the World Bank advising on food subsidies and exchange rates, or the head of a multinational company deciding on the level and whereabouts of its investments. Such a "super-patron" is not a direct member of—but is still a very real participant in— the country's decision-making group.

To recapitulate, the integrative perspective is based on the following building-blocks:

1) Rigorous description and identification of the phenomena to be explained (the foreign policy cluster and its operationalization) comes prior to its explanation;
2) Mono-variable explanations ("power," "economism" or "great man") are mistrusted and excluded;
3) Neither politics nor economics is privileged, but interaction between the two—political economy—is the name of the game;
4) The level of explanation privileged is macro (global) rather than individual or even state-oriented;
5) The framework of international relations is not inter-state but transnational, with an eye on networks across national frontiers—formal and especially informal;
6) The systematic data on determinants and processes of foreign policy can best be interpreted and understood by situating them in their longitudinal context.

CONCLUSION

Since we did not want to limit this chapter to establishing the dearth of material published between 1965 and 1985 on the countries of interest here, it is longer than initially intended. It thus dealt with the difficulties of data-accessibility and the obstacles to conducting field research in explaining Arab and Third World foreign policies. My basic argument, however, is that the main cause of the underdeveloped study of underdeveloped countries is the conceptual lense of comparative foreign policy as it has evolved—or failed to evolve—during the last two decades. By tracing its general chronology to emphasize its conceptual zigzagging but permanence of its main assumptions, the paper showed the ethnocentricity of its models, its overlooking of fundamentals and its noncumulativeness. Briefly, as Wilkenfeld and associates stated in 1980 in justifying the elaboration of yet another foreign policy framework, ". . . foreign policy phenomena have remained embarrssingly mysterious. . . [while]. . . research has been disparate, uneven, and noncumulative."[44]

If any "island of research" has been reasonably consistent, industrious in both data-collection and concept-application, it has been political psychology with its emphasis on individual-idiosyncratic variables. And if its findings were occasionally questioned in their application to some countries, in the case of the Third World, the approach's potency was unanimously accepted. This is why the chapter's section on political psychology submitted this approach to a detailed critical evaluation and questioned its unhealthy monopoly.

Instead of stopping at this point, the chapter reflected on ways to get out of the present impasse. Rather than making a tabula rasa of all that has been achieved in such a relatively short time, the discussion on reformultion of research strategy tries to capitalize on what proved useful while reorienting our approach. To this end, two elements of research strategy are emphasized: a) a clarification of the three main questions of foreign policy analysis (the what, the how, and the why) and the sorting out of available concepts to answer them, i.e.. a research strategy of choosing the best and eschewing the rest; and b) a general conceptual perspective (international political economy) to integrate the promising islands of research and help them to become cumulative rather than criss-crossing.

In this case, we can capitalize on the richness of the relevant applicable concepts of other disciplines and their methodological rigor without sacrificing the issues of substance. While the process of translating this perspective in a researcher's specific framework would necessitate adjustments and "rounding of corners" here and there, the emphasis in this chapter is on the belief that if foreign policy analysis in the Third World is not yet a complete science there is no reason why it should remain a primitive art.

POSTSCRIPT   November 1988

Studies published since this chapter was first written for the conference in Spring 1986 confirm the domination of these conceptual lenses and yet on the other hand a consciousness of their limitation. Thus in an auto-evaluation of the twenty-year history of the American school of comparative foreign policy, the pillars of this field are much more modest about its conceptual achievement and in fact negate what they had said earlier about an "emerging science of comparative foreign policy analysis." Instead of earlier exaggerated self-satisfaction, there is a realization of the incompleteness of the field, a realization that could act as a first step on the road to a mature science of foreign policy analysis. For the new sense of modesty should push people to look around, identify problems and cope with them. Moreover, we are no longer jubilant about an a priori, simplistic affirmation of the sole importance of the personality or idiosyncratic factors. In fact, a whole chapter of this book is devoted to a political economy approach to foreign policy and other chapters emphasize the importance of political units in the shaping of foreign policy decisions. Indeed, increasing space is devoted to the influence of opposition, regimes and other components of the operational environment on foreign policy. Some aspects of the foreign poicy output are treated historically which gives needed longitudinal depth to foreign policy studies. Even in an insistently comparative field, the merits of a serious case study approach are rediscovered, finally leading to the codification of the methodology of comparative case study. In fact, given the empirical difficulties that face analysts of Arab and Third World foreign policies—as documented in the chapter—a series of comparative case studies might well be, at present, the most realistic research strategy to guarantee the collection of needed data and to conduct in-depth analyses of the foreign policies of these countries, thereby providing the basis for the advancement of the comparative foreign policy field conceptually.

In the field of Arab foreign policy analysis itself, advances are also noticeable since this conference paper was written. For instance, at least two studies have been devoted to Libya's foreign policy by authors who combine familiarity with the tools and methods of the social sciences and in-depth knowledge of the country at hand.[45] And major countries that had been under-researched, e.g., Morocco, Jordan, are becoming less so.[46] In fact, Ihrai's study, by concentrating on the role of the state as well as on political parties in dealing with Morocco's foreign policy, makes us aware of the pitfalls of previous work concentrating on the king or the great man in shaping foreign policy.

Even studies of Sadat's Egypt—when this new Pharoah seemed so supreme in power—are increasingly conscious of the limitations of a purely psychologistic approach. Both Goma'a[47] and Zahran[48] in their well-researched and tightly-argued studies give precious data about the social and institutional context of foreign policy-making. Thus Zahran offers minute systematic data on the working of Egypt's national security council, whereas Goma'a, in dealing with the leader's power, situates it in Egypt's societal context and historical evolution (e.g. her tracing of the leader's supreme powers to pharaonic traditions). In other words, leadership's excessive power in Arab and Third World countries is no longer treated as a psychological atom separated from its operational environment but rather as a reflection of it, not as a substitute for the necessary analysis of social dynamics but as its microcosm at the top of the pyramid of political authority. This emphasis on the operational environment and the integration of history in foreign policy analysis is even clearer in the excellent collection of Egypt's foreign policy published by the Center for Political Research of Cairo University.[49]

Last, but not least, yearbooks and specialized journals (e.g., *Yearbook of Strategic Studies*, Cairo, since 1986; *Arab Journal of International Studies*, Washington, D.C., since 1987) devoted to issues of international relations and foreign policy analysis are also published on a regular basis. By their combination of rigor in methodology, interdisciplinary in approach, and relevance in substance, they are bound to socialize an emerging generation in conducting serious studies of Arab foreign policies and advance this subfield generally.

Briefly, from this representative but by no means exhaustive sample of what has been published, it is clear that we are witnessing a stimulating period of transition in the maturing study of Arab foreign policies.

This is a modified version of a paper read at the International Studies Association Convention, Anaheim, California, March 25–29, 1986. This paper is based in part on research funded by the Social Sciences and Research Council of Canada.

NOTES

1. James Rosenau, "Restlessness, Change and Foreign Policy Analysis," in J. Rosenau, ed., *In Search of Global Patterns* (New York: The Free Press, 1976), pp. 370.

2. Charles Kegley & R. Skinner, "The Case-For-Analysis Problem" in J.

Rosenau, ed., *In Search of Global Patterns* (New York: The Free Press, 1976), pp. 303–18.

3. J. Wilkenfeld et al., *Foreign Policy Behavior: The Interstate Behavior Analysis Model* (Beverly Hills and London: Sage, 1980).

4. Bahgat Korany and Ali Dessouki et al., *The Foreign Policies of Arab States* (Boulder, CO.: Westview Press, 1984), p. 10.

5. A. Dawisha, *Egypt in the Arab World: Elements of Foreign Policy* (London: MacMillan, 1976).

6. N. Grimaud, *La Politique Exteriure de l'Algerie* (Paris: Karthala, 1984).

7. R. McLaurin, M. Mughisudin and A. Wagner, *Foreign Policy-Making in the Middle East* (New York: Praeger, 1977).

8. Bahgat Korany, *Social Change, Charisma and International Behavior* (Leiden & Geneva: Sijthoff, 1976).

9. Interview, April 1981.

10. M. Bienen, *Tanzania: Party Transformation and Economic Development* (Princeton: Princeton University Press, 1970).

11. See W. Quandt, *Revolution and Political Leadership, Algeria 1954–1968* (Cambridge, Mass.: M.I.T. Press, 1969); F. Mahmoud, *The Sudanese Bourgeoisie: Vanguard of Development?* (London and Khartoum: Zed Press and University of Khartoum Press, 1984); J. Waterbury, *The Commander of the Faithful: Morocco's Political Elite* (New York: Columbia University Press, 1970); and I.W. Zartman, *Political Elites in Arab North Africa* (New York and London: Longman, 1982).

12. See R. Luckham, *The Nigerian Military* (Cambridge: Cambridge University Press, 1971).

13. J. Frankel, *The Making of Foreign Policy* (Oxford: Oxford University Press, 1963).

14. J. Rosenau, "The Premises and Promises of Decision-Making Analysis," in J. Charlesworth, ed., *Contemporary Political Analysis* (New York: The Free Press, 1967).

15. J. Rosenau, "Pre-Theories and Promises of Decision-Making Analysis," in J. Charlesworth, ed., *Contemporary Political Analysis* (New York: The Free Press, 1967).

16. James Rosenau, "Pre-Theories and Theories of Foreign Policy," in B. Farrell, ed., *Approaches to Comparative and International Politics* (Evanston, Ill.: Nortwestern University Press, 1966). For a table of the different variables of the pre-theory, see B. Korany (with contributors), *How Foreign Policy Decisions are Made in the Third World* (Boulder, CO.: Westview Press, 1986), p. 43.

17. M. Brecher, B. Steinberg and J. Stein, "A Framework for Research on Foreign Policy Behavior," *Journal of Conflict Resolution* 13 (March); for the variables of Brecher's input-output model see B. Korany, *How Foreign Policy Decisions are Made,* pp. 46–47.

18. B. Korany, "Foreign Policy Models and Their Relevance to Third World Countries: A Critique and Alternative" in *International Social Science Journal* 26, no. 1 (March 1974), and B. Korany, "The Take-Off of Third World Studies? The Case of Foreign Policy" in *World Politics* 35, no. 3 (April 1983).

19. Ch. Hermann, "Foreign Policy Behavior: That Which is to be Explained," in H. East et al., *Why Nations Act: Theoretical Perspectives for Comparative Foreign Policy* (Beverly Hills and London: Sage, 1978).

20. As in Steve Smith, "Foreign Policy Analysis," in Steve Smith, ed., *International Relations: British and American Perspectives.* (Oxford: Basil Blackwell, 1985), p. 49.

21. Ibid.

22. Rosenau, "A Pre-Theory Revisited: World Politics in the Era of Cascading Interdependence," in *International Studies Quarterly* 28, no. 3 (September 1984).

23. Rosenau, "A Pre-Theory Revisited," p. 299.

24. See Korany, "Foreign Policy Models and Their Relevance," Rosenau, "Restlessness, Change and Foreign Policy Analysis," and Korany, "The Take-Off of Third World Studies?"

25. Rosenau, "A Pre-Theory Revisited," p. 247.

26. I.W. Zartman, *International Relations in the New Africa* (Englewood Cliffs, N.J.: Prentice-Hall, 1966), p. 65.

27. M. and Ch. Hermann, "A Look Inside the 'Black Box': Building on a Decade of Research," in G. Happle, ed., *Biopolitics, Political Psychology and International Politics* (New York: St. Martin's, 1982), p. 1.

28. Korany, *How Foreign Policy Decisions are Made,* pp. 56–58.

29. Douglas G. Anglim, "Zambia Crisis Behavior," *International Studies Quarterly* 24 (December 1980): 581–616.

30. M. and Ch. Hermann, "A Look Inside the 'Black Box'," p. 30.

31. Rosenau, "A Pre-Theory Revisited," p. 247.

32. K. Holsti, "National Role Conceptions in the Study of Foreign Policy" in *International Studies Quarterly* XIV, no. 2 (1970).

33. See M. Gundevia "La Politique Etrangere de l'Inde," M.A. Dissertation, University of Montreal; Korany, "Foreign Policy Models," and Korany and Dessouki et al., *The Foreign Policy of Arab States.*

34. M. & Ch. Hermann, "A Look Inside the 'Black Box'," p. 30.

35. Korany, *How Foreign Policy Decisions are Made,* p. 171.

36. G. Allison, *Essence of Decision* (Boston: Little Brown, 1971).

37. B. Moon, "Consensus or Compliance? Foreign Policy Change and External Dependence," in *International Organisation* 39, no. 2 (Spring 1985).

38. East et al., *Why Nations Act: Theoretical Perspectives for Comparative Foreign Policy.*

39. J. Wilkenfield et al., *Foreign Policy Behavior: The Interstate Behavior Analysis Model* (Beverly Hills & London: Sage, 1980).

40. P. McGowan and M. Shapiro, *The Comparative Study of Foreign Policy* (Beverly Hills, Calif.: Sage, 1973).

41. M. & Ch. Hermann, "A Look Inside the 'Black Box'," p. 7.

42. K. Booth. *Strategy and Ethnocentrism* (New York: Hohnes and Meir, 1979).

43. B. Korany, "Stratification Within the South: In Search of Theory." *Third World Yearbook,* Vol. II (London: Third World Foundation for Social and Economic Affairs, 1986).

44. Wilkenfeld et al., *Foreign Policy Behavior*, p. 20.
45. See Jane Deeb, *Libya's Regional Foreign Policy* (Boulder, CO.: Westview Press, forthcoming), and Mahmoud Gebril El-Warfelly, *Imagery, Ideology and U.S.-Libyan Relations* (Pittsburgh: University of Pittsburgh Press, 1988).
46. See Said Ihrai, *Pouvouir et influence: Etat, partis et politique etrangere an Maroc* (Rabat: Edino, 1986); and S. Mutawi, *Jordan and the 1967 War* (Cambridge: Cambridge University Press, 1987).
47. Salwa Gomaa, *Egyptian Diplomacy in the 1970s: A Study in Leadership* (Beirut: Center for Arab Unity Studies, 1988) (in Arabic).
48. Gamal Zahran, *Egypt's Foreign Policy* (Cairo: Madbouli Press, 1987) (in Arabic).
49. Ali Abdel-Kader, ed., *Studies in Egyptian Foreign Policy* (Cairo: Center for Political Research, Cairo University, 1987) (in Arabic).

10   Strategic Studies and the Middle East
Periodical Literature in the United States, 1980–1990

P. Edward Haley

No one starts a war—or rather, no one in his senses ought to do so—without first being clear in his mind what he intends to achieve by that war and how he intends to conduct it. The former is its political purpose; the latter is its operational objective. This is the governing principle which will set its course, prescribe the scale of means and effort which is required, and make its influence felt throughout down to the smallest operational detail.

—Clausewitz

IT HAS LONG BEEN fashionable in developing countries to condemn strategic studies. Arab scholars and analysts in particular speak and write of strategic studies as manipulative, biased toward the West and intellectually incomplete. The momentous recent changes in Central Europe and the Soviet Union also pose a challenge to strategic studies, although for different reasons. In a time of *perestroika* and free elections in Czechoslovakia and Hungary, many in Europe, the United States, and Asia increasingly regard the use of military force as irrelevant, as having been supplanted by international trade and investment.

The reasons for taking such positions are understandable, particularly in the Middle East. Given the frustration and suffering that have prevailed in the region for the last century, any individuals or analyses that deal directly and systematically with major political and military problems are bound to be suspect. The view is sometimes justified in specific cases. However, it is

incorrect as a general diagnosis of the field and may have harmful consequences, especially if those who adopt it advise or act on behalf of governments and political movements.

PURPOSE AND METHOD

The aim of this study as originally conceived was to provide a description
of the current state of strategic studies concerning the Middle East. The
method envisioned at the start was to survey all periodical publications intended for the use of individuals with professional and official interests in
Middle Eastern strategic affairs published in English, Arabic and Hebrew
during from 1980 to 1985.

There are a number of reasons why the survey excludes books and
monographs. Serious journals such as those studied for this paper are universally regarded as important in the field of strategic and Middle Eastern
studies. Periodicals are, moreover, a medium in which major developments in the field may, in principle, be most easily expressed, without the
long delays attendant on book writing and publishing. Periodicals are ide-
ally suited to the needs and to the establishment and maintenance of a
community of scholars, analysts and officials. Last, I doubt that the addition of books and monographs to the survey would much change the findings. This must, however, remain the subject of further research.

As the research went forward, it soon became apparent that my difficulties in obtaining comprehensive access to materials in Arabic and Hebrew,
together with practical problems in translating those that could be found,
would force a curtailment of the original design. Initially, the coverage was
restricted to publications in English. This had the virtue of allowing the
inclusion of the impressive body of work published in English by the Jaffee Center for Strategic Studies at Tel Aviv University. However, the Jaffee Center works were dropped from the survey because they belonged
logically to the body of work produced in Israel in Hebrew. Their inclusion among American articles would have been misleading. Therefore, the
decision was made to limit the survey to journals published in the United
States and to include a widely read journal, *Adelphi Papers,* published by
the International Institute for Strategic Studies in London.

There is no hypothesis at the heart of this paper. As a preliminary study,
its approach is descriptive rather than analytical. I do have several hunches.
First, I began with a strong suspicion that most of what is published about

the Middle East, certainly in the United States, has little to do with strategy. My research has led me to suspect that this also applies to strategic studies in the Arab countries. Second, my guess is that most of the research on strategic matters is conducted in Israel in Hebrew. A related hunch is that a strategic studies community exists only in Israel—a group of concerned and informed individuals which is wider than official military, intelligence and diplomatic establishments, whose members regularly exchange views with one another on Middle Eastern strategic matters in ways that are cumulative. Regrettably, the research on which this paper is based can address only the first hunch and offers nothing at all about the second and third.

The research assistants who aided me in the preparation of this paper were instructed to follow Basil Liddell Hart's definition of strategy in determining whether to include an article in their lists. Liddell Hart defined strategy as: "the art of distributing and applying military means to fulfill the ends of policy."[1] The researchers were also asked to count studies about grand strategy, or the coordination and direction of "all the resources of a nation, or band of nations, towards the attainment of the political object of the war—the goal defined by fundamental policy."[2]

The assistants were warned that the destruction of the enemy's armed forces is not the sole or even primary aim of strategy. The responsibility of the strategist is "to seek a strategic situation so advantageous that if it does not of itself produce the decision, its continuation by a battle is sure to achieve this." As Liddell Hart put it: "The perfection of strategy would be to produce a decision without any serious fighting."[3] Consequently, a wide body of writing and study should be counted, which at first glance would appear to be only indirectly related to strategic affairs. An article on Camp David should be counted, for example, if it sheds light on the military, political and economic choices of the combatants and their allies during the 1973 war.

Some examinations of foreign policy issues ought not to be counted. Nations are not constantly at war, even in the Middle East. Their international behavior and, in particular, expert analysis of their behavior cannot easily be related to the ends of strategy and grand strategy. When they were in doubt, I encouraged the researchers to count an article rather than omit it. The result has undoubtedly been to overstate the salience of Middle Eastern strategic studies in the serious periodical literature. The researchers were supervised closely and their work carefully screened and double-checked during the preparation of this report.

THE FIELD OF STRATEGIC STUDIES

A recent survey by the International Institute for Strategic Studies (IISS) observed that the number of research centers worldwide dealing with strategic studies grew from 128 to 167 (30%) in the years 1970 to 1982, while the number of countries with such centers increased from 30 to 44 (47%) during the same period.[4] Further expansion has no doubt occurred in the years since the IISS survey was published. The IISS survey reported that there were centers for strategic studies in Turkey, Egypt and Israel.[5] A new center for strategic studies has recently been established in Jordan.

Part of the reason for the growth in the field surely derives from the prolonged military confrontation between the United States and the Soviet Union. From the most sophisticated systems in outer space, such as the Reagan administration's "Star Wars" and the Soviet Union's latest mobile intercontinental nuclear missile, the SS-X-25, to the operations of *Spetsnaz* and the Delta Force in the Third World, the competition of the superpowers has long been heavily militarized. Because the well-being of all nations is affected by this apparently permanent military contest, there is an understandable need to develop the experts and knowledge needed to comprehend and, where appropriate, to influence Soviet and American policies and behavior. That so much of Soviet and American policy carries a heavy strategic component, particularly in the Third World, is a comment on the times in which we live.

The growth in strategic studies also derives from the existence of major military conflicts other than those involving the Soviet Union and the United States in Western Europe. There are such conflicts between the Soviet Union and China, between China and India, between India and Pakistan, between Vietnam, Thailand and China, between the United States and Cuba, between South Africa and its immediate neighbors in southern Africa, between Iran and Iraq, and, of course, between the Arab states, the Palestinians and Israel. These conflicts are of consuming importance to the parties directly involved. Frequently, the United States, the Soviet Union and other major outside powers intervene. These conflicts and the outside interference they have fostered have given a strong impetus to the growth of strategic studies.

The need of governments to obtain the best possible advice and to coordinate research into strategic matters has helped to expand the field. If it is wise, an impatient and troubled government facing serious problems at home and abroad throws a wide net and draws in academic and other civilian researchers to assist its military and political professionals in their quest for solutions to strategic problems.

Left to their own devices governments and political leaders are apt to "do" strategic studies very badly. Here lies the importance of a community of scholars and analysts wider than the governments concerned. The calculations and proposals of diplomats and soldiers may ignore the interests of their peoples and advance only those of their governments. The reaction of a number of British and American statesmen against just such a development—the Versailles Treaty—led to the foundation of the first foreign policy research centers of the twentieth century, the Royal Institute of International Affairs in London and the Council on Foreign Relations in New York.

Because of their experience, education, or the press of their official responsibilities, members of governments are often devoid of innovative ideas or lack the knowledge of history and of a variety of intellectual disciplines by which to discover them. For domestic political reasons, they may be unable to appear to be proposing controversial ideas, although once they are in the open they may be able to use them to produce a better policy result. An unofficial community can provide a wealth of such ideas and insights.

Finally, strategic studies are attractive because of what might be termed their advocacy value. In pluralistic democracies, the partisans in debates over strategic and foreign policies utilize the research of centers for strategic studies to legitimize and justify their claims. Democratic politicians rely on the centers with which they are politically comfortable to provide rationales and insights that they are unprepared or too busy to develop themselves. In nondemocratic systems this use for strategic studies is circumscribed but surely exists, although the evidence for it is largely anecdotal.

Political leaders will fight to preserve their control of policy. They claim it as their realm, and it is their legal and moral responsibility. But governments that attempt to achieve their ends without the assistance of the ideas and recommendations of a broad and strong community of scholars and analysts work at an enormous handicap. The existence of such a community obviously provides no guarantee against failure, nor are spectacular and costly mistakes a sure sign that no community exists. One suspects, however, that wider consideration within an expert community might have prevented some of the most tragic strategic blunders in recent years—

TABLE 10.1   Articles on Middle Eastern Strategic Affairs in English Published in the United States or United Kingdom, 1980–1985, by Year and Journal

Journal/Year	1980	1981	1982	1983	1984	1985	Total
Adelphi Papers	2	1	0	0	0	0	3
Air Univ. Review	0	0	1	0	2	0	3
Arab Stud. Quart.	2	0	4	*	4	2	12*
Arm. For. & Soc.	0	0	1	0	0	0	1
Arm. For. Journal	*	*	3	5	6	0	14*
Commentary	0	2	3	4	5	2	16*
Foreign Affairs	2	3	2	2	1	1	11
Foreign Policy	0	1	0	0	1	0	2
Int. J. ME Stud.	1	0	1	0	0	1	3
Intl. Security	1	2	3	1	1	0	8
J. Palest. Stud.	0	3	5	6	5	4	23
J. Strat. Stud.	1	0	1	4	0	*	6*
M.E. Journal	0	1	2	1	4	0	8
Military Affairs	0	0	1	0	0	*	1*
Military Review	0	1	1	2	1	2	7*
Orbis	7	6	2	0	2	2*	19*
Parameters	1	4	1	1	0	0	7
Political Quart.	0	0	0	0	2	*	2*
Strategic Review	2	2	1	0	0	1	6*
Totals	19	26	32	26	34	15	152

*Survey incomplete

Iraq's decision to invade Iran, Israel's invasion of Lebanon in 1982, and the Reagan administration's dispatch of the US Marines to Beirut.

THE PERIODICAL LITERATURE ON MIDDLE EASTERN STRATEGIC AFFAIRS

For the original conference, articles published from 1980 through 1985 in nineteen journals intended for use by scholars, government officials and other analysts were surveyed. The results are given in Table 10.1–10.4.

TABLE 10.2   Articles on Middle Eastern Strategic Affairs in English
Published in the United States or United Kingdom, 1980–1985, by
Frequency and Journal

Frequency	Journal
0–4 articles	Adelphi Papers (3) Air University Review (3) Armed Forces and Society (1) International Journal Middle Eastern Studies (3) Foreign Policy (2) Military Affairs (1) Political Quarterly (2)
5–9 articles	International Security (8) Journal of Strategic Studies (6) Middle East Journal (8) Military Review (7) Parameters (7) Strategic Review (6)
10–14 articles	Arab Studies Quarterly (12) Armed Forces Journal (14) Foreign Affairs (11)
15–19 articles	Commentary (16) Orbis (19)
20–24 articles	Journal of Palestine Studies (23)
25 or more	None

In an effort to cover the years between the conference and the publication of the conference papers in this volume, a second survey was carried out during the summer of 1990 for the period 1986–1990 with the aid of a different research assistant. Identical instructions were given and the same journals were surveyed. The results are given in Tables 10.5–10.8.

For the period 1980–1985 a total of 152 articles on strategic matters were published. Only six journals published 10 or more relevant articles: *Arab Studies Quarterly, Armed Forces Journal, Commentary, Foreign Affairs, Journal of Palestine Studies* and *Orbis*. Of these, five—*Arab Studies Quarterly, Armed Forces Journal, Commentary, Journal of Palestine Studies* and *Orbis*—published 12 or more, that is, an average of at least two a year over the six years.

Of the 106 relevant articles published in the five journals 65 deserve at-

TABLE 10.3   Articles on Middle Eastern Strategic Affairs Published in the United States or United Kingdom by Country/Conflict/Issue, 1980–1985

Arab States	1
Britain	7
Iran-Iraq War	7
Israel	22
Nuclear Weapons	1
Oil	5
PLO	3
Saudi Arabia/Gulf	6
Soviet Union	5
Syria	2
United States	10
Western Europe	1
1967 War	1
Total	65

tention as strategic analysis. In the following analysis the 65 articles are categorized by country, conflict and issue, and by level of analysis—grand strategy/strategy, operational strategy, tactics/weapons. I also identify two outstanding articles, writing that advanced the understanding of major strategic problems in the Middle East.

Articles on two countries and one conflict, Israel (22), the United States (10) and the Iran-Iraq war (7), account for more than half the articles (39/65), followed by Saudi Arabia and the Gulf (6). Articles about Israel alone accounted for almost one-third of the total (22/65).

By far most of the articles (45/65) dealt with grand strategy and strategy, with less than one-third about operational strategy (the conduct of battles) (10) and tactics and weapons (10).

There is much good work in these articles. Many are informative. Unfortunately, only two or three of them escape the traps of immediacy or advocacy. The authors and editors responsible have too often settled for quick and easy sketches of recent developments with the choice of topic governed by headlines in the news. Alternatively, they argue in favor of or against an approach to solving a major problem. The United States should

TABLE 10.4   Articles on Middle Eastern Strategic Affairs Published in the United States or United Kingdom by Level of Analysis, 1980–1985

Grand Strategy/Strategy	45
Operational Strategy	10
Tactics, Weapons	10
Total	65

or should not treat Israel as it treats its NATO allies. Israel should or should not withdraw from the West Bank. The United States should or should not deal with the PLO.

Little attention is paid to changing military capabilities. Most important, virtually nothing is said about the relation between military capability and diplomatic behavior. As a result, major diplomatic initiatives and strategic decisions are urged, without concern for their strategic feasibility or desirability. The predominance of articles about Israel leaves many important strategic matters untreated. Grand strategy and strategy also are overexposed.

There is nothing wrong with advocating a solution to a major problem and certainly nothing should be done to limit strategic studies to the conflicts of the distant past. However, advocacy and immediacy carry serious risks. Advocacy often disguises partisanship. The apparatus of scholarly analysis can mask propaganda for a particular nation or cause. Editors can avoid the problem by allowing officials to make propaganda and no one else.

Too close pursuit of the headlines often causes articles to become outdated rather quickly. Authors and editors are aware of the problem and try to counter it by resorting to generalizations, but this risks emasculating the analysis.

Two outstanding articles are by Thomas McNaugher on security in the Persian Gulf and Yezid Sayigh on the military performance of the PLO during the Israeli invasion in 1982.[6] McNaugher argued that a functioning and successful security system exists among the Arab nations of the southern Persian Gulf, despite their inability to defend themselves against outside intervention and that the United States must take care to strengthen

TABLE 10.5   Articles on Middle Eastern Strategic Affairs in English
Published in the United States or United Kingdom, 1986–1990, by
Year and Journal

Journal/Year	1986	1987	1988	1989	1990	Total
Adelphi Papers	0	2	5	1	0	8
Air Univ. Review	2	*	*	*	*	2*
Arab Stud. Quart.	1	1	4	3	0	9
Arm. For. & Soc.	0	2	0	1	0	3
Arm. For. Journal	3	4	1	2	3	13
Commentary	4	1	2	0	0	7
Foreign Affairs	2	4	4	2	1	13
Foreign Policy	2	4	3	2	1	12
Int. J. ME Stud.	0	0	0	0	0	0
Intl. Security	0	0	0	0	*	0*
J. Palest. Stud.	3	1	5	6	2	17
J. Strat. Stud.	8	*	3	2	*	5*
M.E. Journal	2	2	3	6	3	16
Military Affairs	0	0	0	*	*	0*
Military Review	0	1	0	0	0	1
Orbis	3	*	3	2	1	9*
Parameters	*	*	*	0	0	0*
Political Quart.	0	0	0	0	0	0
Strategic Review	*	1	0	*	0	1*
Totals	22	23	33	27	11	116

*Survey incomplete

rather than to undermine it. Sayigh showed that the PLO had never considered, let alone planned, what to do if Israel invaded Lebanon.

By painstaking research these authors were able to avoid the traps of advocacy and immediacy and discover insights of enduring worth.
McNaugher solved the paradox of strength in weakness that plagues Gulf
security questions. In Sayigh's analysis lies much of the explanation for the
failure of the PLO. Its leaders failed to relate their military weakness to their
geopolitical aggressiveness.

During the years 1986–1990, a total of 116 articles on strategic matters
were published. (See Table 10.5.) Five journals published ten or more ar-

TABLE 10.6   Articles on Middle Eastern Strategic Affairs in English
Published in the United States or United Kingdom, 1986–1990, by
Frequency and Journal

Frequency	Journal
0–4 articles	Air University Review (2) Armed Forces and Society (3) International Journal of Middle Eastern Studies (0) International Security (0) Military Affairs (0) Military Review (1) Parameters (0) Political Quarterly (0) Strategic Review (1)
5–9 articles	Adelphi Papers (8) Arab Studies Quarterly (9) Commentary (7) Journal of Strategic Studies (5) Orbis (9)
10–14 articles	Armed Forces Journal (13) Foreign Affairs (13) Foreign Policy (12)
15–19 articles	Journal of Palestine Studies (17) Middle East Journal (16)
20 or more articles	None

ticles: *Armed Forces Journal, Foreign Affairs, Foreign Policy, Journal of Palestine Studies,* and *Middle East Journal.* As in the earlier period, *Journal of Palestine Studies* carried the largest number of articles (17) on Middle Eastern strategic affairs. In a notable change, *Middle East Journal* carried the second largest number (16). (See Table 10.6.)

Once again, articles on Israel and the United States appeared most frequently, accounting for 40 of the 77 articles on the topics specifically examined in the earlier period. In a change from the earlier period, considerably more attention was given to articles about the PLO and strategic affairs: 11/77 as opposed to 3/65. (See Table 10.7.) And once again, articles on grand strategy and strategy were most numerous by a large margin: 53/77. (See Table 10.8.)

TABLE 10.7　Articles on Middle Eastern Strategic Affairs Published in the United States or United Kingdom by Country/Conflict/Issue, 1986–1990

Arab States	3
Britain	1
Iran-Iraq War	7
Israel	18
Nuclear Weapons	1
Oil	1
PLO	11
Saudi Arabia/Gulf	2
Soviet Union	4
Syria	4
United States	22
Western Europe	3
1967 War	0
Total	77

An outstanding article published during the period is Efraim Karsh's "The Iran-Iraq War: A Military Analysis," published by the International Institute for Strategic Studies (London) as number 220 in its *Adelphi Papers* series. In elegantly clear prose, Karsh provided a narrative summary of the first six years of the fighting, evaluated the combat performance of the two sides, and offered an intriguing analysis of the failure of Saddam Hussein's strategy in Iraq's war against Iran. In Karsh's view, the general reason for the Iraqi failure was "a gross misperception of the relationship between the national goals and the means to accomplish them."[7] Specifically, Saddam Hussein failed to recognize that Iraq's limited aim of forcing Iran to abandon its all-out hostility could not be achieved by limited war. The error was then compounded by the decision to halt Iraqi forces while they were still advancing and before they had seized critically important territory or destroyed major elements of Iran's armed forces. Facing these two Iraqi blunders, Iranian leaders had neither the desire nor a strong incentive to refrain from launching general war for unlimited aims in response to the Iraqi attack. A better choice for Iraq, according to Karsh, would have been "either to avoid the war and try to forestall Iranian pres-

TABLE 10.8   Articles on Middle Eastern Strategic Affairs Published in
the United States or United Kingdom by Level of Analysis,
1986–1990

Grand Strategy/Strategy	53
Operational Strategy	10
Tactics, Weapons	14
Total	77

sures by other means (as indeed it did between winter 1979 and summer 1980) or to follow a strategy of general war in pursuit of limited aims."[8]

CONCLUDING OBSERVATIONS

The initial and follow-up surveys suggest that there are serious shortcomings in the manner in which Middle Eastern strategic affairs are treated in the periodical literature in the United States. Despite the significance of military and strategic issues in the contemporary middle East, little attention is given Middle Eastern strategic affairs in the readily available "serious" periodical literature published in the United States. Taken as a whole, the articles that are published provide far more coverage of Israeli and United States strategic concerns than of the other nations and issues in the region. The articles also focus very heavily on grand strategy and strategy to the detriment of operational strategy and tactics.

Of the seven journals that published articles on Middle Eastern strategic issues often enough since 1980 to amount to more than occasional consideration, three, *Arab Studies Quarterly, Commentary* and *Journal of Palestine Studies,* are partisan and cannot be said to treat the issues in a comprehensive, objective manner. Only rarely do the articles even in the seven periodicals accomplish more than an examination of goals and alternative foreign policies that might be followed to achieve these goals.

The articles most often published are "pre-strategic." Typically they propose a "correct" way of looking at the various conflicts in the Middle East. Apparently the assumption is that once the conflicts are seen in the correct way strategy will follow automatically.

This misses two key points: 1) Even if they do not see the conflicts in the region "correctly," the governments involved have adopted strategies by which they hope to achieve their objectives: these strategies are open to criticism and discussion within the terms set by the concepts and objectives of the governments following them (are ends possible, desirable, necessary; are means adequate to ends, etc.?). 2) Even if one assumes that the interested governments will one day see the conflicts "correctly" the strategies they will require to reach their goals are by no means self-evident and should be developed by rigorous analysis and choice based on a rational weighing of costs and benefits.

Precious little of either kind of analysis—the searching scrutiny of existing strategies or the imaginative evaluation of strategies appropriate to different policies—is to be found in the serious periodical literature on a strategic studies published in the United States.

One must conclude that the attentive public in the United States, an important actor in the Middle East, is badly informed about strategic questions in that region. In addition, the findings of the study strongly imply that the United States government and, perhaps, other governments, as well, conduct less research on Middle Eastern strategic affairs than the development of successful strategies for the region would seem to require.

The author wishes to acknowledge the research assistance of John Cook, Clyde Hinshelwood, Sima Kanaan, Carolyn Lacerra, John Ngo, Mark Shpall and Gita in the preparation of this article.

NOTES
1. B.H. Liddell Hart, *Strategy,* rev. ed. (New York: Praeger, 1954), p. 335.
2. Ibid., pp. 335–36.
3. Ibid., pp. 338–39.
4. *Survey of Strategic Studies* (London: International Institute for Strategic Studies, 1982), n.p. IISS defines strategic studies as including "not only research on modern military organization, weapons and battles, but also the study of contemporary international and internal armed conflicts in their political, economic and military aspects; the role of alliances and other security systems; disarmament and arms control; strategic doctrines and national defense policies."
5. In Turkey: Foreign Policy Institute, Ankara. In Egypt: Center for Political Strategic Studies, Al Ahram Foundation, Cairo. In Israel: The Leonard Davis Institute for International Relations, Hebrew University, Jerusalem; Jaffee Center for Strategic Studies, Tel Aviv University, Tel Aviv; Shiloah Center for Middle Eastern and African Studies, Tel Aviv University, Tel Aviv.

6. Thomas McNaugher, "Arms and Allies on the Arabian Peninsula," *Orbis* 28 (Fall 1984), pp. 489–526; and Yezid Sayigh, "Palestinian Military Performance in the 1982 War," *Journal of Palestine Studies* 12 (Summer 1983), pp. 3–24.
7. Efraim Karsh, "The Iran-Iraq War: A Military Analysis," *Adelphi Papers* 220 (Spring 1987), p. 58.
8. Ibid., p. 61.

11 Strategic Studies and the Middle East
A View from the Region

KAMEL S. ABU JABER

THIS DESCRIPTIVE AND ANALYTICAL essay on the state of strategic studies in the Arab World is concerned with the general atmosphere in which specialists in that field operate. Purposely, it concentrates on a consideration of negatives, the existing obstacles to creative thinking needed for the proper establishment of truly creative thinking institutions. For many obvious reasons, the area under discussion is characterised by political instability and military insecurity. The internal and external upheavals constantly faced by the Arab World have resulted in the establishment of a series of authoritarian regimes in most countries of the area where contrary opinions are not usually welcomed or even tolerated. Societal factors, traditional and otherwise, the lack of the scientific and experimental method, sometimes even disdain of innovation are but a few of the factors considered relevant.

If the question of strategic studies was posed in this context it was to generate understanding of the general atmosphere and to focus on major issues rather than on a universal consideration of strategic studies in the area. How can the gulf between the intellectual and the decision-maker be bridged so that their energies will be channeled in the same direction instead of being at odds? How can the product of the intelligentsia be made to aid and comfort rather than frighten the leaders? Books and research seem to continue to frighten the decision-makers for, to them, they seem to contain secrets and mysteries they do not understand. These considerations are vital to all developing societies, for how can modern knowledge, even technology, be transferred without the intelligentsia? To create this atmosphere there is a need for room to manoeuver, space to breath, encouragement, backing and incentive. To create it, it is necessary to set the mind free to speculate, which is precisely what frightens political leaders; for speculation may lead anywhere, even astray!

No doubt the leaders' fear of intellectual speculation and questioning has been buttressed by certain traditional cultural factors as well as the traditional educational system so heavily dependent on the rote memory method. The traditional cultural milieu, though in the process of transition, still discourages dissent, especially in public. The combination of these and other factors has had the effect of stifling creativity. Dissent, even disagreement with the establishment—father, state, religion—has traditionally been viewed as unacceptable, a shame, sinful. The rote system so severely disciplines the mind that it comes to believe only that which is acceptable to society at large. Any deviation or innovation is a departure from the norm, almost heresy. The educational system forces memorization of facts, not *how* to tackle and solve problems. It also inculcates that there are untouchable subjects, taboos beyond human speculation and discussion. Traditionally, most artistic expression, music, poetry, even food and dress, like almost all else in life, had to follow a pattern. In most of the Arab World until recently, it was possible to tell the general area, even the very village from which a man or woman came, simply from their pattern and style of dress. Eveyone had his proper place in the village and the tribe. Children are encouraged to think in patterns; one is encouraged to think like his father, and one can quickly call to mind a proverb, a cliche, a popular saying that can cover any situation thus precluding any serious thinking or consideration. This societal mental "swaddling" of the mind closely follows the traditional way of swaddling the newborn.

These ideas are put forward to suggest why, until now, so few centers of serious research have been established and so little creative thinking produced in the Arab World. It cannot be said that the Arab regimes are still unaware. Perhaps this is the case with all transitional societies venturing a foot tentatively into modernity while the other is still firmly rooted in traditionalism.

Political leadership in the Arab World, for the most part illegitimate, unqualified, or lacking in experience, is not aware of the need for or value of pooling intellectual resources, a team work approach to problem solving. If strategic studies needs anything it is imagination and vision. The inspiration of the leader, where it exists, while necessary, is never quite enough. A community team with a sustained commitment needs to be created to replace sporadic bursts of activity whenever the need for certain information arises.

The present erratic nature of Arab politics means that the area will continue to be open for further exploitation and penetration. Many of the same questions posed by the great Egyptian historian al-Jabarti, who witnessed Napoleon's invasion of Egypt, are still pertinent in the Arab World of today. That first shock in modern times continues to create tremors today. The tragedy is that few answers have been allowed to surface and the soul searching and self-assertion continue in the midst of a confusion which increases each day.

The rapid physical development witnessed by most of the Arab World in recent decades created as many problems as it solved. Physical development, to be effective must, it seems, be accompanied by the development of modern public institutions that will subsume the resulting social and political tensions and attempt to resolve them in a peaceful and orderly manner. Thus far such has not been the case in most Arab countries and the adversity between the political decision-makers and the intelligentsia continues to kill the yeast, fermentation from whence answers and ideas should be forthcoming. The split, schism, the schizophrenia continue. But ultimately who is killed, the individual who questions or the society that causes his intellectual demise?

THE INTELLECTUAL ATMOSPHERE: CONSIDERATIONS

To be effective, strategy should take into consideration both the immediate and the distant future. It should or can be considered as a plan, a conceptualization, a vision. Of necessity, it has to take into account some unforeseen or unknown factors and also include at once the constants and variables. Yet even the constants must have some alternative scenarios rendering the whole more flexible and therefore able to contend with unpredictable factors. An Arabic proverb extoling flexibility within a certain set of principles, a framework, states "Do not be so rigid that you may snap or so soft that you may be squeezed."

But all this requires cool, calculating and a certain amount of relaxed thinking to reduce the level of tension and, to some degree, release the pressure. Such has not been the case in the Arab World where since at least 1948, indeed, since the advent of the twentieth century, the level of tension from internal and external factors has remained at such a high pitch and the pressure so intense that the result has been rampant confusion and logic has almost been totally absent. How can a nation or a country, indeed an individual, plan or even think clearly when he has been so constantly kept on the run?

The question is not an idle one nor is it academic. Nor is it meant to apologise for the seemingly continuous failure on the part of the Arabs in this and perhaps the last century to come to grips with their problems and tackle them properly; a failure that continues to manifest itself in the present dismemberment, confusion, lack of direction, disarray and succeeding debacles of monumental dimensions on the local, regional and national levels. Where else can one look for the reasons but in the lack of a proper strategy, a comprehensive plan, a concept of the future? And why has such a strategy not been contemplated seriously but for the failure of both the intelligentsia and the leadership to come together and delineate a path? Can they?[1]

A cry of anguish has been heard from one intellectual or another in this or previous generations, but the intelligentsia, for a variety of reasons, has rendered itself, or, has been rendered, marginal. In fact, often the majority has been reduced to producing a literature of apologetics for one or another leader, movement or ideology. The state, beleaguered by development pressures from within and concomitant security problems, as well as threats from outside and being ill equipped to deal with them, expanded the security apparatus. The question posed to every leader and every nation throughout history was thrust upon the regimes of the region: Is there anything that takes precedence over stability? The choice was not made simpler, but was in fact dictated by the mounting pressures within, the external challenges and coincidence of historical forces beyond the grasp of the imagination of the rulers of most countries. It is thus that regime security continues to take precedence. And while development has been achieved, though unevenly within the same country, even within the same city, to say nothing of the region as a whole, to a large extent it came about principally as a by-product of the need for stability and security. But then, the purchase of social peace through development is a phenomenon witnessed throughout the world in this century.

Since the day Naploeon's armies landed in Egypt, the region has been trying to "catch up" while attempting to ward off foreign domination in one form or another. Perhaps it is the historical moment that the region has been caught in, or perhaps it takes more than the mere facade of development, its physical attributes, the highways, dams, buildings, schools, universities, street lights, the modern dress, to indicate that a people have changed. The transition is agonizing and difficult both on the individual and the national levels. A people seem to need more time for the new knowledge and tools to be acquired and more time still for these to be digested, absorbed and eventually properly used. It seems that knowledge, when newly introduced, takes time to gain ground, respectability and credibility. Time is, for the region, becoming more precious and dear with the passage of each day. While the security grip of the regimes continues to tighten and become more efficient to cope with the mounting tensions, buildings are being built and other physical changes are taking place changing the very landscape of the region and its horizon.

STUDIES CENTERS

In 1984 the Economic Commission for Western Asia (ECWA) published a two-volume *Dictionary of Research and Studies Centers* in the countries of the region. The *Directory,* which covers all member countries of the Arab League including Palestine but with the exception of Mauritania and Djibouti, includes basic information on 344 such institutions, i.e., specialized government institutions, specialized institutions in both the public and the private sectors, regional United Nations organizations, studies centers, consulting firms and universities. The survey covered areas of knowledge ranging from agriculture, forestation and fisheries, to international trade, housing, science and technology, communications, labor issues, health, economic and social policies as well as planning and business administration, etc.[2]

The Center of Documentation and Information of the Arab League in Tunis lists 73 specialized research centers ranging from the study of drugs and criminology to political, social and economic issues as of April, 1986.[3] The Center, as in the case of the ECWA *Directory* referred to above, acknowledges that their list is only partial. In the listing of the Center of Documentation and Information of the Arab League, Iraq is listed as having 12 centers: Lebanon 9; Algeria, Tunis and Egypt 7 each; Syria 6; Libya 5; Saudi Arabia and Morocco 4 each; Jordan and Sudan 3 each; Kuwait, Palestine, Qatar, South Yemen, North Yemen and the United Arab Emirates 1 each.

In an extensive and insightful study of social science research in the

Middle East, Professor Saad Eddin Ibrahim identified four major areas of research activities: economics, education, science and technology and population and development. These findings were based on interviews he conducted with 86 social scientists from eight Middle Eastern countries where about 450 topics were mentioned as research priorities in the 1980s. The "economics" area, like the three other major areas, was broken down into specific issues such as inflation, subsidies, the taxation system, foreign trade, economics of technology transfer, labor migration, regional economic issues, external organizations, urban economics, real estate, small enterprises, rural economics, changing crop patterns, agrarian reform, small rural enterprises, etc. It is significant that no mention was made of the study of military strategy or military issues.[4] In Appendix B of his study, Professor Ibrahim also gives a partial listing of research centers. Only one center, that of the Center of Strategic Studies of Al-Ahram in Cairo, Egypt is mentioned in the International Institute of Strategic Studies, *Survey of Strategic Studies*. Centers in Turkey and Israel, however, were mentioned.[5]

It is perhaps indicative of the state of the art, that no complete listing of such institutions interested in strategic issues, whether military, economic, social or political, exists. Professor Ibrahim's observation regarding the output of what exists is also worth noting. He says, "First, the quality of their staffing ranges from average to good. Secondly, the volume and quality of their research outputs are inconsistent across subfields and over time.[6] This statement, made in 1982, is to a large degree, still valid.

Al-Khouli lists some 500 college organizations and research centers existing in the Arab World now. However numerous, they are ignored by the decision makers.[7] Zahlan lists only 289 institutions that published research in 1977 and 407 in 1983.[8] Badran mentions that in 1981 there were 50 Arab universities containing 180 colleges and 199 research centers.[9]

There exists no agreement on the number of research centers existing in the Arab World today. That there is little or no communication between them goes without saying, not to mention the lack of coordination or channeling of research in the direction that is most needed. Not even a listing of scientific journals or a listing of books published in the Arab World is available. This truly lamentable state of affairs appears to be yet another symptom of the present socio-economic and political disarray, confusion and relative stagnation in the area.

Research on how much research is done in the area, and by whom, is badly needed, not only for the purposes of coordination and eventual direction, but for the mere assessment of what exists, what does not exist and what is needed.

LITTLE INNOVATION

Because of the pervasive authoritarian atmosphere, the new knowledge and technology have not thus far produced much innovation. Teachers and professors teach, institutions are built, research conducted and papers written but little new ground is broken and little creativity achieved. Is an authoritarian atmosphere anathema to imagination and creativity? Is it possible to achieve within the bounds of the strait jacket of an authoritarian regime or ideology which provides neither incentives nor encouragement?

The question is more momentous for the Arab World now than at any other time, with its present search for identity, its developmental problems and its external challenges. While innovation in the natural and physical sciences is vital, it is the more vital in the humanitarian, philosophical and social sciences because they not only question what was or now is, but peer into the future as well. The Arab World is in the grips of a very deep crisis that, in the words of Khalid Moheiddin, it cannot escape unless it breaks the bonds that tie it to the wheels of outside political, economic and military forces.[10] That is one opinion, albeit a respected one, that does not fathom the depth of the crisis. The crisis is deeper than that: it is perhaps rooted in the very center of Arab life today. It has to do with the question of regime legitimacy: who rules, why, how and how are the problems dealt with?

Surely the question of strategic studies must be related to that of creativity in any given society. The failure of both leadership and intelligentsia, with few exceptions, is a result of societal and historical forces often beyond the comprehension of those caught in their grip. Like any other society, Arab society can and has produced some creative luminaries but most of these, in the words of Professor Saad Eddin Ibrahim, have had to break with the traditions and the web of the authoritarian social fabric engulfing them. Though a few do, the individual in an authoritarian family, society and state cannot always escape. In Arab society, those that have, have done so more in the fields of art, humanities and literature, than in the experimental or technological fields where laboratories and established institutions with an organization, funds and clear objectives are needed. Creativity in the "nonscientific" fields is more individual, more contemplative, theoretical. Even here, creative thinking is sporadic and highly individualistic. For a sustained effort, capable of meeting the challenges, institutions of specialized research and higher studies are needed.[11] The emphasis on stability, on the part of the political leadership, its suspicious nature, indeed in the words of Usamah al-Khouli "its abysmal ignorance of the importance of constructing national scientific technological,"[12] and knowledge capabilities serve to compound the problem. The increasing personalization of political and public life and the increasing tendency towards the cult of the leader have meant that there cannot be systematic attention or analysis on the theoretical level or towards methodological approaches. Life remains personality and event-oriented, with reaction often based more on inspiration than strategy and a conceptual framework.

It is in fact more than ignorance: it is that and also fear. On the part of the society at large creativity means change and nonconformity. The intellectual is thus singled out, isolated and tagged as not abiding by the rules. In discussing this phenomenon, author and writer Ahmad Sudki al-Dajjani relates the observation made by Ibn Fadlan, an Arab traveler, in the tenth century chronicle on his trip to Russia. On his way, and in the regions of some of the Bulgarian and Khazar tribes, they used to kill any person who showed signs of creativity and independent thinking. Their comment on such an occasion was "it is better that he should serve the lord."[13] The mode of killing him was to tie a rope around his neck and hang him on the limb of a tree until he perished. Many creative people of the Arab World today perish by lack of respect and incentive, active discouragment, isolation, containment, marginalization, covert or overt harrassment, active hostility, repression or even violence and some by the trivialization of their opinion or thought. An official's retort to an opinion ventured by an intellectual in a meeting of the establishment may go something like this, "he [the intellectual] learned a few things outside and now he ventures to tell us how to run things!!" Such a retort brings laughter or something else. However daring, courageous or thick-skinned the intellectual is, eventually he becomes timid in venturing a contrary opinion either orally or in writing.

For the leadership, independent thinking is often viewed as a threat to the status quo, a disruption that, in their view, can cause untold damage.

Thus, even if the intellectual is not muzzled or stifled the attempt is not to encourage him but to seek ways in which his energies may be "properly" channeled and the possible effects he may produce contained. Few Arab intellectuals would dispute the need to create a liberal atmosphere permitting the freedom of expression and thought, even on a limited scale, to promote creativity. Such an atmosphere is rare in most countries of the Arab World. A few years ago some Arab intellectuals wishing to discuss the concepts of democracy and popular participation found no place in the Arab World to hold their discussions; they had to hold them in Cyprus.[14]

Professor Nizar al-Zain of the Department of Psychology of the Lebanese University of Beirut complains that "the political authorities do not depend upon the intellectual community to identify the needs and crystallize the objectives" of society. The general societal lack of appreciation for scientific methodology and objectivity was buttressed in "the last two decades by a wave of fundamentalist religious ideology given a certain amount of support by political authorities."[15] While political authorities sometimes patronize them, they in fact basically distrust them, rarely seeking their advice, though on occasion seeking the advice of foreign experts. In the words of Al-Khouli "Of late, all the Arab leaders emphasize in their speeches on various occasions the importance of science, (the scientific approach) in development. The truth of the matter is that such remains a decor"[16] a display for others. Zahlan bluntly puts it "the creativity ability is repressed."[17]

Professor Adnan Badran, former President of Yarmouk University in Jordan as well as Professor Antoine Zahlan go into great detail outlining the various reasons behind the very limited out-put of Arab intellectuals. Both, along with Professor al-Zain, cited above, agree that there has been an increase in quantitative but not in qualitative out-put.[18] Even quantitatively the Arabs lag woefully behind Israel. In his study, Dr. Zahlan goes into great detail contrasting knowledge and scientific productivity between the Arab World and Israel. In one table he shows that in 1978, 3570 Israeli researchers had published works compared to 1618 in the Arab World. Not much change was registered five years later when 4661 Israeli researchers published works compared to 2616 in the Arab World. Worse still is the fact that in 1983 there were 71 independent Arab Universities and "somewhere between 300–1000 Arab research centers."[19] In another work Zahlan adds that in 1976, in Egypt alone, there were 18,000 researchers in addition to 50,000 in the Arab World working as professors in universities or research centers compared to only 12,000 researchers in Israel.[20] It is not a problem of quantity; one has to look elsewhere to explain the lack of productivity.

THE CONCEPT OF STRATEGY: WESTERN AND NON-WESTERN

In contemplating the writing of this paper, several approaches suggested themselves. One was to do a topical survey, basically statistical in nature, concentrating on ascertaining the quantity that exists and the scope of its activities by title. As this paper will amply demonstrate, even the statistics are lacking. No center or university that exists now in the Arab World has a complete listing of all the others. Had such information been available on strategic studies centers, as these centers are defined in the West, one could have divided the subject into the following broad categories of topics of research:

1) Research concerning the theory of Pan Arab national security.
2) Research on the level of the international scene concentrating on the international bi-polarized conflict and its reflection on regional conflicts, principally the Arab-Israeli conflict and its by-products.
3) Research on Arab economic cooperation and complimentarity concentrating on military strategy, industries and efforts in communications and other economic activities relating to the military.
4) Research on the Arab World, the powers and super powers and the countries on the rim of the Arab World.

Another approach would have been a broadly functional one, identifying centers calling themselves "strategic," and the publications, books, or yearbooks they issue and the types of research tackled, concentrating on a content analysis of these publications in the fields outlined above.

Strategic concerns in the Arab World, indeed in the Third World, encompass more than military and spill over to socio-economic and developmental issues. Thus the discussion of this essay will encompass both the western and non-western concerns of strategic thinking.

Strategic studies in the Arab World, where they exist, and perhaps in the Third World in general, are not confined to military strategy and whatever reflects upon it. In the West, interest is focused on military strategic issues where strategy has been conceived as the preparation for war, the waging of war and the possibilities of winning it, and where strategy is ba-

sically defined as the art of military command as well as the projecting and
the directing of a campaign. Webster's *New Collegiate Dictionary* defines
strategy as, "the science and art of employing the political, economic, psychological and military forces of a nation or group of nations to afford the
maximum support to adopted policies in peace or war." T.L. Heyns adds
that this definition "leaves out the nation's technological forces." He adds,
"In the future, the ability of a nation to use its technological capacity for
adopted policies in peace or war will be extremely important."[21] Webster's
New World Dictionary, makes the definition of strategy much narrower:
"1) the science of planning and directing large-scale military operations, 2)
a plan or action based on this, 3) skill in managing or planning, especially
by using strategem."[22] But even in the West there are some who view the
concept of strategy more broadly than just the military. Dr. Harrold
Brown, former United States Secretary of Defense, states that it should
surely "go beyond strategy in the purely military sense. Already and, it
seems, correctly, many have expanded the boundaries of the term to take
in military-political considerations including diplomacy, foreign aid and
even international economics."[23]

The concept of strategy which, of necessity, includes a futuristic conceptualization of the situation, still alien in many parts of the Third World,
including the Arab region, is viewed, where it exists, within the context of
developmental issues. Because of the socio-economic transitional nature of
the situation and the fact that these nations are undergoing various degrees of development labors, the priorities are rarely, if ever, viewed in
purely military security terms alone. In one sense some of the nations of
the area and the Third World may have, unconsciously, stumbled upon developing what may be termed a "grand strategy" whereby they are attempting to control and utilize all the resources of the nation, including
the military, to achieve their vital interests and objectives. The course for
most is still erratic and the objectives vague, but the attempt to integrate
internal and external threats as well as resources is made. Thus, one hears
of food security, labor security, water security, economic security, population studies, etc! In the West, most of these problems have either been
solved or are no longer viewed as top priority for these societies at large. In
fact Western societies have largely moved from the stage of raising the
standard of living to the construction of an index to measure the quality of
life. No such affluence exists in the Arab World, indeed, in the entire Third
World. In the West, life, indeed even change, have adopted a pattern and a
procedure. The dialogue is basically confined to procedure and methodol-

ogy rather than the totality of the broad outlines and goals desired by the given society.

The latter situation is still the case with societies of the Third World. Life in all its aspects is still in an upheaval that transcends military insecurity and spills over into the social, political, intellectual, ideological and economic fields. Regime, even national, insecurity is not always viewed as a function of external forces, military or otherwise. Internally, regime and national insecurity often emanate, not from the military branch, but from the demands for change, for participation and political liberalization in mostly authoritarian regimes as well as from the demands for development leading to the general uplift of the standard of living.

Here technology, mostly imported, is neither understood nor digested, nor has it become part of the pattern of life. This seems to be true even in the military field. The military are an elite class by themselves, isolated or isolating themselves from others, holding onto the "secret" of their power with little meaningful interaction with the society at large. Their top priority seems to be the maintenance of social peace resulting in their often being at variance with the ever expanding aspirations swelling in their societies. Leaders, military, or those closely related to and dependent on the military and they are the majority, thus become more isolated with time. It is thus that many of them become increasingly more suspicious, more distant, more self-reliant. Eventually, inspiration and intuition replace knowledge, depriving leaders and their societies of possible good council. In the process, whatever local talent may exist who could participate in the process of decision-making becomes alienated, frustrated, turns inward upon itself or "drains" abroad.

These observations may not answer all the questions regarding Arab strategic imbalance with the West, indeed with Israel, but the increasing lack of participation and the concommitant isolation of leaders means that fewer and fewer people are thinking in strategic terms. Repeatedly the Arabs have entered battles, both military and political, with Israel, with very little assessment of the existing forces on either side, or even basic knowledge about the adversary.

Thus, the basic strategic questions remain uncontemplated and without answers; questions like how does one develop a national, not to mention a Pan-Arab national strategy in military, food and economic security? The difficulties, in addition to what this paper identifies are many.[24] Is it possible to develop a comprehensive concept of Arab national security in a nation divided into twenty-two states often at odds, sometimes, in military confrontation with one another? How can the proper and appropriate technology be imported, adapted and eventually developed locally? What is the proper equation for striking a balance between the need for stability and the requirements of development and hopefully political liberalization and increased participation? How can the Arabs "modernize" without becoming "westernized," especially since westernization may mean alienation from values viewed precious by the society and are thus viewed with suspicion, even dread? How can the Arabs create the socio-political and economic institutions that will ensure individual and group confidence that may develop into a new social contract? How can the Arabs develop strategic conceptions and policies that may enable them to play a role in an ever changing and dynamic world?

These and many other similar questions will have to wait, it seems, until the general atmosphere changes. The conflicts within each country as well as within the region, in addition to many other tension-causing factors, not only create mistrust and make life dearly expensive, but also lessen the possibilities and shorten the time horizon of planning and forethought.

In conclusion one is bound to ask: Is the very concept of strategic studies in the Western sense of the term, almost nonexistent? Is there anything else taking its place? Are there any strategic studies centers in the broader sense? And finally, what is the general atmosphere in which they and those staffing them exist?

NOTES

1. For a frank if somewhat scathing discussion of the role or Arab leadership and intelligentsia that also draws on the similarly critical writings of Fuad Zakaria and Anis Mansour, see Usamah al-Khouli, "Knowledge and the Imparting of Knowledge," unpublished paper presented at the Center of Arab Unity Conference held in Amman, May 13–16, 1985, pp. 20–24, *passim.* Entitled "The Preparation of the Arab for Scientific Knowledge," the conference was hosted by the Arab Thought Forum.

2. The Arabic version to which the author referred is a more recent follow-up of an earlier English version. It is entitled, *Directory of Research and Studies Centers,* Economic Commission for Western Asia (ECWA) publication (Baghdad, 1984).

3. The computerized list was provided by the Center at the request of the author in a private communication No. 11464, dated April 23, 1986.

4. Saad Eddin Ibrahim, *Social Science Research in the Middle East and North Af-*

rica: Priorities for the 1980s, April, 1982, I.D.R.C. The Middle East Regional Office, Cairo, 1982, (an unpublished paper). See in particular pp. 22–36, *passim.*

5. International Institute of Strategic Studies, *Survey of Strategic Studies* (London, 1982). Other partial listings for some of the countries of the region may be found in, Kay Gill and Anthony K. Kruzas, eds., *International Research Centers Directory 1984,* second edition (Detroit: Gale Research Company, 1984).

6. Ibrahim, *Social Science Research,* p. 69.

7. Al-Khouli, "Knowledge and the Imparting of Knowledge," p. 23.

8. Antoine Zahlan, "Arab Scientific Production," unpublished paper at Center of Arab Unity Conference in Amman, May 13–16, 1985, p. 17.

9. Unpublished comments on Professor Adnan Badran's paper, "The Role of Higher Study Institutes and Research Centers in the Training of the Arabs for Scientific Research," Center of Arab Unity Conference in Amman, p. 17; Zahlan, however, lists the number of Arab Universities as 71 in 1986.

10. See Khalid Mohiedin statements in Paris quoted in *al-Dustur,* Amman, May 17, 1986, p. 22. Mr. Mohiedin was one of the original "Free Officers" who effected the 1952 revolution against King Farouq. Now he is the leader of the National Progressive Unionist Coalition, a contemporary major Egyptian opposition group.

11. See the paper of Saad Eddin Ibrahim, "Family, Society and Creativity in the Arab World," unpublished paper presented at the Center of Arab Unity Conference in Amman, May 13–16, 1985, pp. 18–25, *passim.*

12. Al-Khouli, "Knowledge and the Imparting of Knowledge," p. 14.

13. Unpublished comments presented at the Center of Arab Unity Conference in Amman, May 13–16, 1985, on Saad Eddin Ibrahim's paper at the same conference referred to above in note 3, p. 3. See also the fascinating account in Sami al-Dahhan, ed., *Letter of Ibn Fadlan* (Damascus: The Hashemite Press, 1959), pp. 132–33, *passim.*

14. The seminar entitled, "The Crisis of Democracy in the Arab World," was held in Limassol, Cyprus, November 26–30, 1983.

15. Badran, pp. 3 and 4. This same view is shared by most Arab intellectuals. See also al-Khouli, "Knowledge and the Imparting of Knowledge," p. 23.

16. Al-Khouli, "Knowledge and the Imparting of Knowledge," p. 23.

17. Antoine Zahlan, "Arab Scientific Production," unpublished paper at Center of Arab Unity Conference in Amman, May 13–16, 1985, p. 17.

18. Badran, "The Role of Higher Study Institutes and Research Centers," p. 4 and Zahlan, "Arab Scientific Production," pp. 8–17, *passim.*

19. Zahlan, "Arab Scientific Production," pp. 4 and 5.

20. A. Zahlan, *Science and Science Policy in the Arab World* (London: Croom Helm, 1980).

21. T.L. Heyns, ed., *Understanding U.S. Strategy* (Washington, D.C.: National Defense University, 1983), p. 3.

22. In addition to these two definitions, a summary of Western definitions of

strategy including that of the German strategist Von Clauswitz may be found in al-Kailani, Haitham, *A Study in Israeli Military Strategy* (Cairo: Ma'had al-Buhuth wa al-Dirasat al-Arabiyyah, 1969) (in Arabic).

23. In T.L. Heyns, *Understanding U.S. Strategy*, p. 17.

24. See for instance the article by Jihad Odeh, "The Theory of Arab National Security," *al-Mustaqbal al-Arabi*, no. 78 (1985). Dr. Odeh is currently a researcher at the Ahram Center of Political and Strategic Studies in Cairo.